WE CAME, WE SAW, GOD CONQUERED

The Polish-Lithuanian Commonwealth's military effort in the relief of Vienna, 1683

Michał Paradowski

'This is the Century of the Soldier', Fulvio Testi, Poet, 1641

HELION &
COMPANY

Helion & Company Limited
Unit 8 Amherst Business Centre
Budbrooke Road
Warwick
CV34 5WE
England
Tel. 01926 499 619
Email: info@helion.co.uk
Website: www.helion.co.uk
Twitter: @helionbooks
Visit our blog http://blog.helion.co.uk/

Published by Helion & Company 2021
Designed and typeset by Mary Woolley, Battlefield Design (www.battlefield-design.co.uk)
Cover designed by Paul Hewitt, Battlefield Design (www.battlefield-design.co.uk)

Text © Michał Paradowski 2021
Illustrations as individually credited © Helion & Company 2021
Colour artwork by Sergey Shamenkov © Helion & Company 2021
Maps by George Anderson © Helion & Company 2021

ISBN 978-1-914059-74-2

British Library Cataloguing-in-Publication Data.
A catalogue record for this book is available from the British Library.

For details of other military history titles published by Helion & Company Limited
contact the above address or visit our website: http://www.helion.co.uk.

We always welcome receiving book proposals from prospective authors.

Contents

Acknowledgements

I would like to start with massive thanks to Helion & Company, for allowing me to continue this great adventure with 'The Century of the Soldier' series. Special thanks to series editor Charles Singleton for his constant support and encouragement. I am very glad that I was again able to cooperate with Sergey Shamenkov, whose contribution always brings a lot of the 'wow' factor to each topic he works on.

To Michał Molenda, Dariusz Marszałek and Konrad Pawłowski, many thanks for your kind help in obtaining vital source materials. My eternal gratitude and special thanks goes to Zbigniew Hundert, for his massive support, sharing his passion and great research work into the reign of Michał Korybut and Jan III: Zbyszku, for which I owe you the big one! I am very grateful to E.J. Blaauw for his assistance in the translation of German sources.

Finally, to my wife Patrycja and son Ezra: yet again thanks for all your love understanding and patience ('Dad, can I play my Minecraft now, please?').

Introduction

Venimus, vidimus, Deus vicit! 'We came, we saw, God conquered'. This Latin sentence, paraphrased from the famous saying by Julius Caesar, was used by Polish King Jan III Sobieski in his letter to Pope Innocent XI, announcing that allied side was victorious and had defeated Ottoman forces besieging Vienna in 1683. It was one of the most famous and important battles of the seventeenth century, so it is not surprising that through the years researchers from many countries wrote about the siege, relief of the city and its consequences. The Polish army led by King Jan III Sobieski played a crucial role in the relief of Vienna in 1683, with the famous winged hussars leading a massive charge of allied cavalry at the Battle of Kahlenberg. Earlier Polish experience from waging war against the Ottoman Turks in 1672–1676 made their contribution vital for the coalition's war effort. Sobieski was chosen as overall commander of the joint armies and the Poles deployed on the ancient place of honour in the battle order – on the right wing. There are many works available in English describing the siege of Vienna and the relief action, but unfortunately, they tend to be full of errors and misconceptions about the Polish army and its organisation, strength and activities during the battle. That is why we came up with an idea for this new volume in the 'Century of the Soldier 1618–1721' series, focused solely on the army led by King Jan III, brought from Poland to fight the Turks on the outskirts of Vienna in 1683. In this book, based mostly, but not exclusively, on Polish primary and secondary sources, we will examine many aspects of the Polish-Lithuanian Commonwealth's military system and the role that it played in the allied effort in 1683. While the main part of the book will tell the story of the Polish army at Vienna, we will also investigate other theatres of war. The remaining parts of the 1683 campaign will be covered as well, with both battles of Párkány and some siege operations. The preparations and the arrival of the Lithuanian army, with their marginal operations, will also be covered in a separate chapter. Nor will we forget the organisation and military actions of the troops under the command of Hieronim Augustyn Lubomirski, raised as an Imperial auxiliary division in Poland. This volume will also contain some additional information about Polish and Cossack actions in Podolia and Moldavia, that were previously always under the shadow of main events of 1683.

There are a few additional notes regarding terminology used in the book. Where possible, current geographical names available in their English version are used, usually with the Polish or German name from period as added reference. Polish, German and Latin terms (except personal and geographical names) are written in italics. Certain Eastern European and German words that already are established in English-language nomenclature are not marked in italics, i.e., hetman, haiduks, reiters. For many Polish military words, that do not have an English equivalent, the original form will be used, i.e. *pancerny* or *rotmistrz*.[1] On its first appearance it will be accompanied by footnote explaining its meaning. Currencies mentioned in the text are Polish *złoty* (abbreviated to zl), which was divided into 30 *groszy* (abbreviated to gr). In that period one *grosz* equals 0.27 grams of silver, so one *złoty* was approximately 8.1 grams of silver. If a different currency is mentioned, its equivalent in Polish currency will be given as well.

---

1   While *rotmistrz* is equivalent to a Western European cavalry captain, we decided to keep the original form, especially as in the Polish and Lithuanian military the rank of captain was normally used only in relation to foreign troops.

1

Sources

I would like to start by presenting a list of the main sources that were used in writing this book. As I have relied heavily on eyewitness descriptions of the Polish army and events of 1683, it is important to know and understand their position and point of view, which can explain a certain bias, or lack thereof, by the authors of each. As mentioned before, the focus will be mainly on Polish sources but will be also using those written by foreigners serving in Sobieski's army, those visiting the Commonwealth during that time and German allies from 1683.

During his campaigns, King Jan III Sobieski was in the habit of sending regular correspondence to his beloved wife, Marie Casimire Louise de La Grange d'Arquien, providing her with the details of military actions, descriptions of foreign generals and soldiers and even with some gossip and intimate love-themed confessions. Luckily for us his 1683 campaign was no different in this matter so we can use his letters as a great insight into actions of the Polish army.[1] His son Jakub Ludwik who, despite his young age (he was not yet 16 years old) accompanied his father during the war, also left a diary of the campaign, providing another interesting source.[2]

Another diary was written by Marcin Kątski (1636–1710), General of Artillery and one of the unsung heroes of the battle.[3] One more very important source was written by another eyewitness, Mikołaj Dyakowski (?– after 1722). In 1683 he was Sobieski's court servant and took part in the campaign. In later years he was in fact serving in the Polish army as an officer of light cavalry and after 1717 he wrote his diary of the Vienna campaign.[4] While without doubt his work is an interesting and detailed source, it is also full of bias

---

1   Antoni Zygmunt Helcel (ed.), *Listy Jana Sobieskiego do żony Marii Kazimiery* (Kraków: Biblioteka Ordynacji Myszkowskiej, 1860); *Listy Jana III Króla Polskiego, pisane do krolowy Maryi Kazimiry w ciągu wyprawy pod Wiedeń w roku 1683* (Warszawa: N. Glucksberg, 1823).

2   Jakub Ludwik Sobieski, *Dyaryusz wyprawy wiedeńskliej w 1683 r.* (Warszawa: edited and published by Teodor Wierzbowski, 1883).

3   Marcin Kątski, 'Diarium Artilieriae Praefecti', Franciszek Kluczycki (ed.), *Akta do dziejów Króla Jana IIIgo sprawy roku 1683, a osobliwie wyprawy wiedeńskiej wyjaśniające* (Kraków: Fr. Kluczycki i SP, 1883).

4   Mikołaj Dyakowski, *Dyaryusz wiedeńskiej okazyji Jmci Pana Mikołaja na Dyakowcach Dyakowskiego podstolego latyczewskiego* (Warszawa: Wydawnictwo MON, 1983).

towards Sobieski (due to some post-1683 personal aversion) and he seems to often confuse dates of the events (probably due to his age when he was writing them down) so there are fragments where we need to have in mind Dyakowski's opinions in order to make proper judgements. Former soldier Wespazjan Kochowski (1633–1700) also took part in the 1683 campaign as a privileged historian (*historiographus privilegiatus*) appointed by the King. His official account, written in Latin, was published in 1684.[5] Another official account was attributed to Grand Hetman Stanisław Jabłonowski himself.[6] There were a few others, usually much shorter, written by officers, soldiers and courtiers who took part in the campaign, so further references and explanations will be given in the text. I will also use the writings of soldier and politician Andrzej Maksymilian Fredro (1620–1679) who in 1670 published his theoretical work about the suggested reforms of the Commonwealth's military.[7] It will be interesting to compare his ideas with reality and with the accounts written by foreigners, as they had a unique point of view on the situation. Not forgotten is probably the most famous Polish diarist of the seventeenth century, Jan Chryzostom Pasek (1636–1701). While he was already well past his prime in 1683 and away from the military service, he wrote quite extensively about Sobieski's campaign. It is not surprising as he had a very good source of information. His stepson, Stanisław, served as a companion in the Polish army, fighting throughout the whole campaign. Thanks to his presence there, Jan Chryzostom had some very interesting first-hand interactions, which he was able to record in his diary.[8]

Queen Marie Casimire. Painted between 1676 and 1680 by Jan Tricius (Public Domain)

The Irishman, Bernard O'Connor (1666–1698), arrived in Poland in 1693 and for a year was court physician of King Jan III Sobieski. While O'Connor left Poland for Brussels (and later for London) in the summer of 1694, he was still very much interested in Polish affairs and decided to write a history of Poland. It was published in two volumes in London in 1698, shortly before O'Connor's death. He was a very keen observer, writing lots of interesting

5   Wespazjan Kochowski, *Commentarius belli adversus Turcas* (Kraków: Albert Górecki, 1684).

6   'Relatio a comitiss anni 1683 biennalium gestorum et laborum exercitus…', Andrzej Chryzostom Załuski (ed.), *Epistolarum historico-familiarum*, volume I, part 2 (Brunsberge, 1710).

7   The first edition was published as a part of *Zwierzyniec Ieidnorozcow : Z Przydatkiem Rożnych Mow, Seymowych, Listow, Pism y Dyskursow, tak Polskich, iako y Łacińskich przez Franciszka Glinke Zebrany y Ogłoszon* (Lwów: Drukarnia Jezuitów, 1670). For the purpose of this work we will use Andrzej Maksymilian Fredro, *Potrzebne consideratie około porządku woiennego y pospolitego ruszenia* (Słuck: Drukarnia Radziwiłłowska, 1675).

8   Jan Chryzostom Pasek, *Pamiętniki* (Warszawa: Państwowy Instytut Wydawniczy, 1963).

information about Polish customs, culture and history but also about geography and even military aspects. We can use his comments about the latter,[9] where necessary, adding some additional information, as O'Connor, clearly not military man himself, seems sometimes a little confused about the rather unusual aspects of Polish warfare.

Francois Paulin Dalerac (1626–1689),[10] known also as Chevalier de Beajeu, served as a courtier for King Jan III Sobieski and for his service in 1685, received the Polish *indygenat* (was ennobled during a session of the *Sejm*). After his return to France in 1699, he published a history of Sobieski's reign,[11] which in 1700 was translated into English and published in London.[12] The initial part of his book provides very detailed information about Polish-Lithuanian armies, 'the different sorts of Troops that compose them: Their Pay: Their Arms: and their Manner of Encampment and Fighting'.[13] While he is often very critical towards the Poles, especially when comparing them with the French, his observations are interesting so will be used throughout this volume, especially when describing different elements of the Polish army. Where required, comments and corrections will be provided in footnotes. We will also use the other Polish-themed book written by him, this time under his alias of Chevalier de Beaujeu,[14] as it contains very interesting details of the Royal Guard during the reign of Jan III Sobieski. It is important to bear in mind that he was not a soldier and took part in only one of Sobieski's campaigns, especially when comparing it with the accounts of another, much more military-minded, Frenchman.

The diarist in question, with a much more positive attitude towards the Poles and Jan III Sobieski was Phillipe Dupont (1650 to 1725?) or Phillipe la Masson (he called himself 'du Pont' in Poland and since then was known better under that surname). Unlike Dalerac, he was a military professional and a skilled engineer and artilleryman. He became Sobieski's protégé in the early 1670s, when he joined the Polish army. The young officer served with distinction in the 1672–1676 the war against the Turks and accompanied Sobieski on his march to Vienna in 1683. He was in fact such a trusted confidant of the King that after the relief of the city received a mission to deliver a letter with news of the victory to Queen Marie Casimire back in

---

9   Information will be taken from second volume: Bernard Connor, *The history of Poland. vol. 2 in several letters to persons of quality, giving an account of the antient and present state of that kingdom, historical, geographical, physical, political and ecclesiastical: with sculptures, and a new map after the best geographers: with several letters relating to physick / by Bern. Connor ... who, in his travels in that country, collected these memoirs from the best authors and his own observations; publish'd by the care and assistance of Mr. Savage* (London: J.D., 1698).

10   It is a version of his surname used in Poland and in the English edition of his books, hence the decision to use it throughout the text. French editions of his book are printed under the surname Dalairac.

11   Francois Paulin Dalerac, *Les Anecdotes De Pologne, Ou Memoires secrets du Regne de Jean Sobieski III* (Paris, 1699)

12   Francois Paulin Dalerac, *Polish Manuscripts: or the secret history of the reign of John Sobieski* (London: H. Rhodes, T. Bennet, A. Bell, 1700).

13   *Ibidem*, p.1.

14   Francois Paulin Dalerac, *Mémoires du chevalier de Beaujeu* (Paris, 1698). For the purpose of this work, the author used the Polish translation *Pamiętniki kawalera de Beaujeu* (Kraków: Władysław Markowski, 1883).

Poland. He managed this task so quickly that he even returned to Sobieski's army and took part in the Slovakian campaign. As Dalerac, he also received Polish *indygenat* in 1685. Dupont stayed in Poland until Jan III's death in 1696, after which he returned to France but remained in the service of Marie Casimire. In 1717, after her death, he was in charge of transporting her body to Warsaw, where she was buried next to her beloved husband in the Capuchin church. It seems that Dupont, who idolised Sobieski and was his faithful servant, was really upset with Dalerac's *Les Anecdotes De Pologne* and decided to write his own history of Sobieski's reign, as a complete contrast to his fellow countryman's work. He provides us with very interesting comments on the Commonwealth's military in the 1670s and 1680s, and there were many detailed descriptions of the Vienna campaign.[15] His writing is also additionally beneficial when researching the battle, as he quotes *in extenso* many letters sent by Duke Charles of Lorraine to King Jan III and those sent by the defenders of Vienna to the Imperial army camp. What is interesting however is that Dupont sometimes made direct comments on Dalerac's writing, pointing out inaccuracies of the latter and arguing against him.

Another Frenchman, Gaspard de Tende (1618–1697), who between the 1660s and 1690s spent many years in the Polish royal court, also left a detailed description of the country and its people. Of course he wrote about the army as well, so we can use his observations here. His account was published for the first time in 1686.[16] I will also mention comments written by a few other foreigners like Ulrich von Werdum (Ulryk Werdum) and Laurence Hyde, including some from the Turkish diarists and seventeenth century historians describing the campaign of 1683 from the Ottoman point of view.[17] Some observations and comments from German allies, fighting next to the Polish army in 1683, are also used throughout the book.

One unusual insight into the Polish army on campaign is provided by Bernard Brulig. He was a monk living in the monastery in Rajhradice, 13km south of Brno and 120km from Vienna. During the summer of 1683 he witnessed the Polish army marching through Moravia, as their route took them past his monastery. Every day he made notes of the number and type of troops that paraded by his window. While his counting skills left much to be desired (the number and strengths of units seems to be often exaggerated) he wrote many interesting comments describing the Polish soldiers.[18] In Appendix II is a full list of troops that he recorded, as an example of an interesting primary source from the war.

---

15   Phillipe Dupont, *Pamiętniki historyi życia i czynów Jana III Sobieskiego* (Warszawa: Muzeum Pałacu Króla Jana III w Wilanowie, 2011).

16   For the purpose of this book we will be using the Polish translation from 2013: Gaspard de Tende, *Relacja historyczna o Polsce* (Warszawa: Muzeum Pałacu Króla Jana III w Wilanowie, 2013).

17   Zygmunt Abrahamowicz (ed.), *Kara Mustafa pod Wiedniem. Źródła muzułmańskie do dziejów wyprawy wiedeńskiej 1683 roku* (Kraków: Wydawnictwo Literackie, 1973).

18   Bernard Brulig, 'Pat. Bernard Brulig's Bericht über die Belagerung der Stadt Wien im Jahre 1683'. *Archiv für Kunde österreichischer Geschichts-Quellen*, volume IV, year 3, issue III and IV (Wien, 1850).

Surviving muster rolls and documents from the sessions of the Polish *Sejm*, both in years prior to and after the events of will help in getting a better understanding of the organisation and strength of the Commonwealth's armies. On many occasions existing Polish secondary sources can be relied upon, especially on the research of historians Jan Wimmer, Marek Wagner, Zbigniew Hundert, Konrad Bobiatyński and Radosław Sikora.

2

The Road to War: The Polish-Lithuanian Commonwealth and Ottoman Turkey 1672–1683

The Commonwealth and the Ottomans in the seventeenth century

Throughout the larger part of the seventeenth century direct conflict between Polish-Lithuanian Commonwealth was rare. On most occasions both sides had to deal with their own raiding vassals (Cossacks and Tatars) or waged war by proxy in Moldavia and Wallachia, with interventions by the Polish magnates and Turkish border beys. In the first half of the century there are of course examples of more serious conflict. The Polish attempt to intervene in Moldavia in 1620 ended with a costly defeat at Cecora and the death of Crown (Polish) Grand Hetman Stanisław Żółkiewski. One year later it took the joint effort of Polish, Lithuanian and Cossack armies under the command of Grand Lithuanian Hetman Jan Karol Chodkiewicz to stop the Turkish army led by Sultan Osman II at Chocim (Khotyn). An uneasy peace, full of Cossack raids against Turks and Tatars and (almost) annual Tatar raids into Poland, lasted until 1633. While the main Polish and Lithuanian forces were engaged against the Muscovites besieging Smoleńsk, the Tatars made a new attempt to attack Poland but were defeated by Crown Grand Hetman Stanisław Koniecpolski. A much larger Turkish-Tatar army attempted a new invasion, but in October 1634, defending his camp at Kamianets-Podilskyi (Kamieniec Podolski), Koniecpolski managed to force them to retreat.

Open hostilities ceased for almost 40 years, with the Commonwealth engaged in a series of brutal wars against Cossacks, Muscovy and Sweden, while the Ottomans turned against Persia (1622–1629) and Venice (the Cretan War 1645–1669), and waged a short war against the Holy Roman Empire (1662–1664). There were of course ambitious plans of the Polish King Władysław IV to engage Tatars and Turks in a new war in 1646 but he was forced to abandon these, and after his death the country was too busy with other conflicts to entertain the idea of yet another war against the

Ottomans. Semi-independent Tatars played an important role in the wars engulfing the Commonwealth, initially supporting the Cossacks but later allying with Polish King Jan II Kazimierz against the Swedes and Muscovites. Such activities were normally done with more or less covert approval from Istanbul, as part of the strategy for protecting the Turkish border and political interests. Once the Cretan War ended however, the Ottomans started to look for a new target for their military expansion. This time it was to be Poland, especially the Ukraine, torn between pro-Polish and pro-Muscovite Cossack factions, with their leaders changing allegiances and switching between the warring states. In 1668 the new Cossack Hetman, Petro Doroshenko, who for the time being managed to unite both the Right- and Left-Bank Ukraine, decided to seek help from the Ottomans. In March 1669 the Cossack Council approved his idea of an alliance and in May the same year it was confirmed in Istanbul by Sultan Mehmed IV. Such a change in the political situation could mean only one thing – the outbreak of war between the Commonwealth and the Ottoman Empire.

While initially fighting in the Ukraine was limited to engagements between Poles and pro-Polish Cossacks against Tatars and pro-Turkish Cossacks, it was just a matter of time before the Turks joined the conflict, and on 10 December 1671 the sultan's envoy delivered to Polish *Sejm* a declaration of war. The Commonwealth was not ready for open conflict with the Ottomans. The country was exhausted by long years of war, and the army was small and unpaid. King Michał Korybut Wiśniowiecki was in conflict with many

Dodecameron or Foray against Tartar bands in 1672, Sobieski's campaign against Turks in 1672. Romeyn de Hooghe, 1687 (Rijksmuseum)

powerful magnates, including Crown Grand Hetman Jan Sobieski. None of the neighbouring countries were willing to aid the Commonwealth, yet no one in Warsaw would consider surrendering to Turkish demands.

The summer campaign of 1672 started with a string of Polish defeats. Part of the field army was defeated in July by Cossacks and Tatars at Czetwertynówka/Ładażyn, where they took heavy losses. The important fortress of Kamianets-Podilskyi (Kamieniec Podolski) surrendered in August after just few days of siege – it would not return to Polish control until 1699. Tatar and Cossack raiding groups spread out through large swathes of Poland, taking thousands of prisoners, burning and looting. In the autumn, the city of Lwów survived a siege only because it paid a very large ransom to Turks. Sobieski, leading a small army composed of cavalry and dragoons, tried to stop the Tatars. During the so-called 'Sobieski's expedition against the Tatars' (between 3 and 12 October or 5 to 14 October 1672) his troops covered 450km in a forced march, defeating many Tatar groups and rescuing more than 40,000 captives. Despite this success, the first phase of the war ended with a humiliating defeat. According to the Treaty of Buchach of 18 October 1672, the Commonwealth had to agree to give up a large part of the Ukraine and Podolia, and to pay an annual tribute of 22,000 thalers to the Ottomans. Even worse, Poland was at that point on the verge of a new civil war, with pro- and anti-royal factions very close to open conflict. The conditions of the Treaty of Buchach calmed down the internal unrest, with masses of nobles now seeing the external enemy as a much bigger threat. The Commonwealth did not ratify the treaty and started to raise a much larger

Jan Sobieski as Crown Grand Hetman leading the joint Polish-Lithuanian armies at the battle of Chocim in 1673. Romeyn de Hooghe, 1674 (Rijksmuseum)

army for a new campaign in 1673. In March of that year, when presenting his strategy for the coming war against the Ottomans, Sobieski called for an army numbering 60,000 men, with 30,000 cavalry and 30,000 infantry and dragoons. He wanted at least 6,000 hussars, 'and if there could be more [of them] then it would be better', 30 banners of light horse (so approximately 3,000 horses) with the rest of the cavalry to be composed of *pancerni* 'we do not allow reiters in the army. All *pancerni* should have spears, so it is necessary to increase their pay'. The rest of the army was to be composed of 24,000 infantry and 6,000 dragoons, supported by 80 to 100 cannons.[1] The plan was very ambitious and sadly, considering the fiscal problems of the Commonwealth, unrealistic.

The new year started with strengthened Polish and Lithuanian armies on the offensive, attacking the Ottoman army gathered in Moldavia at Chocim (Khotyn), in the place of the earlier battle in 1621. The new battle, taking place on 10 and 11 November 1673, was a great triumph of the Commonwealth's troops and their leader, Jan Sobieski. The death of King Michał Korybut Wiśniowiecki (he died in Lwów on 10 November, allegedly

King Michał Korybut Wiśniowiecki. Daniel Schultz, 1669 (Wikimedia Commons)

due to food poisoning) did not help the political situation, as Sobieski had to leave the army to attend the election of a new king. Polish garrisons left in Moldavia were gradually forced to abandon their position in January 1674, while the Polish blockade of the fortresses of Bar and Kamianets-Podilskyi was unsuccessful and was unable to cut off Turkish supply lines. Thanks to the victory at Chocim and his growing fame, Sobieski was chosen as the new King on 21 May 1674 but in a rather unusual move he decided to postpone his coronation until the end of the war. He understood that the Commonwealth would soon be facing a new Ottoman counter-offensive, so he focused on preparing his armies for the fight to come.

Turkish operations started in the summer of 1674 but initially they were focused against the Muscovites, who managed to capture a large part of Right-Bank Ukraine: war between those two countries was waged until 1681. Facing a large Turkish field army the Muscovites retreated, hoping for support from the Poles. Sobieski's army managed to recapture the strategic fortress of Bar and a large part of Right-Bank Ukraine, but he was not able to strike at Moldavia, in order to push the war away from Polish borders.

Summer of 1675 brought yet another Turkish offensive, starting (yet again) with the capture of

---

1   Franciszek Ksawery Kluczycki, *Pisma do wieku i spraw Jana Sobieskiego*, volume I, part 2 (Kraków: Akademia Umiejętności), p.1239.

Bar. Sobieski left a large part of his army as garrisons in towns and castles, with the Polish-Lithuanian field army gathered near Lwów. On 24 August 1675 his army managed to defend their fortified camp at Lesienice against the Tatars. At the same time the main Turkish army was unsuccessfully besieging the small fortress of Trembowla and in mid-October decided to return to their own territory.

Attempts at diplomatic negotiations failed again, so in the spring of 1675 Sobieski started to prepare a new army, fully expecting a Turkish offensive in the summer. The Commonwealth was at that point exhausted due the ongoing war, and there was not enough money to pay for strengthening units or raising new ones. The last battle of the war took place at Żórawno (Żurawno) where between 25 September and 14 October the Polish-Lithuanian army was defending their fortified camp against the Turks of Sheitan Ibrahim Pasha and the Tatars under Khan Selim I Giray. The final days of the campaign were fought in very difficult weather conditions, with both armies (especially the Polish-Lithuanian one) suffering due to lack of food. Finally on 17 October 1676 both sides signed the truce of Żórawno (Żurawno), ending the 1672–1676 war. The Commonwealth regained parts of Ukraine and Podolia, but the Ottomans kept Kamianets-Podilskyi. The Turks agreed that the Commonwealth did not have to pay an annual tribute. Later Polish attempts to sign a peace treaty (the embassy of Jan Krzysztof Gniński between 1677 and 1678) failed, as the Ottomans would not agree to the main Polish condition: the return of Kamianets-Podilskyi to the Commonwealth.

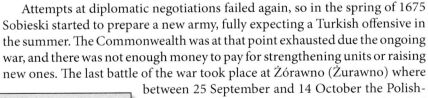

Medal celebrating Jan Sobieski's victory at Khotyn (Chocim) in 1673. Made by Jan Höhn in 1673. (National Museum, Cracow)

The 1680s and a shift in politics

After 1676, there was a rather unusual for the post–1648 Commonwealth period, of seven years of peace, during which Sobieski tried to focus on new external and internal politics, especially against Brandenburg, as they were in a new alliance with Sweden. This led to growing opposition inside Poland and Lithuania, fuelled by money paid by Brandenburg and Austrian envoys. There was even a conspiracy to overthrow Jan III and replace him with Charles of Lorraine. While the plan failed, it clearly showed that the so-called 'Baltic' politics of Sobieski were unwelcome in Poland and her neighbours. Gradually the King shifted his aims towards the southern border, as the Ottomans were not willing to sign a peace treaty and that was the open threat of a new war against them in the future. There was a short-term idea to support the Hungarian *kuruc* rebels in 1677–1678, which was well received (and partially sponsored) by the French. Pro-Austrian factions inside the Commonwealth, with additional support from the Papal Nuncio, managed to put enough pressure on Sobieski to cease his support for the rebels.

Between 1679 and 1680 the Commonwealth attempted to set up a new alliance, hoping to build a new anti-Ottoman front, primarily with Muscovy, France, Spain, the Papacy and the Holy Roman Empire, but also engaging Sweden, Denmark, England, the Netherlands and even the Knights of Malta. Such attempts failed though, as France especially was not interested in waging war against the Ottomans, as they saw them as a perfect counterbalance against the Holy Roman Empire. In 1682 Sobieski started to shift towards the idea of an alliance with Vienna, as the idea of a new war against the Ottomans would be the only one that would be welcomed and supported within the Commonwealth. Of course the plan was not well received in France, and this gradually led to conflict with the French embassy in Poland. Du Vernay-Boucault, the French envoy to Transylvania, and who lived in Poland, was ordered by the King to leave the country and cease his support to the *kuruc* rebels. Nicolas Marie de Vitry, the French ambassador in Warsaw, thought that he could rely on strong support amongst the magnates and nobles who wanted to continue with pro-French politics. He was unaware that Sobieski had inside knowledge of his contacts and his correspondence, as thanks to his one-man 'secret service' – Michał Antoni Hacki – he had access to all Vitry's letters.[2] During the *Sejm* in the winter of 1683 Sobieski managed to push forward his anti-Ottoman agenda and convinced many of the pro-French magnates to support his plans, rewarding them for their support with new offices. He was then able to force through his plan of a new alliance with the Holy Roman Empire (usually known as Polish-Austrian treaty), shifting his attention against the Ottomans. The door to this new phase of Commonwealth-Ottoman conflict was now well and truly wide open.

2   Michał Antoni Hacki (1630–1670) was a monk and Sobieski's secretary, with an amazing knack of breaking cyphers in diplomatic letters. Vitry's correspondence was usually opened and copied in Gdańsk, delivered to Hacki who broke all the cyphers used by Frenchman and provided the King with extremely useful intelligence on the pro-French conspiracy.

3

The Commanders

King Jan III Sobieski

Jan Sobieski (1629–1696) was born into a wealthy family with good political connections. Interestingly, thanks to his mother's – Zofia Teofilia (née Daniłłowicz) – side of the family, he was the great-grandson of the famous Crown Grand Hetman Stanisław Żółkiewski. Young Jan, alongside his older brother Marek (1628–1652), received a good education in Poland and then spent two and half years on the so-called Grand Tour, visiting many countries in Western Europe. He was fluent in Latin, French and German, with some basic knowledge of Italian, Turkish, Greek, Tatar and Spanish. He started his military career in 1648, taking part in battles against the Cossacks and Tatars at Zborów in 1649 and Beresteczko in 1651. He was severely wounded during the second day of the latter battle, and it took him a very long time to recover, so he did not take part in battle of Batoh in 1652, where his brother Marek was taken prisoner, and, alongside many other Polish soldiers, was later killed by the Cossacks and Tatars. Jan continued his military career, taking part in 1653 in the Żwaniec campaign and then in 1654 the battle at Ohmatów. In October 1655, as with majority of the Polish army, he changed sides and joined the Swedish army of Karl X Gustav, where he remained until March 1656. He quickly regained the royal favour of Jan II Kazimierz, as on 26 May 1656 he received the office of Crown Grand Standard-Bearer. Sobieski took part in the three-day battle of Warsaw in the summer of 1656, then continued the campaign with the Polish army, fighting against the Swedes and Transylvanians. In 1660 he served against the Muscovites, fighting at Lubar and Słobodyszcze and then, in 1663, in the unsuccessful Polish offensive towards Moscow.

During 'The Deluge' he met his future wife, the Frenchwoman Marie Casimire Louise de La Grange d'Arquien (in Poland usually called *Marysieńka*). She was serving in the court of Queen Marie Louise Gonzaga, wife to Jan II Kazimierz. It appears that Sobieski and Marcie Casimire fell in love very quickly but in 1658, due to political and financial reasons, she married wealthy magnate Jan Zamoyski. Sobieski still had hopes that she would become his wife in the future, which was one of the reasons he became part of pro-French and pro-royal party in Poland, taking large sums of money from French envoys in the bid to support a French candidate to the Polish throne. The pro-French party in Poland, led by the Queen, was attempting to force *vivente rege* – the election of a new King while the current one was still alive. This did not sit well with the mass of the Polish nobility as it was seen as an unmistakable step towards absolute monarchy. As a supporter of Jan II Kazimierz, Sobieski stood at his side during Lubomirski's rebellion (*rokosz Lubomirskiego*) in 1665–1666, and in 1666 he was nominated as Crown Field Hetman. The Royal army was heavily defeated on 13 July 1666 during the battle of Mątwy, but the huge losses led to a calming down of the situation and the start of negotiations between the rebels and the King. For his role as the royal military leader Sobieski drew down on his head the wrath of the Polish nobles but soon he had the opportunity to show his ability and dedication as the army commander. In October 1667 he successfully defended the fortified camp at Podhajce against a much stronger Cossack-Tatar army and in February 1668 he was nominated as the new Crown Grand Hetman.

As at the same time he was appointed Crown Grand Marshal, and had a huge influence in both the country and among the military. Things also started to look better in his personal life, as in early 1665 he married his beloved Marie Casimire. It happened with a touch of scandal however, as the first (secret) wedding took place on 14 May, just a month after Zamoyski's

Battle of Khotyn (Chocim) in 1673. Anonymous author. (Wikimedia Commons)

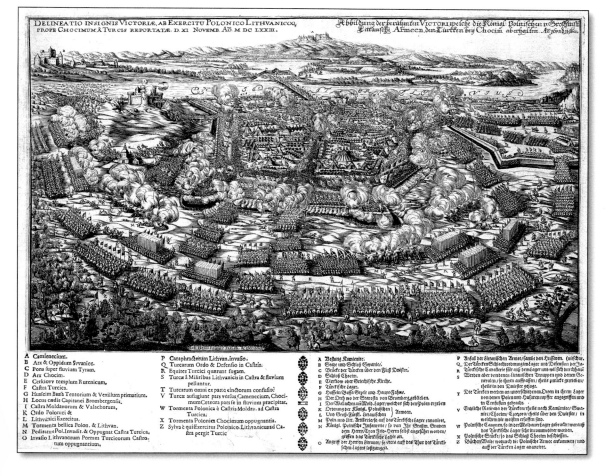

DELINEATIO INSIGNIS VICTORIÆ, AB EXERCITU POLONICO LITHVANICOQ, PROPE CHOCIMUM À TURCIS REPORTATÆ. D. XI NOVEMB. AÑ. M DC LXXIII.

A Camienecium.
B Arx & Oppidum Syvanice.
C Pons super fluvium Tyram.
D Arx Chocim.
E Cerkiovv templum Rutenicum.
F Castra Turcica.
G Husseim Bassa Tentorium & Vexillum primarium.
H Locus cædis Capitanei Brombergensis.
I Castra Moldavorum & Valachorum.
K Ordo Polonici &
L Lithvanici Exercitus.
M Tormenta bellica Polon. & Lithvan.
N Pediratus Pol.Invadit. & Oppugnat Castra Turcica.
O Invasio Lithvanorum Portam Turcicorum Castro-rum oppugnantium,

P Cataphractorium Lithvan. invasio.
Q Turcarum Ordo & Defensio in Castris.
R Equites Turcici quærunt fugam.
S Turcæ à Militibus Lithvanicis in Castra & fluvium pelluntur.
T Turcarum omni ex parte cinctorum confusio?
V Turcæ aufugiunt pars versus Camenecium, Chocimum Cetzora pars se in fluvium præcipitat.
W Tormenta Polonica è Castris Moldav. ad Castra Turcica.
X Tormenta Polonica Chocimum oppugnantia.
Z Sylva è qui Exercitus Polonico-Lithvanicus ad Castra pergit Turcic

death, when Marie should still have been in mourning. The second official wedding took place on 5 July 1665 and was a grand event, with the Papal Nuncio in Poland, Antonio Pignatelli present.[1]

King Jan II Kazimierz abdicated in 1668 and Sobieski was vital to the pro-French party trying to secure the throne for Louis de Bourbon, Prince of Condé and later for Charles-Paris d'Orléans-Longueville, but the nobles elected the Polish candidate, Michał Korybut Wiśniowiecki. It led the Commonwealth to the brink of a new civil war and, with both sides engaged into near open conflict, made Poland vulnerable to Turkish attack in 1672. The period between 1672–1683 has already been covered in Chapter 1 of this book, Sobieski's route to the throne is already known, but it is worth looking into the post–1683 period as well.

In 1684 the Commonwealth joined the Holy League, with Sobieski planning to recapture Podolia and gain new territories, hoping that such victories would lead to his sons taking over the Polish throne after his death. Despite a few large and costly military expeditions into Moldavia and Wallachia, the Commonwealth armies did not achieve any successes. After 1691, due to his failing health, the King remained in Poland, with subsequent military actions led by his army commanders. After a long illness he died of a heart attack in Wilanów on 17 June 1696. Despite his hopes, none of his sons were able to keep the throne, as during the 1697 election, the ruler of Saxony, Fredric Augustus I, became King of Poland and Grand Duke of Lithuania, reigning as Augustus II the Strong.

Sobieski will be always associated with the victory at Vienna in 1683 and his decision to lead the Polish army to the relief of the Austrian capital. While often criticised as a politician and monarch, he is praised as a great military commander, 'specialising' in fighting against Turks and Tatars. He combined the natural ability of Polish 'shock' cavalry – winged hussars – with the fire support of other cavalry and dragoons. His army often fought from a fortified camp, based on the knowledge that it would be very difficult for Tatars to overcome such defences. He increased the number of hussars' banners in the army, seeing them as a vital component in fighting against Turkish cavalry, reviving this formation after its temporary crisis in 1650s and 1660s. At the same time the King understood the importance of infantry and dragoons, not only as support troops but also as formations that could prepare an opening for cavalry to exploit and fight on their own terms (Chocim, Vienna). His armies were well led, as they relied on an experienced officers corps, with many of them serving since the 1660s or gradually raising in the army hierarchy during 1680s and 1690s. Jan III left behind him a legacy of the last of the Polish warrior-kings and is often counted amongst best of the Commonwealth's military leaders in the whole of the seventeenth century.

---

1   Later, between 1691–1700, to become Pope Innocent XII.

Polish and Lithuanian officers

The main officers in charge of the army (if the King was not present) were called hetman. There were four of them in total in the Commonwealth, with a separate Grand Hetman in command of both Polish and Lithuanian armies and their Field Hetman acting as second in command. Throughout the seventeenth century the office of hetman, in both countries, was a lifelong appointment. Following unwritten tradition, once the Grand Hetman died, whether due to natural causes or (rarely) in battle, the Field Hetman was to be promoted to his office and another officer would take over the now vacated seat of Field Hetman. If neither of the hetmen were present with the army (for example, due to their presence being required at the *Sejm*, vacancies due to death or being taken as prisoners) they were normally replaced on an ad hoc basis by a nominated *regimentarz*, who commanded the army until the return of the hetman. Sometimes the officer would keep the rank of *regimentarz* for a longer period, despite the presence of the officially nominated hetman, such as Stefan Czarniecki, who between 1655 and 1665 was in command of his own division in the Polish army. In 1683 the Crown Grand Hetman was Stanisław Jan Jabłonowski (1634–1702), who held the office from then until his death. The Crown Field Hetman was Mikołaj Sieniawski (1645–1683), who died on 15 December 1683 due to sickness on his return from the Vienna campaign. He was replaced in 1684 by Andrzej Potocki (1630?–1691) who in 1683 oversaw the defence of the Commonwealth and did not take part in the Vienna campaign.

Crown Grand Hetman Stanisław Jan Jabłonowski. Portrait by Jean Mariette (Wikipedia Commons)

Crown Hetmen were aided in their day-to-day operations by a small group of officers and officials. The Crown Grand Guard (*strażnik koronny* or, if one prefers, the Latin name of the office, *praefectus excubiarum seu vigiliarum*) was an important member of the hetman's staff, who appeared for the first time in the regular army in the sixteenth century. His traditional role was to support the Field Hetman in securing the border and protecting army lines of communication on campaign, especially in the face of Tatar raids, although gradually it became just an official rank, held by magnates. During Sobieski's reign this office was held by an experienced solder and one of his protégés, Stefan Bidziński (1630–1704), who served in this role between 1668–1696, taking an active role in Sobieski's campaigns. There was also the Military Guard (*strażnik wojskowy*), and his main job was to take care of the important 'leg work' associated with reconnaissance, capturing vital prisoners and protecting the army on the march and in camp. This role was normally held by some minor noble, usually a veteran officer.

In the Polish army in 1683 it was Michał Zbrożek (circa 1630–1691 or 1697), who served in this role between 1668 and 1691. Unlike the Crown Grand Guard, who was nominated by the King, the Military Guard was nominated by the hetman. Another vital member of hetman's staff, also nominated by the monarch, was the Field Clerk (*pisarz polny* or *notaries campestris* in Latin), whose role was to deal with the administration of the army, such as checking muster rolls, dealing with pay and reports on the state of the army that would be submitted to the King and *Sejm*. Despite this being administrative in nature he was in addition obliged to serve as an officer, usually leading his own banner or banners and often overseeing a regiment of cavalry. In 1683 this office was held by Stanisław Czarniecki (d1703), nephew of the famous Stefan Czarniecki (of 'The Deluge' fame), who held this office between 1671 and 1699. He was strongly disliked by Sobieski as the King never forgave him for his role in the 1672 Confederation of Gołąb that, in support of the then-King Michał Korybut Wiśniowiecki, pushed the Commonwealth to the brink of civil war. The Military Camp-Master (*obożny wojskowy*) oversaw the army's camp, from choosing where to place it, through to setting it up and building its defences. He also took care of the army 'tabor' train during the march. In 1683 this office was held by Tomasz Karczewski (circa 1630–1691), who was Camp-Master between 1669 and 1688. The final member of the hetman's staff was the Military Captain (*kapitan wojskowy*) which was a peculiar office in the Polish army. Normally held by a *rotmistrz* of Grand Hetman's Polish-Hungarian (haiduk) infantry banner, he had a dual role. He was in charge of the personal security of the hetman, but he also appears to have been commander of a body of military police, in assisting the military judges during their proceedings. For example, between 1670 and end of 1675 the Military Captain was Adam Siekierzyński, *rotmistrz* of Sobieski's *semeni* banner. In 1676 he was replaced in the office by Piotr Łabęcki (Łabędzki), *rotmistrz* of a haiduk banner of the newly nominated Crown Grand Hetman Dymitr Wiśniowiecki, who continued in this role until the hetman's death in 1682.[2] Once Stanisław Jabłonowski became Grand Hetman, his *rotmistrz*, Jan Franciszek Gładkowski, took the office of Military Captain and held it until 1690. These officials all received regular annual payment (*jurgielt*) from National Treasury:

- Field Clerk – 1,140zł
- Crown Grand Guard – 1,400zł
- Military Guard – 960zł
- Military Camp-Master and Military Captain – 800zł each

---

2   Zbigniew Hundert, 'Pozycja Jana III w wojsku koronnym w latach 1674–1683. Utrzymanie czy też utrata wpływów wypracowanych w czasie sprawowania godności hetmańskiej?', Dariusz Milewski (ed.), *Król Jan III Sobieski i Rzeczpospolita w latach 1674–1683* (Warszawa: Muzeum Pałacu Króla Jana III w Wilanowie, 2016), pp.127–128; Marek Wagner, *Słownik biograficzny oficerów polskich drugiej połowy XVII wieku*, volume I (Oświęcim: Wydawnictwo Napoleon V, 2013), p.177.

This pay was in fact their 'operational budget', from which they had to cover additional costs associated with their office.[3] The Hetman's pay was of course much higher and since 1677 the Crown Grand Hetman received annual pay of 73,800zł and the Crown Field Hetman 48,800zł.[4]

There were additional ranks attached to the hetman's staff, although they did not receive any annual pay. The Military Judge (*sędzia wojskowy*) was, contrary to the name of the function, not linked with enforcing discipline in the army. Instead his role focused on finding so called 'military stations' (*stacje wojskowe*) which were places designated as quarters for the army, especially during winter or periods of peace. Between 1683 and 1687 the office was held by Wojciech Łubieński, *rotmistrz* of a *pancerni* banner.[5]

Finally there was a special office of the General of Artillery. During Sobieski's reign it was held by Marcin Kątski (1636–1710), who oversaw the Polish artillery between 1667 and 1710. Since the reign of Władysław IV, the artillery was organised into a separate corps, with a Master of Ordnance, later called the General of Artillery, in charge of all national arsenals (called *cekhauz*), artillery and engineering staff, and artillery used in the field. To finance the artillery corps, the *Sejm* set up a special tax and each year the General of Artillery had to present detailed accounts, noting all the expenditure including that on wages, the maintenance of weaponry and the arsenals. The general received annual pay of 9,000zł, and additionally, if he campaigned on active service he was eligible for so called 'field pay' of 4,500zł.

Field Hetman Mikołaj Hieronim Sieniawski. Painter unknown, circa 1683 (National Museum, Warsaw)

Stanisław Jan Jabłonowski (1634–1702) had vast military experience, as he started his military career in 1655, on campaign against the Muscovites and Cossacks. During 'The Deluge' he fought against the Swedes and Transylvanians, and, after 1659, against Muscovites and Cossacks once again. From 1666 he served under the command of Sobieski, being part of the pro-French political party. He took a very active part in the 1674–1676 war against the Ottomans, leading Polish troops at Chocim (Khotyn) in 1673. He supported Sobieski in his bid for the Polish crown in 1674. The new King

---

3   Jan Wimmer, *Wojsko polskie w drugiej połowie XVII wieku* (Warszawa: Wydawnictwo Ministerstwa Obrony Narodowej, 1965), pp.339–350; Zbigniew Hundert, 'Strażnicy koronny i wojskowy w dobie Jana Sobieskiego (1667–1696). Kilka uwag o osobach odpowiedzialnych za organizowanie przemarszów armii koronnej', *Acta Universitatis Lodziensis, Folia Historica 99* (Łódź: Wydanictwo Uniwersytetu Łódzkiego, 2017) *passim*.
4   Jan Wimmer, *Wojsko polskie,* p.247.
5   *Ibidem,* p.347.

repaid him by securing his nomination for Field Hetman in 1676. Relations between those two soured in 1681, with Jabłonowski trying to play a more important political role in opposition to the King. Despite this, as he was well liked in the army, and after Grand Hetman Dymitr Wiśniowiecki's death in 1682, Sobieski decided to promote Jabłonowski to the now vacant office. The new Grand Hetman took part in the campaign of 1683, leading the main army towards Vienna and commanding the right flank of the Polish troops during the battle. In the following years he led the field army on campaign, although he was unable to retake the vital fortress of Kamianets-Podilskyi, held by the Turks until the end of the war. After Sobieski's death he had his eyes on the throne for himself, but it was the Elector of Saxony who was chosen in 1697. Jabłonowski served as Grand Hetman until his death in 1702. He was an able field commander, was well liked by his soldiers as he shared in their miseries and depravations on campaign and spent much of his personal money supporting them. He was instrumental in implementing Sobieski's military reforms, and also it was during his tenure as Grand Hetman that the winged hussars' retainers ceased to used lances and a new defensive system against the Tatars was introduced on the border with Podolia.

Mikołaj Hieronim Sienawski (1645–1683) was too young to fight during 'The Deluge', so his first military experience was against the Cossacks and Tatars in the mid–1660s. He quickly became Sobieski's protégé and fought in all his campaigns from 1671, and in 1673–1674 led his division into Moldavia. He also supported Sobieski's candidacy for the Polish throne. In 1682 he became Grand Field Hetman and led the left flank of the Polish army at Vienna. Sadly, he became ill during the later stages of the campaign and died on 15 December 1683 soon after returning to Poland.

There were also many experienced officers at lower levels, from those that were masters of the 'small war' against the Tatars, to those who could lead a 'division' of a few cavalry regiments and infantry as an independent force. Many of them were veterans of wars against Cossacks, Turks, Tatars or even Muscovites and Swedes, providing the army with unique insight into different styles of warfare. When considering the 1683 campaign, it was the most recent fighting from 1672–1676 that was the most crucial, as Polish soldiers gained a great deal of experience fighting against the Turks and Tatars.

The high command of the Lithuanian army was composed of Grand Hetman Kazimierz Jan Sapieha (1642–1720), who held the office since 1683, after the death of his predecessor Michał Kazimierz Pac (1624–1682). His second-in-command was Field Hetman Jan Jacek Ogiński (1619–1684). There were also similar high-ranking offices to those

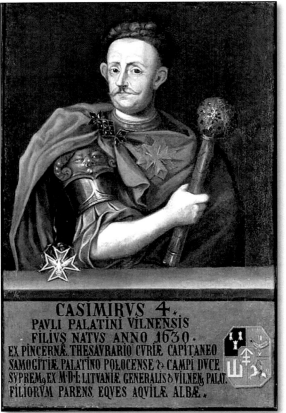

Lithuanian Grand Hetman Kazimierz Jan Sapieha. Author unknown (Wikimedia Commons)

in Poland. Samuel Kmicic (?–1692) was Lithuanian Grand Guard and he was one of the most experienced officers in Sapieha's army, fighting since the early 1650s. Krzysztof Zbigniew Wiktoryn Vorbek-Lettow (1621–1696) was a field guard and had served in the Lithuanian army since 1648. The Field Clerk's office was held by Andrzej Kryszpin-Kirszensztein (?–1704). There was also Lithuanian General of Artillery, and in 1683 this office was held by Maciej Kazimierz Korwin Gosiewski (?–1683). He was yet another very experienced officer, who had served in the army since 1648. Gosiewski held the office from 1673, taking a very active role in the 1672–1676 war. He died in the autumn of 1683 and did not take part in the Lithuanian army's march into Hungary. As with the Polish army, the Lithuanians also had many experienced officers, but military performance was often negatively affected by the inter-Commonwealth politics. Michał Kazimierz Pac opposed Sobieski and during the 1672–1676 war they clashed on many occasions over military plans and the role of the Lithuanian army in them. When Sapieha received the Grand Hetman's office after Pac's death, the situation did not improve. Sobieski was hoping that the new nominee for the office of Field Hetman, Jan Jacek Ogiński, would fall more in line with royal politics but, as will be seen from the Lithuanian operations in 1683, this was not the case. This aspect of the campaign will be discussed in more detail in Chapter 8.

Symbols of office

Even high-ranking officers like hetman were often present in the thick of the battle, therefore it was very important for them to be visible and easily recognisable. Dalerac and Dupont provide us with very interesting descriptions of *buńczuk* (tug) carried next to a hetman as this type of symbol; it was normally called *znaczek hetmański* (hetman's sign). What is more interesting, is that the King also had such sign, with a turban-like ornament, praising his victories against the Turks and Tatars. It can be seen in drawings from the period, both from his time as hetman and as King. Such a symbol was easily recognisable on the battlefield, so other commanders and their messengers could locate the hetman to receive or pass on new orders. Looking at the accounts of our two Frenchmen, to see how they described these signs, reveals much information. Firstly, Dalerac:[6]

> They have both the same Badge of Command, *viz.* a Great Lance, adorned at the end either with Feathers, or Knots of Ribbons, or some other sort of Plume, under a great Ball of some rich Stuff: This the Poles call *Bontchouk* or *Bunczuk*. It is carried by a Man on Horseback before the two Generals, and by its height discovers their Posts at a great distance, either on a March or in Battle. The King hath one of the same sort, with a Plume either of Herons or Eagles Feathers or Knots of Ribbons. But when he is at the Head of the Army, his is only carried aloft, and those of the Generals along by the Horses Neck, in token of their Submission.

6   Dalerac, *Polish Manuscripts*, pp.8–9.

25

Hetman's buńczuk-bearer, equipped in *pancerni* style. Romeyn de Hooghe, 1687 (Rijksmuseum)

And Dupont's account:[7]

When Kings of Poland lead their armies, there is always one noble, mounted on great horse, who is carrying next to the King a type of sign on the top of the long lance. This is called buńczuk. It shows the place where the King is. It makes things very easy for those who would like to speak to the King, ask him for orders, especially when [army] is near the enemy (…). Four Hetman of the Crown [Poland] and Lithuania also have their own buńczuk, with some differences between them. Thanks to that it's easy to find this particular Hetman one is looking for. When [Hetman] approach the King and are near him, their ensigns carrying buńczuk keep them low, leaned on horse's neck and they raise them up only once the Hetman moves away from the King.

What is more interesting is that one Polish source mentions the presence of the Royal battle standard. In his official history of the war, Kochowski mentions that part of Sobieski's entourage during the battle of Vienna were a herald carrying shield with the *Janina* coat of arms of the Sobieski family and a hussar holding a lance with the royal standard, with feathers from falcon wings attached to it.[8]

Another symbol, that we can see on many portraits, was an ornamented mace called a *buława*. It seems to be more often used in the time of peace, when the hetman was in front of the *Sejm* or the King himself, as it was clearly a badge of office. Another quote from Dalerac draws a comparison to similar items used in France:[9]

The Generals have likewise a Baton of Command, which is given them by the King, together with their Office, as is done to the *Mareschals of France;* It is a Mace of Arms very short, having a great Ball at one end, either of Silver or Vermillion gilt, sometimes adorned with Jewels. This Baton is called *Boulaf* or *Bulawa*, is seldom carried, but only represented in their Pictures to denote their Charge, as is done in the Pictures of the *Mareschals of France.*

A less ornamented mace, that could also be used as weapon, was called *buzdygan*. Its head had usually six to eight so-called 'feathers', normally in the shape of a triangle or semi-circle. It was a symbol of the rank of the officers such as colonel, *rotmistrz* and lieutenant in the cavalry and Polish-Hungarian infantry.

---

7   Dupont, pp.285–286.
8   Kochowski, p.30.
9   Dalerac, *Polish Manuscripts*, p.9.

4

The Army: Organisation, recruitment, pay and overall strength in 1683

Organisation and recruitment

A letter of recruitment (*list przypowiedni*)[1] was always approved by the King and issued by the chancellery. It would normally state the name and rank of the chosen officer, the type and size of the unit, details of his quarterly or monthly pay (per horse in the cavalry and per portion[2] in the infantry) and conditions of service – when and where the unit was to muster and for how long it was due to serve. We can also often find details of equipment needed for the unit, although sometimes the description is vague, stating just 'proper [winged] hussars' equipment' and so on. When in April 1683 the *Sejm* decided to raise a larger army to support the Imperialists, official documents issued by it stating that 'in those recruitment letters [that will be send out] there should be put down order and equipment [required], in the way that we will agree with hetman of both nations.'[3]

By the time of Sobieski's reign, many *rotmistrz*-level officers, especially in winged hussars, were just nominal positions, held by wealthy nobles and important officials. Because of this, the main job of recruiting to the banners was in the hands of a lieutenant (*porucznik*), who was second in command of the unit and usually led the troops on the campaign. The letter of recruitment

---

1   The process of recruitment did not change much from first half of the seventeenth century, and readers can find parts of the text are similar to the one from author's previous book, *Despite Destruction, Misery and Privations…* (Warwick: Helion and Company, 2020).

2   In the Polish-Lithuanian Commonwealth infantry was always counted as 'portions' (*porcje*), understood 'as units of pay' instead of men. Officers and NCOs were normally paid the equivalent of a number of portions, so the actual strength of a unit was always lower than the number of portions. This system will be explained in more detail in the section covering foreign infantry. A similar system was in place for the cavalry and dragoons, where the number of horses recorded on the paper strength of the unit was always higher than the number of men.

3   Kluczycki, Franciszek (ed.), *Akta do dziejów Króla Jana IIIgo sprawy roku 1683*, p.85.

was registered in the local court[4] of the district he was planning (or was allocated) to raise the unit in. The letter was then added to the district's record, in a process called *oblatowanie*, which made it official. It gave the officer the right to look for volunteers, and described the timeframe within which he was expected to raise the unit. Candidates for joining the unit as 'companions', in junior officer ranks, were looked for in many ways: from amongst people known to the officers (and their families), former soldiers from previously disbanded units, and finally amongst local nobles looking for a possible military career.

The recruiting officer could look for candidates during any gatherings or meetings of nobles, and would sometimes even appeal for volunteers in church during Mass. Those that agreed to join the unit and were accepted, received a sum of money in lieu of their pay and had to provide their own retinue (*poczet*), composed of retainers called *pocztowi*. One of the companions was designated as standard-bearer (*chorąży*), who would carry the unit's standard, although he was not treated as an officer. In case of the absence of the *rotmistrz* and lieutenant, one of these companions was normally appointed as the deputy (*namiestnik*) in charge of the troops. Retinues in each banner were part of a so-called *rolla*. It was the list of all retinues written down in order of the status of the companions: so starting with the *rotmistrz*'s and lieutenant's retinues, but the next places would be taken by wealthier or somehow more important companions, not necessarily by the standard-bearer. It was all part of the delicate social structure of the unit, where in theory officers could only ask their soldiers to follow their orders as, because all officers and companions were nobles, they were (at least in theory) equal. The position in the banner's *rolla* could help in future promotions (i.e. to replace the lieutenant or standard-bearer), and the higher one was in the hierarchy the better the chance to become a deputy or the unit's envoy sent to pick up and deliver pay. There are even examples of the duels between companions, fighting for a better place in the *rolla*. On 15 September 1660, the Lithuanian soldier and diarist Jan Poczobut Odlanicki had to defend his position in a hussar banner in a duel against another companion, Kazimierz Jurewicz. It led to a general melee between companions from several units, but in the end Poczobut Odlanicki was able to keep his position in the *rolla*.[5]

Recruitment of the foreign infantry and dragoons was slightly different. Colonels of the

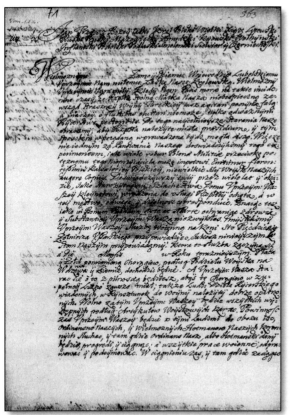

First page of a recruitment letter for a banner of 150 (winged) hussars, issued in 1683 to Marcin Zamoyski (AGAD, Warsaw)

---

4   So called *sąd grodzki*.
5   Jan Władysław Poczobut Odlanicki, *Pamiętnik Jana Władysława Poczobuta Odlanickiego* (Warszawa: Drukarnia Michała Ziemkiewicza, 1877), p.37.

units, known under the Germanised term *oberszter*, received a recruitment letter but rarely dealt with the unit itself. By the 1670s large numbers of such regiments were allocated to magnates and court officials, especially to those that were at the same time *rotmistrz* of hussar banners. As equipping and keeping those cavalry units in service was expensive, simultaneously holding the rank of infantry or dragoon colonel meant the officer could claim some part of a unit's nominal strength as his pay (so called 'dead pay') and was a way of rewarding him and providing some unofficial, yet well-known, means of reimbursement. Additionally one fifth of each soldier's pay was deducted to go towards the colonel's pay; such a process was known under the German name of *kopfgeld*.

As with many cavalry banners, recruitment and organisation of infantry and dragoons was handed over to the second-in-command, usually the lieutenant colonel (*oberszter lejtnant*) or major. Usually the colonel signed a special document called a capitulation (*kapitulacja*) with such an individual, where they specified the conditions under which the second-in-command would then recruit the regiment, i.e. special pay, the period within which unit needed to be fully recruited, etc. From thereon in, the lieutenant colonel took over and looked for lower ranking officers to help him raise the regiment. Despite being called 'foreign', these units were recruited locally in Poland and Lithuania, although many officers and NCOs were indeed foreign, especially German (in the infantry) and French (in the dragoons). This aspect will be discussed in more detail in Chapter 5. Volunteers could officially only be looked for on royal and church lands, and it was forbidden to recruit from amongst peasants living on magnates' and nobles' lands, although many fugitives from such areas still ended up in the ranks. Sometimes a magnate, to quickly rebuild or bolster the strength of the unit, would look for recruits on his own lands, although this was rare in practice. Troops were recruited by the method of the 'free drum', with officers leading recruitment parties into the area designated in their recruitment letter and announcing their search for new soldiers.

When thinking about Polish and Lithuanian armies and their organisation, one further element cannot be forgotten about. It did not play a big role in combat but was essential from a logistical point of view, especially when fighting in hostile territory. Each retinue in the cavalry had a number of servants, called *luźna czeladź*. It was their duty to take care of horses and tabor wagons, look after their master's belongings and find provisions and water for both men and horses of the whole retinue. All those servants were armed and in time of need they could, if forced, engage in combat, for example in the defence of the camp or on foraging missions. During the main fighting they would lead spare horses for companions and retainers, take care of the wounded and of course were always on the lookout for opportunities for looting on the battlefield, in the enemy camp and the baggage train. Numbers of servants varied, depending on the personal wealth and needs of each of the companions. Hussars could have as many as a dozen or so, while companions in Wallachian banners relied on perhaps just two or three. In the diary of Michał Polanowski, who served as a winged hussar companion in banner of Wojciech Urbański, is an interesting note about the numbers of servants. He and his brother Jan, also serving as a companion in the same unit, took part in the campaign of 1683, where on 1 November Jan died due to sickness at Esztergom.

At the end of the campaign Michał wrote in his diary 'we did not have any other losses other than my brother and the finger I lost from my hand, [we] did not lost anyone from amongst the servants, so together I returned with mine and my brother's [retinues] of 23 men and 36 horses'.[6] Considering that both brothers most likely served in three-horses strong retinues (so in total two companions and four retainers) we can see that there were an additional 18 servants that were officially not accounted for as soldiers and had to be paid from the companions' own pockets. John Stoye in his *The Siege of Vienna* mentions one Silesian news sheet, called *Neu-Ankommender Krieg-Currier,* where eyewitnesses described the Polish army as 50,000 men, 6,000 wagons and 28 cannon. Stoye pointed out that 'the first figure is incredible, the third sounds plausible'.[7] The figure of 50,000 actual soldiers is likely to be an exaggeration. But assuming that there were up to 10,000 Polish cavalry and knowing about the large number of servants who were also mounted and armed, we can see how everybody in such a large force could easily be mistaken as soldiers; a servant, with a sabre and a firearm, would look very similar to an unarmoured *pancerny* or light horseman.

There were also likely to be additional functionaries attached the banner, paid directly by the *rotmistrz* and officially not part of the unit. They could be mentioned in the *rolla* but not as part of the retinue's muster roll, only as supernumeraries. These could include extra musicians, surgeons and chaplains. The latter, often monks, were usually found within hussar banners, some of them also accompanied the most important dignitaries as part of their entourage. Sobieski's confessor, Jesuit Adam Przyborowski, went with him during all his campaigns and took part in the relief of Vienna but died due to the plague on 6 October 1683, 'taking all opium and dying in his sleep'.[8] Ulryk Werdum mentioned the military appearance of such chaplains, as seen by him in 1671. 'Monks, who celebrated Mass in the army, were usually mounted, with breviary [kept] under their right and the sabre under their left hand'.[9]

National cavalry was normally formed into regiments (*pułki*) that were a combination of different banners, usually with hussars and *pancerni* as its core. There were no regulations dictating the size of such units, as regiments could vary between two and 20 or more banners. Light horse were normally attached to different regiments for the duration of the campaign, often being

---

6   Marek Wagner (ed.), *Źródła do dziejów wojny polsko-tureckiej w latach 1683–1699* (Oświęcim: Wydawnictwo Napoleon V, 2016), p.19.

7   John Stoye, *The Siege of Vienna* (London: Birlinn, 2000), p.171. The author of all accounts published in *Neu-Ankommender Krieg-Currier* was Albrecht Leopolod Paczyński, see Marcin Kopiec, *Król Sobieski na Śląsku w kościołach w drodze pod Wiedeń* (Mików: Spółka Wydawnicza Karola Miarki, 1920), p.11.

8   Antoni Zygmunt Helcel (ed.), *Listy Jana Sobieskiego do żony Marii Kazimiery, p.*401, Jan III do Marii Kazimiery, 7 Octobris; na samemu się ruszeniu ku Parkanom, które miejsce jest na końcu mostu przeciw Strigonium, alias Gran, na tej Dunaju stronie.

9   Ulryk Werdum, *Dziennik podróży 1670–1672. Dziennik wyprawy polowej 1671*, p.124.

part of the regiment led by officers in charge of the vanguard or reconnaissance missions. As an unwritten rule, regiments under the name of the King, Grand Hetman and Field Hetman were the largest, with the highest concentration of hussars' banners in the army. Each regiment was named after its colonel, who was normally a high ranking official (King, Hetman, Army or Court official, important Voivode), whose banner/banners were always part of the regiment itself. As they were often commanders in just name only and not even present with the army, in the field regiments were usually led by the lieutenant of the colonel's hussar banner, further highlighting the importance of this cavalry formation in the army. Often such a lieutenant was also called colonel, usually as 'Colonel of His Royal Highness'. However, it should be noted that such regiments did not have a proper command structure like their Western European counterparts, and that their composition was very flexible. It could vary from campaign to campaign, with banners changing their commanders, being disbanded, upgraded (or even downgraded) or switched between regiments. Often units could be detached (i.e. for garrison duties) or more troops could be attached to the regiments – from light horse to dragoons, and there are examples of such vast differences and variety of the size and composition of these regiments.

In 1673 the Crown army had 22 regiments of national cavalry (of just hussars and cossack cavalry/*pancerni*). The Royal regiment of King Michał Korybut Wiśniowiecki was composed of 10 banners (including one of hussars), Grand Hetman Jan Sobieski had 16 banners in his (including four of hussars) and Field Hetman Dymitr Wiśniowiecki 11 banners (including one of hussars). Six more regiments had one banner of hussars each (under

A hussars unit, including the standard bearer. Romeyn de Hooghe, 1687 (Rijksmuseum)

the nominal command of regiment's colonel) and between three and seven banners of cossack cavalry. The remaining regiments were composed of cossack cavalry alone, usually between four and six banners, with the smallest made up of just one banner. Light horse and *arkabuzeria* were not officially part of the regiment, only attached to them on an ad hoc basis during the campaign.[10]

At the end of 1678 there were 17 regiments of national cavalry, again composed of hussars and cossack cavalry/*pancerni*, while light horse and *arkabuzeria* were not included in their structure. The Royal regiment of King Jan III Sobieski had 20 banners: seven of hussars and 13 of *pancerni*. The regiment of Grand Hetman Dymitr Wiśniowiecki was composed of four banners of hussars and 11 banners of *pancerni*, while Field Hetman Jabłonowski had four banners of hussars and 11 banners of *pancerni*. Hussars, one banner each, were also present in five other regiments: four of them had also four banners of *pancerni*, while one had only two such banners. The remaining nine regiments had only *pancerni*, of between one and six banners.[11]

Information about the structure in 1683 can based on the list of units in winter quarters in 1683/1684, which gives a good insight into the army structure.[12] There were 13 cavalry regiments in total. The Royal regiment of King Jan III Sobieski was the largest, with 11 banners of hussars and 10 banners of *pancerni*. The Grand Hetman had five banners of hussars and 11 banners of *pancerni*, while the Field Hetman had five banners of hussars and six of *pancerni*. Three further banners of hussars were spread, one each, between three regiments, accompanied by between three and five banners of *pancerni*. The remaining regiments were composed of *pancerni* alone, between two and six banners. An added 10 banners of *pancerni* were detached from the main army and not the part of regimental structure, as they were units that stayed in Poland. As is often the case in such documents, light horse and *arkabuzeria* are recorded separately. A detailed list of these regiments can be found in Appendix IV.

In 1686 hussars and *pancerni* were divided into 12 regiments.[13] The Royal regiment of King Jan III Sobieski had seven banners of hussars and 10 of *pancerni*. Royal Prince Jakub Sobieski had in his regiment three banners of hussars and seven of *pancerni*. Grand Hetman Jabłonowski had under his command the largest regiment in the army, with seven banners of hussars and 15 banners of *pancerni*, while Field Hetman Andrzej Potocki had under his command six banners of hussars and 15 of *pancerni*. Two other regiments had one banner of hussars each, one accompanied by three, the other by five

10 Zbigniew Hundert, *Husaria...*, pp.431–434.

11 AGAD, Archiwum Skarbu Koronnego, II, 64, Rachunki generalne sejmowe – na sejm walny grodzieński – pro die 12 Decembris w roku 1678 złożony – od skarbu koronnego podane, pp.92v–100.

12 BCzart, no 2589, pp.97–102.

13 Zbigniew Hundert, 'Komputowe oddziały rodziny królewskiej w kampanii mołdawskiej 1686 roku w świetle rozkazów i sprawozdania sejmowego hetmana wielkiego koronnego Stanisława Jabłonowskiego', Dariusz Milewski (ed.), *Jarzmo Ligi Świętej? Jan III Sobieski i Rzeczpospolita w latach 1684–1696* (Warszawa: Muzeum Pałacu Króla Jana III w Wilanowie, 2017), pp.167–168.

banners of *pancerni*. The rest of the regiments were composed of *pancerni* banners, each having between two and seven units. As in 1683, other banners of cavalry were only assigned to regiments on an ad hoc basis.

In 1690 there were also 12 regiments of national cavalry. The Royal regiment of King Jan III Sobieski had eight banners of hussars and 10 of *pancerni*, while Royal Prince Jakub Sobieski's regiment had three banners of hussars and eight of *pancerni*. The very large regiments of both hetmans this time included light cavalry as well. Grand Hetman Jabłonowski's was composed of seven banners of hussars, 16 banners of *pancerni* and five banners of Wallachians, while Field Hetman Andrzej Potocki had under his command five banners of hussars, 14 of *pancerni* and two of Wallachians. Additionally there were hussars present in two more regiments: one had two banners of hussars and two of *pancerni,* while the other had just one banner of hussars and four of *pancerni.* The remaining six regiments again varied in strength, between two and seven banners of *pancerni.* The rest of the light horse, 18 banners of Wallachians and six of Tatars, were not attached to the regiments. *Arkabuzeria* were also not part of the any regiment.[14]

Crown Grand Hetman Jan Sobieski and the victory at Chocim in 1673. Ferdinand van Kessel and Andreas Stech, 1674–1679 (Wikimedia Commons)

Pay

Through the large part of seventeenth century the regular army was traditionally paid in two ways, depending on the type of the troops. Up to 1652 the core of the Polish army was the so-called 'quarter army' (*wojsko kwarciane*), financed by the special tax drawn from the income of the Crown estates. The tax, established in 1563, was set at the rate of one quarter of all income, hence the name of the army.[15] In the case of a larger conflict or a

---

14   Zbigniew Hundert, Jan Sowa (ed.), 'Komput wojska JKM i Rzeczpospolitej koronnego na sejmie anni 1690 ad numerum 30,000 redukowany i spisany, Przemysław Smolarek *Kampania mołdawska Jana III roku 1691* (Oświęcim: Wydawnictwo Napoleon V, 2015), pp.90–94.

15   As early as in 1567 the tax rate was changed from one fourth to one fifth of the income, but the name of the troops was not changed.

longer campaign, supplementary troops were raised to support the 'quarter army' or even to fight as the main force, if the latter was engaged elsewhere. Such a new army was paid from the taxes agreed during the session of the *Sejm* (parliament), which was normally gathered every two years (ordinary session) but, in time of need, could be assembled in extraordinary sessions. Unfortunately agreeing and (especially) the collection of the taxes that were to be used to finance the war were always problematic, as the local *Sejmiki*[16] would often disagree with the proposed rates and even the purpose of the tax. Add to this the almost constant state of war since 1648, loss of large parts of the country to Cossacks, Swedes or Muscovites and the wide destruction and human loss amongst the population, it can only be imagined how huge the problems were that had to be overcome in attempts to pay and equip Polish and Lithuanian armies in the second part of the seventeenth century. The 'quarter army' ceased to exist in 1652, when it was merged with supplementary troops into a regular army known as *komput*. Its size could vary, depending on the political and military situation, while the army was to be now fully financed by quotas set up, proportionate to their size and wealth, by each Polish region (as agreed by local *Sejmik*) , supported by payments from the Crown estates, previously used to finance the 'quarter army'. Additionally there was another tax from Crown estates, used solely to pay for the artillery corps.[17]

The Lithuanian establishment was different from the Polish one insofar that it never had a 'quarter army', and instead troops were raised based on the current military needs, although since 1654 there was usually a regular *komput* in constant service. They were also paid from taxes from each land and voivodship and, as in Poland, here there were also the constant problems of gathering the required funds on time and paying the soldiers. In 1661, when the troops started to mutiny, known in the Commonwealth as confederations (*konfederacje*), Polish soldiers alone were owed the huge amount of 24,076,727zł, for the period they were unpaid between 1653 and 1661. To show this sum in perspective, all taxes (including tolls and other special fees) gathered in Poland between 1659 and 1661 totalled just over 7,000,000zł.[18]

In 1667 the system of financing a standing army in Poland (but not in Lithuania) was changed, with the introduction of a distribution system known as *repartycja*. All voivodeships and lands in Poland were assigned several army units (banners and regiments) that they were required to pay. Of course the wealthiest areas of Poland, like the voivodeships of Cracow or Poznań, had to support more troops than the others. Additionally a few banners of hussars were supplied via quarter tax, previously used for paying the 'quarter army'. Tax for artillery upkeep was also kept in place. A few examples how many troops had to be paid by some lands are shown below:[19]

---

16 A kind of local parliament of each estate and voivodship, that prior to the *Sejm* assembly elected its own deputies to be sent there, with their own local agendas and plans.
17 The so called 'new quarter' (*nowa kwarta*), established in 1637. As this tax was not enough to cover all expenses, especially during wartime, there were usually also special payments, set up during each *Sejm*.
18 Jan Wimmer, *Wojsko polskie*, p.136.
19 Zbigniew Hundert, *Między buławą a tronem. Wojsko koronne w walce stronnictwa malkontentów z ugrupowaniem dworskim w latach 1669–1673* (Oświęcim: Wydawnictwo Napoleon V, 2014),

Voivodeship of Cracow: one banner of hussars (100 horses), five banners of cossack cavalry and light horse (440 horses), *arkabuzeria* (400 horses), two regiments of dragoons (600 horses), two regiments of foreign infantry (500 portions)

Voivodeship of Poznań: nine banners of cossack cavalry and light horse (810 horses), four regiments of foreign infantry (1,000 portions)

Dobrzyń Land: one banner of light horse (60 horses)

Voivodeship of Prussia: one regiment of foreign infantry (250 portions), one regiment of dragoons (250 horses), one banner of Hungarian infantry (50 portions)

Voivodeship of Płock: one regiment of foreign infantry (150 portions)

To ensure that lands avoided paying for 'dead men's pay' and non-existent units, each local *sejmik* was to receive the means to control and monitor the soldiers attached to them. Nominated commissioners were to receive up-to-date muster rolls of each assigned unit and compare it with earlier muster rolls lists, to avoid any overpayment. It was then up to the local *sejmik* to raise enough taxes to be able to pay for the soldiers that they were responsible for. Such changes in the way that the army was financed, following the recently ended Lubomirski Mutiny (*rokosz Lubomirskiego*) also had a political aspect. Thanks to the 'regional' way of supplying the troops, they were taken from under direct royal control, giving nobles a new way to affect the internal politics of the country. Such a fiscal system was kept during the reigns of both Michał Korybut Wiśniowiecki and Jan III Sobieski. Of course numbers and strengths of the units assigned were fluid, depending on changes in the structure of the army. When in May 1683 initial plans to increase the Polish army were signed off by Grand Hetman Jabłonowski, they listed types and numbers of each formation assigned to each voivodeship or other area of land. Banners and regiments were not only to be paid by such regions but also each was to be the main recruiting ground for reinforcements and newly raised units. It is possible to compare the same areas listed earlier in 1667 with their obligations for 1683:[20]

Voivodeship of Cracow: 550 horses of hussars, 2,340 horses of *pancerni*, 144¼ horses of light cavalry, 1,236 portions of foreign infantry, 200 portions of Hungarian infantry, 480 horses of dragoons

Voivodeship of Poznań: 470 horses of hussars, 1,000 horses of *pancerni*, 230 horses of light cavalry, 100 horses of *arkabuzeria*, 2,495¾ portions of foreign infantry, 92½ portions of Hungarian infantry, 700 horses of dragoons

Dobrzyń Land: 100 horses of *pancerni*, 132½ portions of foreign infantry

Voivodeship of Prussia: 200 horses of hussars, 300 horses of *arkabuzeria*, 1451¾ portions of foreign infantry, 107½ portions of Hungarian infantry, 1,300 horses of dragoons

Voivodeship of Płock: 100 horses of hussars, 350 horses of *pancerni*, 94 horses of light cavalry

---

pp.49–68.
20   Jan Wimmer, *Wiedeń 1683*, pp.160–163.

Trumpeters and drummer from the entry of the Polish embassy to Rome in 1683. Pieter van Bloemen and Niccolò Codazzi (Author's archive)

As was seen through the whole of the seventeenth century, in 1683 rates of pay in the army varied, depending on the different formations and part of the Commonwealth. A comparison in the pay for both the Polish and Lithuanian armies can be made:[21]

Formation	Pay in Polish army (per quarter)	Pay in Lithuanian army (zl per quarter)	Notes
Hussars	51	51	
Arkabuzeria	51	-	
Pancerni	42	-	Units of Lithuanian *petyhorcy* not equipped with lances would be paid as pancerni
Petyhorcy	-	46	Officially present only in Lithuanian army but some *pancerni* units in Polish army could also be equipped same way
Light horse	32	41	
Foreign infantry	46	42	
Hungarian infantry	46	39	
Garrison infantry	36	-	
Dragoons	56	45	

Due to the sudden increase in the army, the typical Polish fiscal system was unable to generate enough money to pay for all the new troops or their provisions, clothing and equipment. Both officers and companions had to on many occasions take out loans or letters of credit to help with raising units and recruiting soldiers. It comes as no surprise that other ways of supplementing the available funds had to be found. There were four types

---

21 Jan Wimmer, *Wiedeń 1683. Dzieje kampanii i bitwy* (Warszawa: Wydawnictwo MON, 1983), p.164.

of foreign subsidies paid out to support the military preparations of the Commonwealth, all as part of building the anti-Ottoman alliance.

First, there was support from Italy, the largest of which was that provided by Cosimo III de'Medici, Grand Duke of Tuscany, who sent a total of 200,000 florins. Other smaller donations were received from Papal Cardinals. All 'Italian' payments amounted to approximately 250,000 florins, which was roughly 550,000zł. The money was not paid directly to the Poles but through the Papal Nuncio in Poland, Opizio Pallavicini.[22]

Secondly was the Papal subsidy, which was sent in a few tranches to Pallavicini. There were delays in passing it on to the Poles, as Rome insisted that the money was to be paid only once the Polish army moved towards Vienna. As can be imagined, such a policy was not received warmly by the Poles, as funds were needed at once to raise new troops, and for the purchase of equipment, weapons and horses. After the Nuncio supported the Polish stance in this respect, he finally received permission from Rome to disburse some of the money. Official accounts from the Polish *Sejm* that was in session between 16 February and 31 May 1685 mentioned that in 1683 and 1684 Polish officials received a total sum of 382,761zł and 50gr, including 100,000zł for the artillery and 189,633zł for 'the recruiting of the foreign regiments', which in this case means foreign *autorament* of Polish army, including the dragoons. A small part of this last amount, 3,562zł, was also used towards recruiting new men for the Polish infantry banners of the Grand and Field Hetmen.[23] There were also additional funds paid by the Nuncio towards 'the provisions and clothing of Zaporozhian Cossacks' as well as a supplement for existing units. As this money was not issued via the Polish Treasury but paid directly by the Nuncio, the *Sejm* did not mention it in its accounts.[24] Other Papal funds, up to 400,000zł, were also paid towards the preparations of the Lithuanian army.[25]

Thirdly was the Imperial subsidy for the Commonwealth, which is mentioned in the *Sejm*'s accounts as being 800,000zł[26] but it had been rounded up as a more detailed list of payments shows that it was in fact 793,427zł. It was paid towards supplementing existing units and raising new ones, so therefore payments varied depending on the type and size of a unit or planned numbers of reinforcements. Hussars received a payment of 102zł per horse (i.e. 20 horses of supplement equals 2,040zł), *pancerni* 42zl per horse, *arkabuzeria* 125zł per horse, light cavalry 32zł per horse, foreign infantry 8.9zł per portion and dragoons 40zł per horse. Polish-Hungarian infantry was not included, as it did not receive any supplements. If we divide total Imperial subsidies by each formation of the Polish army, we can find following amounts.[27]

---

22 Jan Wimmer, *Wiedeń 1683*, p.204.
23 AGAD, ASK, II, 68, *Rachunki sejmowe na sejm 1685*, pp.5v. 17v–19.
24 *Ibidem*, pp.5v–6.
25 Jan Wimmer, *Wiedeń 1683*, p.232.
26 AGAD, ASK, II, 68, *Rachunki sejmowe na sejm 1685*, p.6.
27 *Ibidem*, pp.11–17v.

Formation	Total amount paid
Hussars	153,510 zł
Pancerni	333,900 zł
Arkabuzeria	50,000 zł
Light horse	75,560 zł
Foreign infantry	73,657 zł
Dragoons	106,800 zł

It is probable that some further money from the Imperial subsidy (which was promised as 1,200,000zł) was in fact paid via the Papal Nuncio, as he would receive part of the Papal support to Austria as money that was to be forwarded to the Poles, but any figures showing the scale of such support are unknown.

Finally, a further 70,000 florins (circa 210,000zł) were paid by Zierowsky directly into the hands of Polish magnates and high-ranking nobles, as so called *largicje* (gifts). For example Grand Hetman Jabłonowski received 6,000 florins (circa 18,000zł) and Field Hetman Sieniawski 3,000 florins (circa 9,000zł).[28] While one may think of these as bribes, Polish historian Kazimierz Konarski[29] points out that the way in fact it was offered was as support to nobles who were raising units in the Polish army and who, as it was often the case in the history of the Commonwealth, were 'wealthy people without cash', badly needing coin for their soldiers and equipment.

King Jan III Sobieski was heavily involved in financing the organisation of the army and at least some of such payments can be traced by *Sejm* accounts in 1685. There is 95,551zł that was described as 'spent on different public expenses', which was in fact used to raise units of Cossacks. Another 110,000zł from the royal treasury was spent on advance payments for raising new units for the Polish army. Jan III also spent large sums on equipping banners of hussars under his name and the names of his sons, his squadron of *arkebuzeria*, banner of *pancerni* (in the Polish army) and *petyhorcy* (in the Lithuanian army). He also sent some money to be used to increase the fortifications of Lwów. The King also paid from his own pocket for his household troops, with some units taking part in the expedition to Austria and some being left in Poland, to protect royal-owned territories. Overall, Jan Wimmer estimated that Sobieski spent more than 500,000zł from his own treasury to support the preparations of the army.[30]

Very difficult to establish is the amount of personal wealth spent by different officers on their own units – both those that were part of the regular army and those raised privately. This would be for upfront payments to help soldiers buy equipment and horses, and the additional sums paid to officers to deputise for them (i.e. the nominal *rotmistrz* paying his lieutenant to lead the banner). Then there was also the money spent by the companions

28   Franciszek Kluczycki (ed.), *Akta do dziejów Króla Jana IIIgo sprawy roku 1683*, p.160.
29   Kazimierz Konarski, *Polska przed odsieczą wiedeńską 1683 roku* (Oświęcim: Napoleon V, 2017), p.150.
30   Jan Wimmer, *Wiedeń 1683*, pp.204–205.

themselves to hire and equip their retainers and servants. As a lack of cash was quite common even amongst magnates, many soldiers ran into debt or had to offer their possessions as collateral for loans. For example a noble named Miciowski registered in the local court in Oświęcim a receipt for 5,000zł that he took as a 'loan, in this dire need, against the Enemies of the Holy Cross'. This money was used by him to buy horses and equipment, probably as a part of his service as a hussar.[31] The scale of private expenditure across the whole country can only be imagined and had to run to hundreds of thousands of złoty and is something that should not be forgotten when taking into consideration the effort and cost of equipping and preparing the Polish and Lithuanian armies.

Overall army strength in 1683

At the beginning of 1683, Polish army serving 'in the time of peace' was composed of:[32]

> 21 banners of hussars – total 2,100 horses
> 49 banners of *pancerni* – total 3,130 horses
> One company of *arkabuzeria* – 100 horses
> 14 banners of Wallachian light horse – total 690 horses
> 20 regiments of foreign infantry – total 4,340 portions
> Two banners of Hungarian infantry – total 320 portions
> Four regiments of dragoons – total 1,500 horses

In total there were 111 units, with a total of 12,180 horses and portions. Most cavalry banners, except the royal and hetman's units, were small, with 50-60 horsemen, often with smaller than usual retinues (i.e. many one-and-half or one horse-strong) to allow them to keep larger numbers of companions in service.

> At the same time Lithuanian army was composed of:[33]
> Four banners of hussars – total 540 horses
> 21 banners of *petyhorcy* – total 2,600 horses
> One company of reiters – 100 horses
> One banner of cossack cavalry – 120 horses
> Two banners of Tatar light cavalry – total 320 horses
> 13 banners/free companies of dragoons – total 1,450 horses

---

31   Kazimierz Konarski, Kazimierz Konarski, *Polska przed odsieczą wiedeńską 1683 roku*, p.162.
32   Jan Wimmer, *Wiedeń 1683, passim*; Jan Wimmer, *Wojsko polskie*, pp.196–97, Zbigniew Hundert, 'Wykaz koronnych chorągwi i regimentów w okresie od 1 V 1679 do 30 IV 1683. Przyczynek do organizacji wojska koronnego w dobie pokoju 1677–1683, *Studia Historyczno-Wojskowe*, Volume V (Zabrze-Tarnowskie Góry: Wydawnictwo Inforteditions, 2015), pp.274–287.
33   AGAD, AZ, 3112, pp.583–586; Zbigniew Hundert, 'Projekty komputów wojska Wielkiego Księstwa Litewskiego z lat 1683–1684. Przyczynek do badań nad problemem rywalizacji Jana III z Sapiehami o wpływy w wojsku litewskim w latach 1683–1696', *Rocznik Lituanistyczny*, volume 3, year 2017 (Warszawa: Instytut Historii Polskiej Akademii Nauk, 2017), pp.110–112.

Five units of foreign infantry – total 1420 portions
Five banners of Hungarian infantry[34] – total 600 portions

In total there were 52 units, with a total of 7,150 horses and portions. Unlike in the Polish army, Lithuanian cavalry banners were at full strength, with the majority having 120 horses. Quite a large part of the whole military establishment was composed of foreign units, although they were mostly spread between individual banners and free companies, not entire regiments.

 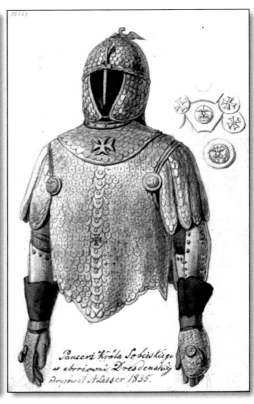

Jan III Sobieski's armour, from the collection in Dresden. XIX-century drawing by Aleksander Lesser, 1835 (National Museum, Warsaw)

As a part of the alliance with the Holy Roman Empire, the *Sejm* of the Polish-Lithuanian Commonwealth agreed during the session in April 1683 to expand the standing army to 48,000 horses and portions, with 36,000 in Poland and 12,000 in Lithuania. The new military establishment in Poland was to be as follows:[35]

4,000 hussars
16,000 *pancerni*
4,000 light horse
9,000 infantry
3,000 dragoons

---

34 Including one janissary banner.
35 *Akta do dziejów Króla Jana IIIgo*, pp.81–83.

while the new expanded Lithuanian army was to consist of:[36]

1,000 hussars
3,000 *petyhorcy*
1,500 light horse (cossacks and Tatars)
4,400 foreign infantry
1,500 dragoons
600 Hungarian infantry

All new units were to enter service from 1 May 1683[37] and were to be mustered by the beginning of June. Any units that were late to such musters would have their pay for the first quarter of their service (May–July) withheld and would only be paid starting from the next quarter, beginning on 1 August.[38] The majority of Polish units already in service were to be strengthened by the so-called supplements, by which commanding officers were to receive new and updated recruitment letters, stating the planned strength of the unit and conditions of service. In the cavalry, banners were usually enlarged by between 20 to 50 horses, in some cases even 80 or 100. In the infantry, regiments were to receive a larger number of reinforcements, in most cases doubling their size. For example Aleksander Cetner received from the King a new recruitment letter on 27 May 1683.[39] The colonel already had a 120-men strong regiment and according to the royal letter he was to expand it to 280 men. On 3 June 1683 Crown Field Hetman Mikołaj Hieronim Sieniawski issued orders to the officers of his foreign infantry regiment to recruit soldiers around Lwów and Halicz.[40] His unit was to be expanded from 180 to 590 portions, as it was planned as one of the largest regiments in the Crown army. We mentioned before that in Lithuania banners were kept at full strength, but some cavalry banners were increased from 120 to 150 horses, while companies of dragoons and infantry were strengthened usually by 20 men (i.e. from 80 to 100). Additionally a few new banners were to be created but on a much smaller scale than in Poland.

At the same time the *Sejm* had already established, that once the conflict with Ottomans ends, 'once God will give us victories', the Polish army would revert to an establishment of 12,000 horses and portions, although with a slightly different composition from the pre-war army:[41]

4,000 hussars
2,400 *pancerni*
600 light horse

36 Władysław Semkowicz, *Udział wojsk litewskich Sobieskiego w kampanii 1683* (Wilno: Zakłady graficzne Znicz, 1934), p.1.
37 That would be beginning of the first quarter of their service, that they would be paid for.
38 *Akta do dziejów Króla Jana IIIgo*, p.82.
39 *Akta grodzkie i ziemskie z czasów Rzeczypospolitej Polskiej z archiwum tak zwanego bernardyńskiego we Lwowie, volume X: Spis oblat zawartych w aktach grodu i ziemstwa lwowskiego* (Lwów, 1884), p.349.
40 *Ibidem*, p.349.
41 *Ibidem*, p.83.

3,000 infantry

2,000 dragoons

The overall strength of the Polish forces taking part in the relief of Vienna was, and probably always will be, a matter of debate between modern researchers, with estimated figures varying between 13,000 and 34,540 soldiers. There are a large number of sources providing a fairly large range of numbers, and additionally it is also important to adopt the appropriate approach when interpreting these sources. Some of those available are shown here, after which they will be compared with most important research in the field, followed by some observations.

On 16 August 1683 Imperial Commissioner Tobias Joseph Eidtner wrote in his letter to *Hofkammer* that there were 16,000 Polish soldiers marching towards Silesia from Cracow. It was a number based on reports sent from Cracow by Imperial envoy Hans Christoph Zierowsky.[42] The Papal Nuncio in Poland, Opizio Pallavicini, writing from Cracow on 12 August, described the Polish army as being made up of 2,000 hussars, 13,000 good and experienced cavalry and a few thousands of infantry.[43] Tommaso Talenti, secretary of King Jan III, in a letter to Cardinal Carlo Barberini dated 18 August, wrote that the Polish army that was on the march had approximately 13,000 to 14,000 men, with other troops, especially a large part of the Lithuanian cavalry and 4,000 Cossacks, left behind.[44] The Tuscan ambassador at the Imperial court, Giovanni Baptiste Pucci, writing from Lintz in 31 August, estimated that 'with the servants of the nobles [number of Poles] will be 20,000 to 23,000, a number much lower that was expected here in [Imperial] Court (…) but composed almost completely from veterans accustomed to fight with Turks'.[45]

The French ambassador in Vienna, the Marquise du Sèbeville, in his letter from 25 September, gives a figure of 14,000 to 15,000 men.[46] A very high number is provided in a Saxon report of the allied forces, mentioning 28,200 men, divided into 7,800 hussars and *pancerni*, 4,200 light horse, 6,000 dragoons and 12,200 infantry.[47] Brulig, who was counting the Polish troops marching past his abbey in Moravia, calculated all forces (including those that were late for the main battle) as 37,360 cavalry, 11,260 dragoons and 17,280 infantry; in total 66,000 men.[48] Dupont estimated the size of the army gathered near Cracow at 25,000.[49] Dalerac lowered the figure of the Polish army to 18,000.[50] Kochowski mentioned the size of the Polish army as 24,000.[51] Jan Dobrogost Krasiński, who served as *rotmistrz* of a hussars'

---

42 Franciszek Kluczycki (ed.), *Akta do dziejów Króla Jana IIIgo*', p.260,

43 *ibidem*, p.249, Relatio Nuntii Aplici, ad Secretarium Status.

44 Augustin Sauer, *Rom und Wien in Jahre 1683* (Wien: K. Hof- und Staatsdruckerel, 1883), p.38.

45 Franciszek Kluczycki (ed.), *Akta do dziejów Króla Jana IIIgo*', p.324.

46 As mentioned in Johann Newald, *Beiträge zur Geschichte der Belagerung von Wien durch die Türken im Jahre 1683*. Part II (Wien: Verlag von Kubasta und Voigt, 1884), p.90.

47 *Das Kriegsjahr 1683: nach Acten und anderen authentischen Quellen dargestellt in der Abtheilung für Kriegsgeschichte des K.K. Kriegs-Archivs* (Wien, 1883), p.235.

48 See Appendix II for detailed list and additional comments.

49 Dupont, p.182.

50 Dalerac, p.47.

51 Kochowski, p.24.

banner in Grand Hetman Jabłonowski's regiment, estimated the fighting strength of the Polish army as 20,000 men.[52] An anonymous Imperial officer, whose account was published in 1684 in French, described the Polish army as 12,000 cavalry and 3,000 infantry.[53] Turkish estimates, based on the accounts of prisoners captured in early September, were that Sobieski brought with him 35,000 cavalry and infantry.[54] Hasan Esiri, who did not take part in the campaign of 1683, said that Sobieski had '16,000 iron [armoured] cavalry, alongside the other troops'.[55] Another author of a chronicle from the period, Sary Mehmed Pasha, wrote about 24,00 Polish cavalry and infantry, led by the King, and the Grand and Field Hetmen.[56]

Winged hussars in sketches by Martino Altomonte, made after 1684 (Author's archive)

In the nineteenth and early twentieth centuries German and Polish historians clashed over the real size of the Polish army at Vienna, with German researchers having a tendency towards estimating the figure as 18,000–20,000 men while some decreased it to even as low as 13,000–14,000 men. The Polish academics tended to provide higher numbers, based mostly on Polish primary sources, giving the size of the army as between 25,000 and 34,540 men.[57] For English-speaking readers it may be interesting to see the estimates of those authors who wrote in English. John Stoye mentioned

52 'Relatia seu descriptia wojny pod Wiedniem, pod Strygoniem i dalszej kampaniej A. 1683', Otton Laskowski ed.), *Przegląd Historyczno-Wojskowy*, volume II, part 1 (Warszawa: Główna Księgarnia Wojskowa, 1930), p.163.

53 *Journal de tout ce qui s'est passé entre les Impériaux et les Turcs: durant la campagne de l'année 1683 et 1684* (Leyden: Pierre Du Marteau, 1684), p.103. Many fragments are similar to writings of François le Bègue, secretary to the Duke of Lorraine, so it is possible that there is another version of his journals.

54 Silahdar Mehmed Aga z Fyndykły, 'Diariusz wyprawy wiedeńskiej i kronika związanych z nią wydarzeń w państwie osmańskim od 21 stycznia 1681 do 28 lutego 1684 r', Zygmunt Abrahamowicz (ed.), *Kara Mustafa pod Wiedniem. Źródła muzułmańskie do dziejów wyprawy wiedeńskiej 1683 roku* p.155.

55 Dżebedżi Hasan Esiri, 'Wspomnienia i refleksje o wyprawie wiedeńskiej', Zygmunt Abrahamowicz (ed.), *Kara Mustafa pod Wiedniem. Źródła muzułmańskie do dziejów wyprawy wiedeńskiej 1683 roku*, p.231.

56 Defterdar Sary Mehmed Pasza, 'Wyprawa wiedeńska i związane z nią wydarzenia w państwie osmańskim od lutego do czerwca 1684 roku', Zygmunt Abrahamowicz (ed.), *Kara Mustafa pod Wiedniem. Źródła muzułmańskie do dziejów wyprawy wiedeńskiej 1683 roku*, p.294.

57 For the full list of authors and their estimates, see Jan Wimmer, *Wiedeń 1683*, pp.217–218.

16,000 leaving Cracow in August and up to 20,000 fighting at Vienna.[58] The latter number is also used by Simon Millar.[59] Andrew Wheatcroft uses a much lower estimate, mentioning just 2,000 hussars, 10,000 other cavalry and enigmatically, a 'few foot soldiers'[60] although while depicting the battle itself he wrote about 'almost three thousand *hussars*'.[61] The most detailed research, yet at the same time somehow the most controversial, comes from Thomas Barker. In his *Double Eagle and Crescent: Vienna's second Turkish siege and its historical setting*, published in 1967, he analysed many German and Polish sources, at the same time disagreeing with some of the Polish estimates. He concluded that by the time Sobieski arrived at the Danube crossing, he had with him no more than 18,000 soldiers.[62] Barker challenged the earlier research of Polish historian Jan Wimmer[63] and his estimate of 27,000 soldiers, claiming that this number 'is based upon muster rolls which were apparently even more inflated than those of the Austrian army, surely more than the ten percent Wimmer is willing to concede'.[64] Barker seems also to favour the very low estimate of the number of Polish infantry at Vienna, giving it as only 3,000 men. As will be seen shortly, those claims are based on incorrect assumptions and came from the combination of the lack of proper access to Polish sources and errors in the interpretation of the other source material.

Jan Wimmer writing in 1983 to commemorate 300th anniversary of the battle, published in Poland his in-depth study of the siege and the relief action, *Wiedeń 1683. Dzieje kampanii i bitwy*. The book was based on many primary and secondary sources, including such important documents as the muster rolls of the units. Wimmer commented on Barker's approach, pointing out that American researcher knew only of selected Polish sources and that he did not properly understand the system of 'dead pays' used in the seventeenth century Polish army (which explains the 10 percent figure used by Wimmer to lower the strength of the units). As such, the American researcher was drawing conclusions that the difference between the paper and real strength of the units should be much larger, further lowering the numbers of Polish soldiers.[65] Another mistaken assumption made by Barker, points out Wimmer, was the conclusion that there were only 3,000 Polish infantry at Vienna. This was based on incorrect understanding of the passage of text from Kochowski's account, where he mentioned that newly-raised regiments were late for the battle. Wimmer pointed out, also using

---

58   John Stoye, *The Siege of Vienna* (London: Birlinn, 2000), pp.168, 208.

59   Simon Millar, *Vienna 1683. Christian Europe repels the Ottomans* (Oxford: Osprey Publishing, 2008), p.60.

60   Andrew Wheatcroft, *The enemy at the gate. Habsburgs, Ottomans and the Battle for Europe* (New York: Basic Books, 2009), p.167.

61   *Ibidem*, p.184.

62   Thomas Barker, *Double Eagle and Crescent: Vienna's second Turkish siege and its historical setting* (Albany: State University of New York Press, 1967), p.306.

63   Jan Wimmer, *Wyprawa wiedeńska 1683 roku* (Warszawa: Wydawnictwo MON, 1957).

64   Thomas Barker, *Double Eagle and Crescent*, p.427.

65   Jan Wimmer, *Wiedeń 1683*, p.218.

Kochowski's account, that there were in fact no less than 21 regiments of infantry present at Vienna as part of Sobieski's army.[66]

So what was Wimmer's final estimate of the strength of the Polish army? Based on primary sources, taking a basic paper strength from the muster from 1 August, and lowering it by 10 percent for 'dead pays', he suggested the following:[67]

Formation	Number of units	Paper strength as of 1 August	Real strength
Hussars	23	2965	2670
Arkebuzeria	3	590	530
Pancerni	53	5674	5100
Light horse	26	2112	1900
Zaporozhian Cossacks	1	-	150
Dragoons	7	3110	2800
German infantry	21	7962	7150
Polish-Hungarian infantry and janissaries	3	520	500
Artillery crew	-	-	150
Total:		**22,933**	**20,950**

The final total had to be lowered due to losses on the march, mostly through sickness and desertion, which Wimmer estimated as between 600 to 700 infantry. He did not indicate any losses amongst the cavalry, as the army was accompanied by volunteers and private units, which could be used to 'make up' the numbers of any cavalry lost from the ranks. This leaves approximately 20,000 Polish soldiers present during the battle outside Vienna, including those units that were delayed and did not initially march with the Sieniawski's vanguard and the King and Jabłonowski's main army but still managed to join them prior to the battle. Further units, including contingents of Cossacks and more infantry regiments, joined later during campaign and their overall strength is estimated at 4,000 to 5,000 soldiers. This would give the total strength of the Polish army present during campaign as approximately 25,000 soldiers.

Wimmer's research tends to be used as a baseline for any subsequent Polish studies. Recently Radosław Sikora, in his study of Polish hussars taking part in the battle,[68] suggested that there were in fact 24 banners of hussars at Vienna, although he incorrectly identified that one missing from Wimmer's list was the unit of Stefan Branicki.[69] Later studies by Zbigniew Hundert proved without a shadow of doubt that it was in fact the banner of Władysław Denhoff. [70] In his book Sikora presented the theory that the

---

66   *Ibidem*, p.236.
67   *Ibidem*, pp.235–236.
68   Radosław Sikora, *Husaria pod Wiedniem* (Warszawa: Instytut Wydawniczy ERICA, 2012).
69   *Ibidem*, p.86.
70   Zbigniew Hundert, 'Organizacja husarii koronnej na kampanię wiedeńską 1683 roku', *"W hetmańskim trudzie". Księga Pamiątkowa ku czci Profesora Jana Wimmera* (Oświęcim:

number of 'dead pays' in Polish units should be higher than the 10 percent suggested by Wimmer and should be taken as between 20 and 25 percent of the paper strength. While this is definitely an interesting theory, the author does not provide enough source-based evidence to support it, giving only one example from 1671 and a few from the early eighteenth century.[71] As such, caution should be used when applying such a large reduction to the strength of the Polish units and it is preferable to use the 10 to 15 percent suggested in Wimmer's research.[72] Additionally, Zbigniew Hundert's research into the banners of Polish hussars in the period 1673–1676, where 'dead pay' due to the *rotmistrz'* retinues was usually around 12 per cent can also be considered. To date there is no similar study into other cavalry units from this period, so hopefully this is an area where more focus from Polish researchers may be seen in the future.

Battle of Khotyn (Chocim) in 1673. Romeyn de Hooghe, 1674 (National Library, Warsaw)

Additional units continued to join the main army after the battle of Vienna, so some of them took part in both battles of Párkány and the latter part of campaign. A large group of Polish units that were late for the Vienna campaign abandoned the long march through Silesia and Moravia, and instead, at the beginning of October 1683, accompanied the Lithuanian army entering Upper Hungary (Slovakia).[73] These were the *pancerni* banner of Mikołaj Daniłowicz (who was in charge of this 'division'), the hussar banners of Stefan Branicki and Franciszek Bieliński, the *pancerni* banner of Józef Mniszech, and at least one or two more *pancerni* banners. With them marched a Cossack contingent of three mounted *sotnias* and six *sotnias* on foot, Rafał Leszczyński's foreign infantry regiment and Jan Koniecpolski Hungarian infantry banner.[74] Finally there was an *ad hoc* banner of 150 horses, composed of cavalrymen from different units that had not joined

Wydawnictwo Napoleon V, 2017), pp.166–196; Zbigniew Hundert, 'Jeszcze o organizacji husarii koronnej na kampanię wiedeńską 1683 r', *Przegląd Historyczno-Wojskowy*, no 3 (269) (Warszawa: Wojskowe Biuro Historyczne, 2019), pp.9–24.

71 Radosław Sikora, *Husaria pod Wiedniem*, pp.79–81.

72 With the latter number often applied to units of foreign infantry and dragoons.

73 'Djarjusz kampanji węgierskiej in Anno 1683', Otton Laskowski (ed.), *Przegląd Historyczno-Wojskowy*, volume VI, part 2 (Warszawa: Główna Księgarnia Wojskowa, 1933), p.263; Marcin Kątski, 'Diarium Artilieriae Praefecti', Franciszek Kluczycki (ed.), *Akta do dziejów Króla Jana IIIgo'*. p.613.

74 A private unit.

their original units on time and now were part of this delayed 'division'. Most of these soldiers[75] joined the Polish army at the very later stages of the campaign, meeting them in Hungary on 5 November, while the rest arrived with the Lithuanians. As such, they had no opportunity to take part in the major battles of the campaign but at least they were able to strengthen the field army, at that point badly weakened by losses.

---

75 Without the infantry regiment and some Cossacks, that marched alongside the main Lithuanian army.

5

Lances, sabres and muskets

This chapter will present in more detail the organisation, equipment and tactics of all formations of the armies in the late seventeenth century Commonwealth. Again, the focus will be placed on the Polish army, as directly involved in the relief action, although much of the information will be equally relevant to the Lithuanians. To date English-speaking readers could find some insight into Polish military organisation in works of Thomas Barker[1] and Simon Millar[2] but unfortunately their portrayals are full of errors, mostly due to a lack of access to proper Polish sources and the language barrier. A much more detailed and accurate picture of Sobieski's armies is presented below.

(Winged) Hussars

It is only fair to start the description of the army formations with the most iconic element of Polish-Lithuanian Commonwealth's military establishment, the famous winged hussars. For this work we will be using the term hussars, as wings were not always worn during their battles and were not normally used in the Polish names for this formation, such as husaria or usaria. While during the first half of the seventeenth century hussars could form up to half of the whole cavalry in the standing army, their numbers were quite drastically reduced during the 1650s, when, during the battle of Batoh in 1652 eight banners of hussars were destroyed and completely disappeared from the ranks of the regular army. Between 1654 and 1667, through 'The Deluge' and different stages of the war against Muscovy, the number of banners remaining in service was small. For example in the summer of 1655, at the start of the war against Sweden, there were just six banners of Polish and six banners of Lithuanian hussars. In 1667, at the end of these conflicts, the Polish army still had only six, while the Lithuanians had five banners. The 1672–1676 war against the Ottomans brought an increase in numbers

---

1   Thomas Barker, *Double Eagle and Crescent*, pp.182–187.
2   Simon Millar, *Vienna 1683. Christian Europe repels the Ottomans*, pp.23–24.

of this formation, as it was seen as a crucial element in combating Turkish cavalry and infantry. By 1672 Poland already had 11, while Lithuania had five. Gradually the Polish 'corps' of hussars was strengthened by upgrading existing units of cossack cavalry/pancerni, so at the end of the war in 1676 there were 21 banners in service. Lithuania, with a much smaller army, retained a steady number of five banners.

As elite shock cavalry, hussars were always the best equipped and armed, with expensive weapons, clothes and horses. At the same time, service in their units, especially those where nominal command was held by royalty and high-ranking officers (like hetmen), could open doors to military promotions and a political career. It is no surprise that there are so many detailed descriptions of how splendid hussars appeared. These are full of very interesting and detailed observations. Clearly the sight of the hussars always made huge a impression on visitors, especially when seeing them for the first time.

Lance-armed hussars and a musket-armed retainer or dragoon. Romeyn de Hooghe, 1687 (Rijksmuseum)

Laurence Hyde, visiting Poland in the autumn of 1676, provides an interesting description of a rather unusual banner of hussars:

All the rest of the army is foot, and not extraordinary, but this troop is the finest thing that ever was seen; they were about eighty horse, admirably mounted, and most of them with embroidered housings their horses; they usually have back and breast [plate] and head-piece: but these had only head-pieces, that is pots, and on their bodies as it were a net of steel, which preserves them against the arrows. Everyone carries a long spear, and at the end of it a long red and white flag with a swallow tail, and when they charge, they run full speed with these spears couched, so that nothing can stand before them. I never saw a more beautiful sight.[3]

3   Samuel Weller Singer (ed.), *The Correspondence of Henry Hyde, Early of Clarendon*, volume I (London: Henry Colburn, 1828), p.607.

This unit was equipped with *misiurka* helmets and chainmail, because the banner in question was Marcin Zamoyski's hussars, that until the spring that same year had served as *pancerni*. The unit was upgraded to hussar status (so called pohusarzenie), but it appears that the soldiers did not have chance to fully change their equipment by the time Hyde had an opportunity to see them. The crucial part of their armament – lances – had already been delivered, as had the pennants that were attached to them, which helped to identify soldiers from the same banner on the battlefield.

Writing about the hussars, Frenchman Gaspard de Tende mentioned that they are an elite force, 'brave and fearless' and that they were armed with lances. He also pointed out the famous wings, 'some of the cavalry units is composed of the horsemen, carrying on their back wings made of bird's feathers, usually white, that are supposed to scare horses of the enemies that are not used to it. All of them [soldiers] are dressed in rich attire, with pelts of tigers, panthers or leopards. Their horses are very noble and well equipped. It can be said that it is the most beautiful and the best cavalry in the world and it would be invincible if it would have better discipline and if their pay would be better'.[4]

Hussar using pistol in melee. On his back a very distinct pair of wings. Romeyn de Hooghe, 1687 (Rijksmuseum)

Dalerac wrote an extensive description of late 1690s hussars, with details of their equipment, weapons and tactics. It is an interesting point of reference to the other foreigners writing about the hussars, and gives a good insight into Dalerac's work and his comments about Poles. While his writing describes the situation a decade after relief of Vienna, most of it is still very relevant to 1683, and a large part of it follows here:[5]

The Hussars are the first Gens d'Arms of the Kingdom, as the Guard du Corps are in France, and without Contradiction the finest Cavalry in Europe in respect of the Mein of the Men, the Goodness of the Horses, and their Magnificent and Noble Apparel. Their Name is Hungarian, and common to all the Cavalry of that Country, but in its proper Signification it signifies Brave, for 'tis supposed, that the Touariches[6] ought to be so by way of Eminence. In France we suppose that the Hungarian Cavalry was called Hussars from their Cry of War in time of Battle, where 'tis alledged they cry, Houssa! Houssa! as we say, Tue! Tue! kill, kill; and the Turks cry, Alla! alla! But this Etymology is unknown in Poland, where they animate one another by crying Bi-zabi;[7] i.e. Strike, strike him to death.

---

4   Gaspard de Tende, *Relacja historyczna o Polsce*, p.227.
5   Francois Paulin Dalerac, *Polish Manuscripts*, pp.14–20.
6   (Pol.) *Towarzysze* is a word used to describe companions in all cavalry units.
7   (Pol.) *Bij, zabij*, that can be literally translated as 'Strike, kill'.

The Hussars never keep Guard, do not go out on any Parties, Convoys, &c. and much less in the Strageniks[8] Detachments. They are reserved only for Battles and other distinguishing Actions. But the present Grand General[9] being discontented with this sort of Gens d'Arms, who are become more effeminate and less valiant than formerly he began in the Campagne of 1689, to take away their Lances to arm them with Musquetoons, and to make them serve like ordinary Troopers on Convoys, Vanguards and other Fatigues of the Camp without distinction, a certain evidence that those Troops are much degenerated from their Ancient Splendor, else they would never have endured it.

They are composed of handsome Men, mounted on the finest Horses of the Kingdom, with divers other Led-Horses, richly capparisoned, their Bridles adorn'd with Plates and Nails of Silver or Vermillion gilt, embroidered Saddles with gilt Boys, great hanging Houzes, according to the Turkish Manner, with Fringes of Gold and Silver: A Falchon or very rich Sword fixed to the left-side of the Saddle under the Horseman's Thigh. Formerly the Polish Cavalry had no Pistols, but now they are used amongst those fixed Troops. But the Vallachians, Cossacks, and even abundance of Poles, have none at the Saddle Boys, no more than the Turks, but carry one or sometimes two at their Girdle behind.

The Equipage of the Hussars is as much distinguished as their personal Habit. They have two or three Waggons, a great number of Servants, and fine Tents, so that a Troop of them takes up a great deal of Ground in the Camp, because the Streets must be large for their Equipage, which is placed in the Intervals, and not in the Rear, as in France and Elsewhere. The Hussars are armed with Back and Breast, a scaled Head-Piece adorn'd on the sides, and behind with Pendants of Iron Plates quilted, which come down to their Shoulders, where they have another separate Piece of Armour, with Braces reaching over their Neck to which there is fixed a sort of a Gantlet of Mail, which covers the back of the hand only, the Poles not knowing the Use of Gloves, nay, not so much as on Horseback. Overall this they wear a great Leopard or Tigre's Skin, in form of a loose Coat made in a Warlike Fashion, which is a very fine Ornament to the Gens d'Arms. The Lances they carry are no less Ornamental to the Body of the Troops in general: they are longer than the French great Pikes, round, pointed with Iron, made of a light Wood; the upper part adorn'd with a Streamer of Taffata, in form of a Standard, and three or four Ells in length, painted and gilt from one end to the other. They carry 'em in a Boot fixed in the Saddle, which supports 'em also when they make use of them in Battle, otherwise there were no making use of this Machine, because of its Weight. Nor is the effect of it, so terrible as was imagined. I have seen those Hussars in Action, and likewise at muster in the Camp, and always found they had a great deal of Trouble in making use of their Lance, and that their Impetuosity is not so considerable when particularly enquired into. 'Tis true indeed, that they never retire, they ride at full speed, as if they were running at the Ring, so that they break through all that oppose them.

---

8   (Pol.) *Strażnik,* Guard mentioned in description of the army officers.
9   Grand Hetman Jabłonowski.

The Hussars have each two Servants arm'd, and in pay, who are called Pacolets;[10] they are mounted much like their Masters, armed with Head-Pieces and Lances, but without Back and Breast, and Leopards Skin; instead of which they have the Skin of a White Wolf made like a Coat; and behind their back a very great Wing made of Eagles Feathers, which gives them a fierce and savage Mein: Formerly they had two Wings; and we see them painted so in Pictures of old Wars. I am of opinion that they are very useless, but the Poles pretend that the whistling they make in the Air terrifies the Enemy's Horses and helps to break their Ranks. They left off one of them by degrees, and it's hoped that the Great General, who hath lately eased 'em of their Lances, will likewise take away this Accoutrement, which is good for nothing but to frighten little Children.

Those Troops form themselves into Squadrons, like ours, three Men deep, and seventy in Front, more or less, according to the number of the Gens d' Arms and Pacolets; for every Hussar may have three but no more. The first Rank consists all of Masters, the other two of Pacolets: And when a Hussar has the Guard of the Standard, he fixes his Lance by it, and hangs the Wings of his Servants round it, according to their number, for some have three, and others but one, and they are paid in proportion.

As those Companies are very expensive, the Republick entertains but few of them, and give them little enough Pay; but the Lords who have them, make this up by an augmentation of Pay, as a sort of Pension; and thus they make themselves Creatures of the Touarizes, and of the Lieutenants that command them, who are always Men of Note, and fit for Service, to whom they give at least a Pension of 6,000 Francs to bear their charge, because those Officers are oblig'd to keep a Table in the Army. The Captain Lieutenant of the King's Hussars, called Polanoski,[11] was one of the Candidates for the Crown when Casimir abdicated; by which the Reader may understand that those Places are fill'd with Persons of Merit and Quality.

The King hath a Company of those Gens d' Arms; Prince James and Prince Alexander have likewise each of them one; the Chief Senators, the Bishops and Ministers of State, who will be at the expence of it, have the same: They cost the Captain above 25,000 Francs, besides the Pay of the Commonwealth. The King makes them a compensation for this Expence, by giving them Regiments of Foot or Dragoons in the Foreign Army, which cost them little, and bring in a great deal, as I shall shew afterwards. The Standard of those Companies is very high, and almost as large as that of a Company of Foot. The Lance has a gilt wooden Ball upon the upper end, like that on the Stern of a Ship. The Drums and Trumpets are plac'd round the Standard, in March as well as in Battle: For other things the Order is much the same as ours, only their Trumpets never found any Charge, or point of War, but always a Fanfare even when on a March. They have this peculiar in their way of Encampment, that the Officers are always at the Head of the Company, close to the Standard, and all the Baggage in the Streets or Intervals, which is the same in all the other Troops of the Kingdom.

---

10 He describes here the retainers, known as *pocztowi* in Polish. The word he uses is a version of *pacholkowie*, also sometimes used to described retainers and servants.

11 Aleksander Polanowski, Lieutenant of King's hussars banner.

Later in his writing he added a passage regarding lances:[12]

I must not forget one Circumstance relating to the Hussars, which is that every Year they had new Lances given them at the beginning of the Campaign; for it was supposed for their Honour, that they had broken those of the preceding Year; and indeed formerly nothing more shameful could befall and Hussar, than to bring back his Lance from an Engagement, and therefore new ones were always carried in Waggons with the Camp to supply those that were broken.

Winged hussars' *szyszak* helmet, dated between 1680 and 1700. (National Museum, Cracow)

Dupont, was also very impressed with hussars, and described them as follows:[13]

They are elite amongst nobles – with their look, weapons and horses and the wealth of their equipment they exceed everything that ancient authors wrote about Persian, Greek and Roman wars, and everything that could be seen in Europe and Asia.

Service in the hussars leads to [promotion for] all offices and functions in the kingdom. No noble, no matter how important his family is, would not dare to apply for any office if he would not previously serve as soldier [in hussars]. All Poles are by nature tall and well built. Let's try to imagine such man wearing ornamented armour. There's rivalry between them, as each want to surpass the others with the wealth of their weaponry. This man had his arms protected [with armour] to the wrists, and the beautiful helmet on his head. His armour is covered with beautiful panther pelt, fastened over the left shoulder, with the rest [of the pelt] covering back and attached at the bottom on right hip. Armoured in such way, the man is mounted on the most glorious horse one can only imagine, with its tack covered with small lamellas of enamelled gold, often covered with precious gems. In right hand he had lance [kopia], painted and gilded, 14 to 15 feet[14] long, supported on

---

12   Francois Paulin Dalerac, *Polish Manuscripts*, pp.36–37.
13   Dupont, pp.80–82.
14   Dupont most likely wrote about *pied du roi,* which was 32.48cm, giving his measurement for the lance as 4.5 to 4.9 metres.

small saddlebow.[15] On its top there is a pennant with two tails, each between eight and nine feet long. Each banner [company] have different colour [of pennants] and that how unit [and its] commander can be recognised. One should not just think about those pennants as simple decoration. No enemy [cavalry] squadron can keep their order, when these pennants will start to flicker in the eyes of their horses and the sound of it makes [lots of] noise when hussars are charging at the full speed. Hussar is carrying one sabre at his side and the other[16] attached to the saddle under his left thigh, [also] brace of the pistols. In each company there are 100 companions and 100 archers,[17] that forms second rank of the squadron. [Retainers] Have same horses and same weapons as the others [as companions], the only difference is that instead of panther pelts they have white wolves pelts. Hussars' companies are led by governors of the provinces and main officials of the country. Archbishops and majority of the bishops also have their companies, that they partially finance and pay high salary to their lieutenants. I will dare to say that there's no more beautiful and glorious troops than hussars, especially when they muster across the plain on fine day. When marching, there's large herd of beautiful horses preceding the company, as each hussar own few horses, each covered with long, embroidered shabrack and [with] beautiful tacks.

Bernard O'Connor described winged hussars in 1694. Despite his observation being written down 11 years after the Vienna campaign, nothing really changed about the equipment of these troops:[18]

The former are 1. The Hussartz[19], which, with their Horses, are both in close Armour. And 2. the Tovarzysz[20], which have only a Breast-Plate, Helmet, and Gorget. These are both choice Men, and the latter are so named from a word in Polish which signifies Companion. The first of these are Armed with short Lances, Sabres, and Pistols, and the second, with Carabines, Bows, and Arrows[21], &c. These short Lances are called by the Poles, Kopye[22], whence also the Body of Men that uses them is term'd Kopiynick[23]. These Kopiie are about 6 Foot long, and tied to the Horsmen's Wrists with strings of Silk. When they come near their Enemy, they dart their Lances with all their Force against them, and if they miss their Bodies, they suddenly snatch back the Lance, by help of the Silken string, but where they have mortally wounded any, then they slip the Silk, and leave the Lance in their Bodies, till such time as they can ride up to them to cut off their Heads with a broad well temper'd Sabre, which always hangs by their Saddles.

---

15 Probably he is thinking about the leather *wytok* tube, attached by straps to the belt. Hussars put the bottom of their lance into it.

16 This second weapon will be an estoc (*koncerz*) or pallasch.

17 In this case, Dupont used the word to describe retainers.

18 Bernard Connor, *The history of Poland*, vol. 2, letter VI, pp.9-10

19 (Pol.) *Husarz.*

20 O'Connor clearly gets confused here with Polish terminology. What he described as *Hussartz* will be a noble leading the retinue, called companion (*towarzysz*), while *Tovarzysz* from the Irishman's account refers to the retainers (*pocztowi*) serving in companion's retinue.

21 Bows would be used by companions in pancerni and light cavalry but highly unlikely by retainers in winged hussars' banners.

22 (Pol.) *Kopie.*

23 (Pol.) *Kopijnicy.*

Both the Hussartz and Tovarzysz, with their Horses, look frightfully, being stuck all over with Wings of Storks, Cranes, Turky-Cocks, &c. and Cloath'd over their Armour with skins of Leopards, Tygres, Bears, Lyons, &c. all which they do to make themselves the more terrible to their Enemy. These Cavalry for the most part set themselves also off wilh various Partycolour'd Mantles, which oftentimes shine with Jewels, Gold and Silver. Of the Hussartz there are but 5 Companies in Poland, every Company consisting of about 300 Men, all Arm'd Cap-a-pe. They have but one Lieutenant in each Company, which they call Poruczknik[24], and one Korazy, or Trumpeter, with a particular sort of Trumpet, which they call Koronzy.[25]

Winged hussar's breastplate, end of the seventeenth/ beginning of the eighteenth century. (National Museum, Cracow)

Andrzej Maksymilian Fredro, writing his theoretical treatise in 1670 wanted to have hussars on 'excellent horses' and equipped with 'full armour, which is half-cuirass,[26] eight ells-long lance[27] without pennant, with good handgun(s)'.[28] It is very interesting that he was an opponent of the pennants being attached to the lances. He mentioned that it added unnecessary weight to the weapon, causing added fatigue for soldier and horse alike. It could also be a hindrance when the unit was trying to march through woods, and, when hiding from the eyes of the enemy, hussars should lower their lances. Finally, and especially when the situation required a large number of new units to be raised, pennants would just be an added and avoidable cost .[29] Fredro saw the lance as an important shock weapon, useful against 'German pikemen, Hungarian hussars and Turkish spears [of the cavalry] as it can break them and have advantage due to length'.[30]

An unnamed burgher living in Cracow in 1676 wrote in his account of Sobieski's coronation on 30 January 1676 about units present and that entered the town, that 'all these were followed by Company of Hussars, with white and blue Coats, with large white Wings on their backs, lined with Fur of Leopards and Panthers. There followed after these one of the like Companies, with sky-colour'd and black Cassocks furr'd alike'.[31] Other Polish

---

24 (Pol.) *Porucznik*.
25 The Polish word *chorąży* means standard-bearer/ensign, so O'Connor used it incorrectly here. A trumpeter would be called *surmacz* or *trębacz*.
26 In this case: breast and backplate.
27 As in old Polish ell (*łokieć*) which was 59.6cm, which means that Fredro's lance was to be around 480cm long. In a different part of his book he mentioned slightly longer lances of eight-and-half ells.
28 Andrzej Maksymilian Fredro, *Potrzebne consideratie*, p.43.
29 *Ibidem*, p.34.
30 *Ibidem*, p.35.
31 *A True Relation of the Manner of the Coronation of the present King of Poland* (London, 1676), pp.4–5.

accounts describing the entry of Jan Sobieski into Cracow for his coronation provide information about pennants used by three banners of hussars present there. The unit of Lithuanian Field Hetman Michał Kazimierz Radziwiłł had a combination of black and white, which seems to be a nod to the colours of Radziwiłł's coat of arms (black eagle on yellow background). Royal Prince Jakub's banner used white and blue, while the Royal banner had a combination of white and red.[32] There are also short descriptions from the Turkish side, giving some insight into how the hussars looked during the relief of Vienna. One of the Turkish diarists mentioned 'armoured Polish cavalry', that was all 'in iron [armour]'. One of the units was supposed to have red and white pennants on their lances, a second one blue and white, while the third one had black and white.[33] Another Turkish diarist, when describing the allied Catholic forces, mentioned what seems to be a description of the Polish winged hussars, 'army of infidels, all wearing armour, with lances in their hands, [looking] robust and mounted on horses [fast] as hawks'.[34] In November 1684, Bishop Stanisław Wojeński, writing about the campaign of 1684, described 'hussars, all nobles, wearing full armour, so [they] seems like unbreakable iron wall, [and] with tigers [pelts] on their shoulders they can strike terror [amongst the enemy], being the strongest and undefeated army in the world'.[35]

Another example of a hussar with his distinctive wings; also note the animal pelt on his armour. Romeyn de Hooghe, 1687 (Rijksmuseum)

Wespazjan Kochowski's official account of the campaign includes a short description of Polish hussars. He wrote that companions had leopard and tiger pelts, while retainers wore wolf pelts. Regarding equipment he mentions helmets and iron breastplates; with all hussars armed with a 10 foot lance with a silken pennant, sabre and long sword used for thrusting, and firearms.

---

32 Biblioteka Zakładu Narodowego im. Ossolińskich we Wrocławiu, no 337, *Opisanie wjazdu J. K. M. do miasta stołecznego Krakowa na koranotią Anno 1676*, p.1.

33 Dżebedżi Hasan Esiri, 'Wspomnienia i refleksje o wyprawie wiedeńskiej', Zygmunt Abrahamowicz (ed.), *Kara Mustafa pod Wiedniem. Źródła muzułmańskie do dziejów wyprawy wiedeńskiej 1683 roku*, pp.226–227.

34 Husejn Hezarfenn, Historia wyprawy wiedeńskiej, Zygmunt Abrahamowicz (ed.), Kara Mustafa pod Wiedniem. Źródła muzułmańskie do dziejów wyprawy wiedeńskiej 1683 roku, p.256.

35 *Compendiosa e veridical relazione di quanto ha operato nella scorsa campagna l'armata del re di Polonia contro quelle de' Turchi e Tartari nella Podolia* (Bologna, 1685), pp.12–13.

What is interesting is that he did not write anything about wings being used by these soldiers.[36] They are mentioned in other short accounts, however. In his report to *Neu-Ankommender Krieg-Currier* an eyewitness who had the chance to see Polish troops in Silesia mentioned that 'hussars have large wings, and wear wolf pelts, turned with raw hide outside out. They were armed with lances, pistols, sabres and carbines'.[37]

Brulig was impressed with the hussars marching through Moravia, giving the following evidence: 'Otherwise as far as concerns their martial discipline, equipment and marching, the officers present kept good order and good intention, also seem the nobility to be a polite people, and were beautifully equipped both in clothing as weapons and horse; especially those over 2,000 nobility worthy to watch, who were each winged with two eagle wings from the helmet on their heads down to the knee in beautiful armour, armed with two pairs of pistol, a musqueton or drawn short handgun[38], sabre and kopia lance, on extraordinary strong, big and beautiful horses, also decorated with shining armour, in good order, with kettledrums and trumpets [they looked] more parading as marching'.[39]

An anonymous Imperial officer taking part in the campaign of 1683 (possibly Francois le Bègue), described hussars as follows: 'hussars or otherwise called lancers, which are the best men in the Kingdom, richly dressed, equipped with cottes de mailles [chainmail] and a tiger skin which covers this coat, and we can say that it is the most beautiful sight in the world and they are the bravest people'.[40] It seems that some of the hussars, even in the 1680s, were still using chainmail as additional or even the sole type of armour, probably due both to better mobility and cost. Another account definitely written by Francois le Bègue, described hussars equipped with 'cottes de mailles' (chainmail) and it is unlikely that he would mistake pancerni for hussars.[41] Another anonymous account probably written by an English or Irish officer in Imperial service, also mentioned that Polish hussars 'were all well-armed with Coats of Male'.[42]

When the very delayed Lithuanian hussar banner of Jan III Sobieski arrived at Cracow at the end of October, a group of 20 companions were allowed to visit and kiss the hand of the Queen. Eyewitnesses mentioned that they were 'in leopards and bracers (arm-guard)', which he found unusual, as hussars were not supposed to wear them in front of royalty when not on campaign. Clearly, they wanted to present themselves properly at the court.[43] Odd fashion choices when it came to additional clothing and pelts

36   Wespazjan Kochowski, *Commentarius belli adversus Turcas*, p.23.
37   Marcin Kopiec, *Król Sobieski na Śląsku w kościołach w drodze pod Wiedeń*, p.15.
38   Brulig uses term *stutz* which is equivalent of Polish *krócica* – meaning pistol with short barrel.
39   Bernard Brulig, '*Pat. Bernard Brulig's Bericht über die Belagerung der Stadt Wien im Jahre 1683*', pp.430–431.
40   *Journal de tout ce qui s'est passé entre les Impériaux et les Turcs: durant la campagne de l'année 1683 et 1684*, p.103.
41   Radosław Sikora, *Husaria pod Wiedniem 1683,* pp.90–91.
42   *A true and exact relation of the raising of the siege of Vienna, and the victory obtained over the Ottoman army. The 12th of September 1683* (Dublin: Joseph Ray, 1683), p.6.
43   Władysław Skrzydelka (ed.), *Listy z czasów Jana III i Augusta II* (Kraków: Drukarnia Wincentego Kirchmayera, 1870), p.45, Jan Kaczanowski do Benedykta Sapiehy, Z Krakowa 2ego listopada

could be very confusing to allied German troops and officers. Dyakowski mentioned a situation from the feast in Vienna, where Ernst Rüdiger von Starhemberg hosted the King and his most important commanders and chosen companions. The former was wearing a simple overcoat known as burka[44] while the latter had pelts from exotic cats. While inviting the Poles to the table, Imperial officers said *Domini Tigrides ad primam mensam* and *Domini Tapetes ad secundam mensam*: 'Gentlemen in tigers [are welcome] to the first table' and 'Gentlemen in sheets [are welcome] to the second table'. As none of the Polish soldiers moved seats, the confused Imperials asked what the problem was. The King and the high-ranking officers started to laugh, explaining that 'those in sheets are leading those in tigers'.[45]

Sobieski, both during his service as Hetman and later during his reign as King, wanted to have a strong corps of hussars in the army, understanding how important they were when facing the Ottomans. He put much emphasis on having the correct equipment – especially lances – and of training the soldiers. Even in a time of peace, between 1676 and 1683, he kept a core number of hussar banners as a part of the regular army, which gave them plenty of opportunities to improve their skills, on both an individual and unit level. After the relief of Vienna, when the Polish army was visited by the Emperor, Leopold I asked to see soldiers exercising with the lance. Sobieski ordered Jabłonowski to prepare the show by choosing experienced men, 'to show honour of our army'. The Hetman chose 24 officers and companions from different banners, even supplying some of them with his own horses if their mounts were not ready. The detachment was then divided into two groups of 12, who were ordered to charge against each other and, at the moment where they were near the point of their lance hitting their opponents' breast, to suddenly put their weapons up, avoiding the blow. Even though the hussars did not have time to practice such an unusual manoeuvre, they succeeded without any incidents. The Emperor was very pleased with the show and one can only assume that Sobieski and Jabłonowski were as well.[46] The previously mentioned English or Irish officer described it as follows: 'having viewed the whole Polish Army, the great Mareschal [Grand Hetman Jabłonowski] commanded the said Hussars to make the course which they are used to make, when they go invest the Enemy, wherewith his Imperial Majesty was highly pleased'.[47]

Through the whole of the 1680s the lance was still the primary weapon for hussars, although a new trend began to appear at the end of this period, when in 1689 Grand Hetman Jabłonowski ordered retainers to abandon lances and use bandolets (carbines) as their primary weapon. This was directly connected with fighting against the Tatars as their main opponents, where firearms were much more useful in the 'small war' against them. In

---

1683.

44 Popular during Jan III Sobieski's reign, they were made from camel wool. Used as travelling coat, giving protection against the rain, and the fashion came to Poland from the Tatars.

45 Mikołaj Dyakowski, p.69.

46 *Ibidem,* pp.73–74.

47 A true and exact relation of the raising of the siege of Vienna, p.6.

1693 all companions and retainers that were to serve in the fortress of Okopy Świętej Trójcy[48] (today the village Okopy in western Ukraine) were to be equipped with 'leopard [pelts], armour, arm-guards, with long firearm (…) on good horses [and] with brace of pistols'.[49] Such an order is not surprising considering that the main role of this fortress was to block supply lines between Turkish-held Kamianets-Podilskyi and Moldavia, where supply convoys were always escorted by Tatars. Even when not equipped with lances, hussars were still well armed, with a combination of melee weapons (sabre, estoc or pallasch) and firearms, making them formidable opponents in fights against the Ottoman and Tatar cavalry.

Karacena armour of Crown Grand Hetman Stanisław Jabłonowski, dated between 1680 and 1700. (National Museum, Cracow)

Service in a hussar banner was a very expensive matter, as each companion had to buy equipment, weapons and horses not only for himself but also for his retainers and servants. There were only certain items that were provided by either the national treasury or, more often, by the *rotmistrz* himself, such as a unit's flag, lances, lanceheads (bought separately) and pennants. In 1676, when *rotmistrz* Jan Gniński signed a contract with his Lieutenant Jacek Boratyński, their agreement mentioned that Gniński would provide 5,000zł 'above what will be paid by Commonwealth' to purchase lanceheads, and that he will purchase in Lwów 'flag, lances and pennants' for his unit.[50] During the campaign of 1683 the King ordered lances for his hussar banners

---

48   Which translates as Ramparts of the Holy Trinity.

49   Jan Sowa, 'Ludzie niezwalczeni'. Rejestry chorągwi jazdy autoramentu narodowego w Okopach Św. Trójcy, 1693–1695, *Studia nad staropolską sztuką wojenną*, volume II (Oświęcim: Wydawnictwo Napoleon V, 2013), p.265.

50   Zbigniew Hundert, *Husaria koronna w wojnie polsko-tureckiej 1672–1676* (Oświęcim: Wydawnictwo Napoleon V, 2012), p.251

(in both the Polish and Lithuanian armies), and probably also for those units under his sons' names.

There are many examples of hussar banners' muster rolls, showing us the composition of the units and strengths of the retinues. A few of these from the first quarter of 1676, during the final stage of the 1672–1676 war with Ottomans can be analysed to understand the structure of the units. Considering that the *romistrz* was usually just an honorary position and he was not in fact present with the banner, we can see how a fairly large percentage of unit's strength was wasted on so called 'dead pay'.

King Jan III Sobieski's banner under Lieutenant Aleksander Polanowski[51]

Number of horses in retinue	Number of retinues of that type in banner	Additional comments
24	1	*Rotmistrz* retinue
1	1 (see comments)	Lieutenant's retinue
3	1 (see comments)	Standard-bearer's retinue
3	57	

Total: 60 retinues with 199 horses.

Royal Prince Jakub Sobieski's banner under Lieutenant Michał Kozubski[52]

Number of horses in retinue	Number of retinues of that type in banner	Additional comments
15	1	*Rotmistrz* retinue
1	1 (see comments)	Lieutenant's retinue
1	1 (see comments)	Standard-bearer's retinue
3	34	
2	1	

Total: 38 retinues with 120 horses (in fact 121).

51 *Ibidem*, p.118.
52 *Ibidem*, p.118.

Szczęsny Potocki's banner under Lieutenant Remigian Strzałkowski[53]

Number of horses in retinue	Number of retinues of that type in banner	Additional comments
15	1	*Rotmistrz* retinue
4	1 (see comments)	Lieutenant's retinue
4	1 (see comments)	Standard-bearer's retinue
3	33	
2	4	
Additional staff (not counted towards retinues)	See comments	Chaplain, surgeon, drummer, other musicians (trumpeters)

Total: 40 retinues with 131 horses (in fact 130).

Andrzej Potocki's banner under Lieutenant Mikołajzłotnicki[54]

Number of horses in retinue	Number of retinues of that type in banner	Additional comments
16	1	*Rotmistrz* retinue
3	1 (see comments)	Lieutenant's retinue
3	1 (see comments)	Standard-bearer's retinue
3	30	
2	4	
Additional staff (not counted towards retinues)	See comments	Chaplain, surgeon, drummer, other musicians (trumpeters)

Total: 37 retinues with 120 horses.

For the purpose of the new war against the Ottomans, the hussar corps was enlarged, by creating new units and by strengthening existing ones. Those banners already in service were to be expanded by the addition of between 20 and 50 horses. Thanks to surviving documents and the further work of modern researchers[55] the composition of this formation in 1683 can be reconstructed:

53 *Ibidem*, p.120.
54 *Ibidem*, p.121.
55 Jan Wimmer, *Wiedeń 1683,* pp.219–221, 235–236; Radosław Sikora, *Husaria pod Wiedniem, passim;* Zbigniew Hundert, 'Organizacja husarii koronnej na kampanię wiedeńską 1683 roku', pp.166–196; Zbigniew Hundert, 'Jeszcze o organizacji husarii koronnej na kampanię wiedeńską 1683 r.', pp.9–24.

Rotmistrz	Lieutenant (if known)	Paper strength	Muster from 1 August 1683	Notes
King Jan III	Aleksander Polanowski	200	159	
Royal Prince Jakub	Mikołaj Złotnicki	200	184	
Royal Prince Aleksander	Zygmunt Zbierzchowski	200	149	
Crown Grand Hetman Stanisław Jabłonowski	Michał Florian Rzewuski	200	200	
Crown Field Hetman Mikołaj Hieronim Sieniawski	Nikodem Żaboklicki	200	200	
Jan Małachowski	Stanisław Małachowski	120	118	
Stanisław Dąmbski (Dąbski)	Konstanty Kaliński	100	97	Kaliński died during the first battle of Párkány 7 October 1683
Andrzej Potocki	Stanisław Potocki, after him Krzysztof Skarbek	150	121	Stanisław Potocki died during the battle of Vienna 12 September 1683
Szczęsny Kazimierz Potocki	Krzysztof Skarbek, after him probably Kazimierz Chrząstowski	120	120	
Marcin Zamoyski	Stefan Stanisław Ważyński	150	150	
Samuel Prażmowski,	Jan Zygmunt Strzałkowski	120	108	
Wacław Leszczyński,	Unknown	120	91	
Franciszek Bieliński	Unknown	120	118	
Władysław Denhoff,	Jarosz (Hieronim) Rosnowski	80	-	Unit was late for battle of Vienna. Denhoff died during the first battle of Párkány 7 October 1683
Stanisław Herakliusz Lubomirski	Maciej Radzimiński (Radzymiński)	120	120	
Jan Gniński	Jacek Boratyński	120	118	
Jan Wielopolski	Krzysztof Łasko			
Wojciech Urbański	Andrzej Siemianowski	120	112	Siemianowski died during the first battle of Párkány 7 October 1683
Jan Dobrogost Krasiński	Kazimierz Minor	150	128	
Rafał Leszczyński	Unknown	150	133	
Michał Warszycki,	Jarosz (Hieronim) Lipiński	150	135	
Józef Karol Lubomirski	Władysław Wilczkowski	150	124	Wilczkowski died from dysentery after the battle of Vienna
Stefan Branicki	Unknown, possibly Jędrzej (Andrzej) Siemianowski	150	144	
Marcin Cieński	Unknown	100	71	
Stanisław Myszkowski	Possibly Mikołaj Radecki,	100	96	
Aleksander Cetner	Andrzej Kamiński or Jerzy Konstanty Kamiński	100	100	

There is a crucial question to be answered – what were the hussars' tactics, how they were deployed and how did they fight? By the time of Sobieski hussars tended to fight in two ranks, with companions placed in first one, although as seen in Dalerac's description he said that they deployed in three ranks. As hussars were shock troops, relying on the impact of the charge and long reach of their lances, they gradually increased the speed of their attack, starting with lances held up and normally lowered mid-way to the enemy. While they could deploy in loose ranks, especially when facing heavy firepower, the charge itself was performed in close order ranks, 'knee to knee'. Once the lances were shattered on impact, the hussars switched to their secondary weapons, which of course could vary, depending on the opponent, i.e. estocs against infantry, heavy pallasch or sabre against horsemen.

Royal Prince Jakub Ludwik Sobieski, who took part in the campaign, mentioned the very interesting practice of joining hussars and pancerni into combined squadrons. The King 'mustered his hussars [banner] and other

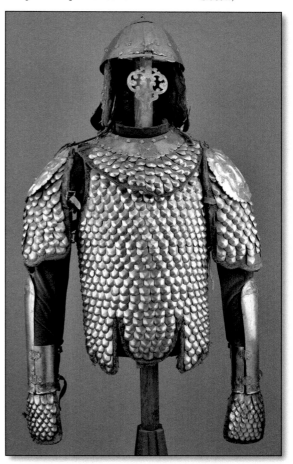

Karacena armour of Crown Field Hetman Hieronim Sieniawski. (National Museum, Cracow)

that were looking at it were told to do what he ordered; dividing them into two ranks, with first one moving slowly in close order, where [soldiers'] feet were touching each other and with two banners of pancerni joining them: they marched in this way and cover large ground'.[56] Dupont also mentioned that each hussar banner was fighting in two ranks, always with two banners of pancerni on its flanks.[57] It was a technique used previously during 1672–1676 war against Turks and Tatars, with a banner of hussars having a banner of pancerni on each flank. Thanks to this deployment hussars received additional fire cover from the attached pancerni, while the latter could take advantage of the success of the lance-armed hussars and more effectively utilise their own combination of weapons. As will be seen in the description of the Battle of Vienna, when Sobieski attached some of his cavalry to the Imperial troops fighting on the left flank of allied army, he seems to have followed the squadron structure as mentioned in Royal Prince Jakub's diary, by sending three banners of hussars and six of pancerni, in effect providing his allies with three battle squadrons. Of course if needed, the hussars could operate on their own, without the support of other cavalry units but as will be evident from the early stages of the battle of Vienna this could lead to high and often unnecessary losses.

56   Jakub Ludwik Sobieski, *Dyaryusz wyprawy wiedeńskliej w 1683 r*, p.9.
57   Dupont, p.196.

Pancerni, petyhorcy and cossack cavalry

By the time of the Vienna campaign, *pancerni* cavalry were the most common formation in the Polish army. The name means 'armoured', and it became more commonly used from 1640s, initially to highlight better-equipped units of cossack cavalry, then gradually, and especially from the 1670s, it was used as a new name for cossack cavalry as a whole. Interestingly, the term 'cossack cavalry' was still sometimes used as an alternative to *pancerni* and to distinguish some units not as well armoured or equipped as the others. In the Lithuanian army there were *petyhorcy* cavalry, equipped in a similar way to *pancerni* in Poland, with the main difference being the lance or half-lance used by Lithuanians (see below for more on this subject). *Pancerni* were easily recognised due to their distinctive chainmail armour *(kolczuga)*, with some, especially officers, using plate or even scale armour as well. Of course the requirement that all soldiers were equipped with chainmail was often hard to follow, especially during a long campaign, so cavalry banners often presented a mix of armoured and unarmoured soldiers. The round eastern shield *(kałkan)* was also very common, despite not being part of the official equipment. Their main weapons were sabres, a brace of pistols and either a bow (used only by companions) or long firearms (carbine, bandolet or musketoon). As in the case of the hussars, other additional weapons

Polish *pancerni* cavalryman, equipped with a horseman's pickaxe and carbine. Romeyn de Hooghe, 1687 (Rijksmuseum)

were used as well: horsemen's picks, axes, sometimes even estocs. One interesting insight into the organisation and equipment of early *pancerni* cavalry comes from September 1671, when nobles from Halicz (part of the Ruthenian Voivodship) decided to raise two banners of provincial troops to protect their territory. Units were to be composed 'of good nobles, not Wallachians, [with] proper equipment on good horses with good retainers, all with [chain] mail [and] with good firearms'.[58]

The spear, known usually under the Polish name of *rohatyna* or *dzida*, became widely used in the 1670s. In 1673, during the battle of Chocim (Khotyn), the majority of Lithuanian cavalry were already equipped with spears. In March 1676 King Jan III Sobieski, in his document describing requirements for further war against the Ottomans, mentions that all 'cossack[59] and light cavalry should be equipped with *dzida* spear, as it is weapon that seems to be better,

---

58   *Akta grodzkie i ziemskie z Archiwum Ziemskiego we Lwowie. Lauda sejmikowe halickie 1575–1697, volume XXIV* (Lwów: Towarzystwo Naukowe, 1931), p.327.

59   By which he means *pancerni*, as both names were still used alternatively.

more needed and easier in use that [those] used by petyhorcy'.[60] While it is possible that all pancerni and light cavalry banners planned for 1683 were also to be equipped with such weapons, it is more than likely that at least some of them had carried them on the march to Austria. It appears that there were many logistical problems with equipping troops with the correct weapons. At the end of August 1683 Jan III wrote in his letter to the Queen about this; 'there are many banners without lances and spears here. I gave away many of those that belong to me; even Lithuanian ones,[61] as no one heard about those rogues here'. He had to improvise and 'order, on my own cost, to make spears and [make] pennants [for them]; I will give them away to other banners'.[62] He repeated his sentiment on 9 September, writing 'no lances, nor spears were sent to us [from Poland]'.[63]

When describing armour and weapons of *pancerni,* it is important to remember that even officers, those in rank of *rotmistrz* and lieutenant, could be equipped in this way. Andrzej Modrzewski, Crown Court Treasurer, during the 1683 campaign was *rotmistrz* of a *pancerni* banner. As a volunteer he joined a reconnaissance party with Prince Aleksander's winged hussars and, as he attacked ahead of the rest of troops, he was surrounded and killed by the Turks. His servant Stanisław Chróściński, in a detailed account of his master's last fight (which will be explored later) mentioned that Modrzewski had chainmail and a *misiurka* helmet, with his weapons being a spear, a brace of pistols and a sabre.[64] Stanisław Potocki, who was leading his own *pancerni* banner, was also described as wearing chainmail, when he died supporting banners of hussars during another similar incident.[65]

As with hussars, there are some interesting comments made by foreigners about such cavalry. Dupont described *pancerni* in the campaign of 1673 as follows:

'it numbers between 15,000 to 16,000. Instead of armour, those soldiers have chainmail worn over clothes, also [chain] hoods and chain gloves. Main weapon is spear. During the march soldiers place the end of it in the left stirrup and lean it over left shoulder. This spear is 12 feet long. On its end there is a taffeta pennant, five to six feet long, in the colour chosen by [the unit's] commander. *Pancerni* also have a sabre and a brace of pistols. Each banner is composed of 100 companions and 100 archers.[66] Their horses are as beautiful as the hussars' ones, and they also

60 'Sposoby i porządek obrony Rzpltej podczas wojny tureckiej (marzec 1676 r.)', *Przegląd Historyczno-Wojskowy,* volume II, part 1 (Warszawa: Główna Księgarnia Wojskowa, 1930), p.146.

61 Prepared for the Lithuanian units of which the King was nominal *rotmistrz.*

62 Antoni Zygmunt Helcel (ed.), *Listy Jana Sobieskiego do żony Marii Kazimiery,* p.376. Jan III do Marii Kazimiery, Z Heiligenbron, mil 3 od Tulmu, gdzie most budują, ultima Augusti.

63 *Ibidem,* p.381, Jan III do Marii Kazimiery, Za Dunajem u mostu pod Tulnem, 9 Septembera, rano o piątej.

64 Filip Friedman (ed.), 'Nieznana relacja o batalii wiedeńskiej 1683 roku', *Przegląd Historyczno-Wojskowy,* volume VII, part 1 (Warszawa: Główna Księgarnia Wojskowa, 1935), p.136.

65 Dalerac, *Polish Manuscripts,* p.96.

66 In this context he means retainers, who would not normally be equipped with bows.

have grand horse tacks. Only nobles are allowed to serve here. All magnates that oversee the company of hussars, also have a *pancerni* banner'.[67]

The German Ulrich von Werdum (Ulryk Werdum), who spent two years – between 1670 and 1672 – in Poland as part of the spy mission of Jean de Courthonne (aka 'Monsieur Beauval'), had many occasions to see the Polish army in action. He mentioned 'cuirassiers, known by Poles as *pancerni*, because instead of armour they have chainmail (Jacque de Mailles) and instead of helmet a flat cap with mail around the head, falling down on shoulders'.[68]

Another oft-quoted Frenchmen, Dalerac, provides a very detailed description of this formation, based on his experience from the 1680s:

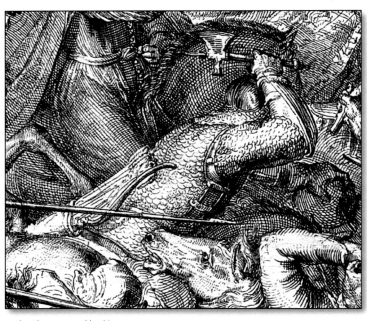

A rather unusual looking hussar or pancerny, with 'karacena' armour, armed with bow and short axe. Romeyn de Hooghe, 1687 (Rijksmuseum)

The second sort of Gens d'Arms is the Pancernes, who are somewhat inferior to the Hussars, but much higher than all the rest of the Cavalry. They are called so from their Armour, which is a Coat of Mail, in the Polish Tongue Pancernick, with an Iron Cap, encompassed with Net-work of the same, which covers all to their Shoulders, and shewing [showing] only half of Visage, makes them look like Satyrs, because of the great M[o]ustaches ordinarily worn by the Poles. Those Pancernes are arm'd with Falchons[69] and Musquetoons, like Light Horse, as well mounted as the Hussars, but not so richly equipped. They are upon all Guards that require fatigue, are form'd into Squadrons as the other, with a Standard of the same form, their Drums are also the same; but in lieu of a Trumpet they have a certain little Instrument of Copper, not much bigger than a Flagelet, crooked and hollow like a Cornet, which makes the thrillest and most Savage Noise imaginable. It is supposed to be the Lotuss of the Ancients. Those Companies have less Pay than the Hussars but are on the same footing as to their Servants, who make up the two last Ranks, and are also called Pacolets. They pass however for Light Horse, that is to say, Lightly Armed, for in other respects they are true Gens d' Arms by their dignity, and commanded by Lords, the King himself and the Princes having each of 'em a Company in the two Armies.[70]

---

67   Dupont, p.83.

68   Ulryk Werdum, *Dziennik podróży 1670–1672. Dziennik wyprawy polowej 1671* (Warszawa: Muzeum Pałacu Króla Jana III w Wilanowie, 2012), p.123.

69   By which he means sabres.

70   Dalerac, *Polish Manuscripts*, p.20.

What is more interesting, Dalerac also wrote about the Lithuanian *petyhorcy* cavalry, pointing out their difference from hussars and *pancerni*:[71]

> Besided these two sorts, ther is a third in the Great Dutchy of Lithuania, armed like Pancernes and having Lances as the Hussars, but not quite so long; nor are their Streamers so large; and from this difference, they have different Names: Those of the Hussars are called Kopies, from the Latine word Copia, Forces; and those of the other are call'd Gides,[72] which is a Word in use in that Country, and also amongst the Turks, as it likewise that sort of Lance. I saw only four Companies of them in the Lithuanian Army, that of the Crown having almost none of'em, but there's nothing finer than those I saw in that Dutchy, the Hussars not being more magnificent in either of the Armies. At present they have left off their Gides and are upon the same footing with the Pancernes, they are call'd Peteores, and are likewise honoured with the Quality of Tourachies.

Pancerny or *petyhorzec* from Jakub Kazimierz Haur's *Skład albo skarbiec znakomity sekretów o ekonomiej ziemianskiej*, published in Cracow in 1693 (National Library, Warsaw)

Brulig had seen all types of Polish cavalry marching through Moravia in 1683 and he noted the wide variety in their equipment and weapons. Some, which clearly sound like well-equipped *pancerni*, were composed of armoured nobles, and amongst their different weapons also used bows, while their musicians 'kept partly with kettledrums and trumpets and partly with drums and shawms' and were marching in good order. Many banners had a large range of weaponry, 'bow and arrow, carbine, sabres, and kopia[73] lances', with some 'without kopia lance and carbine, only with pistols and bow and arrow' and other 'with kopia lance and single pistol instead of carbine'.[74] Such a description clearly matches Polish sources which also mention the problems of equipping troops with spears and is further proof of the rather loose approach of Polish cavalrymen towards any regulations regarding weaponry in their units.

O'Connor, writing in 1694, confirmed that *pancerni* and Lithuanian *petyhorcy* used chainmail, while as their weapons he mentioned 'Darts[75] and Sabres'. He added some interesting detail saying that 'if they please, they may wear Wings and Feathers'.[76] It is interesting to observe, that in the Lithuanian units of *petyhorcy* that were not equipped with lances they tended to be called *pancerni* (to add further to the confusion in terminology) and they received lower pay (than the *pancerni* in Poland).[77]

71   Dalerac, *Polish Manuscripts*, pp.21–22.
72   (Pol.) *Dzida*, meaning spear.
73   Most likely spears, not lances. It is unlikely that *pancerni* were equipped with lances.
74   Bernard Brulig, 'Pat. Bernard Brulig's Bericht über die Belagerung der Stadt Wien im Jahre 1683', p.431.
75   These had to be spears, used as a main weapon.
76   Bernard Connor, *The history of Poland*, vol. 2, letter VI, p.10.
77   The author would like to thank to Zbigniew Hundert for highlighting this issue.

Trumpeter and kettle-drummer of the Polish cavalry. Romeyn de Hooghe, 1687 (Rijksmuseum)

Andrzej Maksymian Fredro, who wrote his theoretical work in 1670, shows a clear disregard towards the cossack and *pancerni* cavalry. He did not agree with cavalry using a combination of bows and short spears, claiming that these were weapons most useful for skirmishing and they should be abandoned by cavalry fighting 'knee to knee' in ranked formations. His theory was to rely instead on *petyhorcy,* whom he also called light hussars. Their main weapon should be *rohatyna* spear, five to seven ells long and, as with hussars' lances, it should not have pennant. He described it as good against 'German reiters, [Zaporozhian] Cossacks on foot and mounted Tatars, as being a light weapon, one can easily use it when manoeuvring'.[78] Such *petyhorzec* should have good horse, and 'helmet, breastplate or good padded jack and arm-guards'. As well as the *rohatyna,* each man should be equipped with a bandolet (long firearm) and at least one pistol.[79] Fredro mentioned that if a soldier was unable to have armour, he should at least have *kałkan* shield. As headgear, especially to replace normal caps, he suggested the use of a small *szyszak* helmet, with some extra cloth inside, 'as it provides better protection (especially with cheek guards) and it is warmer than caps during winter weather and will not distract the soldier [by moving] during the fight'.[80] Kochowski wrote a short passage about this cavalry in his history of the war of 1683, in which he explained that they were categorised this way, as their main equipment was chainmail, quae Lorica alias Pancerz, hinc Pancerne Roty.[81] The Papal Nuncio Antonio Pignatelli also highlighted the connection of equipment and the name of the formations, writing that 'they are known as Pancerne in Polish, Loricati in Latin and what can be described in Italian as covered in [chain] mails'.[82] In November 1684, Bishop Stanisław Wojeński, writing about the campaign of 1684, mentioned 'Panzerni, also [composed of] nobles, wearing Giacco[83] and chainmail, and as almost as formidable as the others [hussars]'.[84]

The *kalkan* shield was a common item in the cavalry (except the hussars), but Dalerac mentioned it in his book as something already going out of

---

78   Andrzej Maksymilian Fredro, *Potrzebne consideratie,* p.35.
79   *Ibidem,* p.42.
80   *Ibidem,* pp.34–35.
81   Wespazjan Kochowski, *Commentarius belli adversus Turcas,* p.23.
82   Franciszek Kluczycki (ed.), *Akta do dziejów Króla Jana IIIgo sprawy roku 1683,* p.316.
83   It seems to be the word used to describe the outer garment or coat, so it probably in this case meant *kontusz* or *żupan.*
84   *Compendiosa e veridical relazione di quanto ha operato nella scorsa campagna l'armata del re di Polonia contro quelle de'Turchi e Tartari nella Podolia,* p.13.

fashion in the 1690s, and used mostly by officials. While this is contrary to other sources, as we know that the shield was still employed by companions and retainers alike until the end of Sobieski's reign, it is interesting to see what Dalerac wrote about them, especially in context of 1683:[85]

Pancerni charging Tatars.
Romeyn de Hooghe, 1687
(Rijksmuseum)

The Poles had formerly Bucklers of Ozier, cover'd with Skins, of a round Figure a little rais'd, pointed in the middle, where there was a piece of Iron, the use of which is now almost abolished. I have seen some Lords carry them in a day of Review or Battle, not so much for Defence as for Ornament; for on such Occasions they fix them to the Saddles of their Led-Horses. When the King march'd to the Relief of Vienna, he had a mind to review his Cavalry in the Plain of Tarnovitz, the first City of Silesia, before Count Caraffa, who was sent by the Emperor to receive his Allie at the entrance of his Dominions. The King drew them up in Order of Battle the morning before his March, that the Emperor's Ministers might see the Beauty of his Troops. The Polish Senators, who had there their Troops of Hussars or Pancernes, appear'd at the Head of 'em with all the Warlike Ornaments of the Nation; their Rich Murrions, Gilt Harness, Magnificent Houzes, splendid Coats of Mail, and some of them had Bucklers of great price, for so I think we may call 300 Ducats of Gold for a Buckler of Ozier. It's true they alledge that they are proof against Shot, but for anything that appears by them, there's nothing to commend them but a pleasant variety of Colours, and a Satin Quilt in the inside.

It was noted earlier that *petyhorcy* were usually slightly better equipped than *pancerni*, using a sort of lance, which could lead to confusion amongst eyewitness, especially those not well versed with the military customs of the Commonwealth. Radosław Sikora points out that a few German accounts from the battle of Vienna, including one written by Francois le Bègue and another by Johann Georg II, Prince of Anhalt Dessau, mentioned 30 companies of hussars – more than were known to be present there – and that some of those accounts described hussars as equipped with chainmail. This could suggest that some of those 'hussars' were in fact *petyhorcy*.[86] The main problem with such sources is that it is known that there were no Lithuanian units present at Vienna and that officially none of Polish *pancerni* units were

---

85   Dalerac, *Polish Manuscripts*, pp.31–32.
86   Radosław Sikora, *Husaria pod Wiedniem 1683*, pp.90–94.

equipped with lances as were the *petyhorcy*. It is possible that there were some private units armed this way or even that some of the officers equipped their pancerni banners with lances, but unfortunately so far, no evidence of such practice has come to light.[87]

As with the winged hussars, some of the muster rolls for banners of *pancerni* from the 1670s, give an interesting insight into the structure and organisation of their units.

Pancerni banner of Crown Field Hetman Stanisław Jabłonowski, 1 May 1678:[88]

Number of horses in retinue	Number of retinues of that type in banner	Additional comments
15	1(see comments)	*Rotmistrz* retinue
3	1 (see comments)	Lieutenant's retinue
3	1 (see comments)	Standard-bearer's retinue
3	15	
2	27	
Additional staff (not counted towards retinues)	See comments	Musicians (no further information)

Total: 45 retinues with 120 horses.

Pancerni banner of Szczęsny Potocki, 1 May 1677:[89]

Number of horses in retinue	Number of retinues of that type in banner	Additional comments
7 ½	1(see comments)	*Rotmistrz* retinue
4	1 (see comments)	Lieutenant's retinue
2	22	
1 ½	1	
1	3	
Additional staff (not counted towards retinues)	See comments	Trumpeter, surgeon, drummer

Total: 28 retinues with 60 horses. The unit did not have a designated standard-bearer.

---

87   Zbigniew Hundert, 'Kilka uwag na temat chorągwi petyhorskich w wojskach Rzeczypospolitej w latach 1673–1683', *W pancerzu przez wieki. Z dziejów wojskowości polskiej i powszechnej*, Marcin Baranowski, Andrzej Gładysz, Andrzej Niewiński (ed.) (Oświęcim: Napoleon V, 2014), p.141.

88   AGAD, ASW, dz. 85, no 115, pp.45–45v.

89   AGAD, ASW, dz. 85, no 115, pp.61–61v.

Pancerni banner of Andrzej Sierakowski, 1 February 1679:[90]

Number of horses in retinue	Number of retinues of that type in banner	Additional comments
6	1 (see comments)	*Rotmistrz* retinue
3	1 (see comments)	Standard-bearer's retinue
2	19	
1	1	
Additional staff (not counted towards retinues)	See comments	Surgeon, drummer

Total: 22 retinues with 48 horses but the banner was paid for 50 horses. The unit did not have a designated lieutenant.

Pancerni banner of Stefan Czarniecki, 1 February 1679:[91]

Number of horses in retinue	Number of retinues of that type in banner	Additional comments
12	1 (see comments)	*Rotmistrz* retinue
3	1 (see comments)	Lieutenant's retinue
3	6	
2	26	
1	7	
Additional staff (not counted towards retinues)	See comments	Drummer, trumpeter

Total: 41 retinues with 92 horses but the muster was recorded as 100 horses despite the numbers not matching. This unit did not have a designated standard-bearer.

Based on surviving documents and modern research[92] it is possible to try to reconstruct all the banners serving in the Polish army in 1683. There were also a few additional units, probably raised as private banners and outside of the official army register, that served in 1683 either as part of the relief force or in the defence force left in Poland and that later became part of the regular force. Some units below seem to have been planned, and even received their initial pay, but for various reasons never entered service.

---

90   AGAD, ASW, dz. 85, no 115, p.117.
91   AGAD, ASW, dz. 85, no 115, pp.144–144v.
92   Jan Wimmer, *Wiedeń 1683*, pp.221–229, Marek Wagner, *Słownik biograficzny oficerów polskich drugiej połowy XVII wieku, volume I, passim*, BCzart, no 2589, pp.97–102, AGAD, ASK, II, 68, Rachunki sejmowe na sejm 1685, pp.12–14v.

Rotmistrz	Lieutenant (if known)	Strength	Muster from 1 August 1683
King Jan III Sobieski	Aleksander Wronowski	200	190
Grand Hetman Jabłonowski	Roman Linkiewicz (Lenkiewicz)	200	192
Field Hetman Sieniawski	Prokop Jan Granowski	200	200
Andrzej Potocki	Mikołaj Poniatowski	150	111
Szczęsny Kazimierz Potocki	Michał Liniewski	150	107
Michał Jerzy Czartoryski		100	121
Konstanty Wiśniowiecki		150	145
Mikołaj Sapieha		120	92
Hieronim Augustyn Lubomirski	Stanisław Świeżyński	200	123
Franciszek Dzieduszycki		120	90
Jerzy Wielhorski		150	150
Stanisław Karol Łużecki	Jakub Rozwadowski	150	131
Stefan Czarniecki		150	121
Stefan Bidziński		150	134
Marcjan Ścibor Chełmski	Krzysztof Dobiński	150	90
Józef Słuszka	Michał Wilkoński	120	98
Mikołaj Daniłowicz		120	118
Michał Warszycki		150	112
Andrzej Modrzewski		150	119
Wojciech Prażmowski		120	90
Aleksander Chodorowski	Maciej Dobrosławski	120	95
Józef Lubomirski	Stefan Garbowski	150	140
Józef Stefan Zahorowski		120	109
Atanazy Miączyński	Andrzej Gęsicki	150	136
Władysław Morsztyn		120	81
Stanisław Potocki		120	86
Piotr Daniłowicz	Franciszek Suchodolski	150	147
Adam Mikołaj Sieniawski		150	134
Remigian Strzałkowski		120	104
Franciszek Sebastian Lubomirski		150	68
Tomasz Karczewski	Rafał Aleksander Janicki	150	114
Michał Zbrożek	Rajecki	150	128
Stanisław Cetner		100	81
Jan Andrzej Sierakowski		120	118
Marcin Bogusz		120	117
Stanisław Sariusz Łaźniński		120	91
Jan Koniecpolski	Konstanty Koźmiński	120	107
Andrzej Miączyński		100	78
Jan Franciszek Stadnicki		120	104
Bogusław Potocki		100	84
Stanisław Miączyński		100	72
Andrzej Rzeczycki	Aleksander Garczyński	120	105
Michał Florian Rzewuski		120	119
Stanisław Tarło		120	96
Stanisław Opaliński		120	108
Melchior Grudziński		120	118
Stanisław Druszkiewicz		120	105

Jan Łącki		120	119
Jerzy Jan Wandalin Mniszech		120	117
Kazimierz Widlica Domaszewski		100	100
Franciszek Makowiecki		100	100
Aleksander Łaszcz		100	95
Jakub Rokitnicki		100	65
Nikodem Żaboklicki		120	111
Aleksander Przyłuski		100	100
Jan Stanisław Giżycki		100	100
Tomasz Bogusz/Dymitr Zabokrzycki		100	100
Marcin Ubysz		100	100
Michał Wasilkowski		100	92
Jerzy Skarżyński		100	100
Wiktoryn Bykowski		100	81
Adam Radliński		120	73
Kazimierz Grudziński		120	101
Teodor Tyszkiewicz		100	87
Kazimierz Ledóchowski		100	91
Wojciech Łubieński		100	100
Tomasz Kazimierz Głuski		100	96
Aleksander Bogusz/Józef Szumlański		100	88
Dymitr Jełowiecki (Jełowicki)		100	97
Felicjan Białogłowski	Stefan Horodyszczyn	100	98
Stefan Andrzej Dymidecki	Aleksander Chomentowski (Chomętowski)	100	91
Krzysztof Modrzewski		100	74
Stanisław Potocki	Tyszkowski	100	92
Stefan Grudziński		60	60
Stanisław Witwicki		100	90
Mikołaj Szczawiński		100	90
Wojciech Stępkowski		100	85
Aleksander Drzewicki (Drzewiecki)	Mikołaj Belczycki	100	92
Marcin Zamoyski		120	120
Hieronim Lanckoroński		100	99
Jakub Czarnowski		120	120
Franciszek Koryciński		120	120
Wojciech Dąbski		100	?
Hieronim Siemiaszko		100	85
Dominik Potocki		70	Probably not raised or serving as private unit
Jan Bogusław Zbąski		70	Only serving until November 1683, no strength
Michał Franciszek Czartoryski		100	
Jan Gałęzowski		100	Only serving until November 1683, no strength
Piotr Bielawski		100	
Adam Bełzecki		100	

Pancerni tactics have already been briefly mentioned, when describing their attachment to the hussars. Unfortunately no written regulation describing how this formation was supposed to fight has been found, and it is possible that no such document was ever created during the seventeenth century. Period sources tend to be very vague when describing the fighting methods of *pancerni,* with overall notes stating that 'they charged', 'they hit the enemy', 'they gave fire', etc. The organisation of the banners and size of retinues indicates that, as with hussars, both *pancerni* and *petyhorcy* were deployed in two, or a maximum of three ranks. They could form joint squadrons with the hussars or operate in squadrons only composed of their own type, depending upon the situation and available troops. With their varied range of armament, *pancerni* were in fact a sort of jack-of-all-trades, as they could act as shock cavalry employing their spears, as fire support with bows and firearms or even as skirmishers, engaging Turkish and Tatar horse. While *petyhorcy* seem to be slightly more specialised, being seen as 'light hussars' when using lances, they could of course be employed in the same way as *pancerni.*

Arkabuzeria and reiters

It is interesting to note that in the 1670s and 1680s the Polish army officially did not have any units of Western-style cavalry, known in the Commonwealth as reiters. They were still present however, with a token representation of one banner of 100 horses in the Lithuanian army. Unofficially, the reiters were still part of the Polish army, disguised under name of *arkabuzeria*. In the first half of seventeenth century such a term was used to describe an unusual type of cavalry, armoured as Western European cuirassiers, armed with 'three firearms' but recruited in the same way as Polish cavalry, with retinues made of companions and retainers. In the 1660s the name was reintroduced as a disguise for the few units of reiters that remained in the Polish army. Masses of the nobility were strongly against employing Western-style cavalry, seeing in them, as foreign troops, an element that could be used by the King in their struggles against the nobles. Additionally, reiters were very expensive troops, in the late 1660s being paid 14zł more per month than hussars (reiters: 65zł, hussars: 51zł).[93] Despite strong pressure to disband all of their units, one regiment of *arkabuzeria* was kept in the Polish army after 1671, thanks to the political connections of its commander Maciej Ścibor Chełmski (as one of Hetman Jan Sobieski's faction) and possibly due to the forthcoming war against the Ottomans. The odd dual terminology of this cavalry formation can be even found in King Michał Korybut Wiśniowiecki's proclamation about keeping the unit in service, where it was called a 'reiter regiment [of] *arkabuzeria*'.[94] A few new units were created during the 1672–1676 war against

---

93   Mirosław Nagielski, 'Organizacja rajtarii i arkebuzerii koronnej w XVII wieku, Karol Łopatecki (ed.), *Organizacja armii w nowożytnej Europie. Struktura-urzędy-prawo-finanse* (Zabrze: Inforteditions, 2011), p.197.

94   Zbigniew Hundert, *Między buławą a tronem*, p.238.

the Ottomans, but at the end of the conflict, after the army reduction in 1677, only one small squadron of 100 horses under the command of Jan Górzyński (Górzeński) was left in service.[95] The unit became part of Jan III's guard and as part of the preparations for the campaign of 1683 was expanded to 300 horses. Additionally, two new companies, under the nominal command of each hetman, joined the army:

Nominal commander of the unit	Strength	Notes
King Jan III	300	Guard squadron under Jan Górzyński. Mustered on 1 August 1683 with 293 horses.
Grand Hetman Jabłonowski	100	Under Lt. Colonel Joachim Wilhelm von Venediger and Captain Jerzy von Glasenapp
Grand Hetman Sieniawski	100	Mustered on 1 August 1683 with higher strength of 197 men

All three units took an active part in relief of Vienna, fighting in the all the main battles. Colonel Jan Górzyński died on 12 September 1683, while an unknown reiter from the guard squadron sacrificed himself while saving Sobieski's life during the first battle of Párkány (see Chapter 7 for more details on this action). As part of the preparations for the defence force left in Poland, Michał Radziejowski, Bishop of Warmia, declared that he would raise, as private units, two companies of 100 reiters each,[96] although there is no evidence to confirm if they were in fact created.

While muster rolls of the *arkabuzeria* from 1683 cannot be found, one from the summer of 1685 does exist, showing the structure of the unit.[97] It is the muster roll of the company of Crown Field Hetman Andrzej Potocki, who replaced Sieniawski after he died at the end of the 1683 campaign. The company was composed of 125 horses, and it is noticeable that it was much smaller in reality, as there were only 64 soldiers, with the remaining 61 horses (used mostly as 'dead pay') divided between the staff of just eight men, giving a total strength of the unit as 72 men. The staff was divided as follows (in brackets are the number of horses per rank):

Medal celebrating the victory at Vienna in 1683, depicting what seems to be lance-less hussars or even *arkabuzeria* fighting the Turks. The central horseman has armour and a helmet, and is using an estoc to thrust, and there is sabre or pallasch under his saddle. The second soldier, also with a helmet, is armed with pistols. (National Museum, Cracow)

---

95   Mirosław Nagielski, 'Organizacja rajtarii', p.288.
96   Franciszek Kluczycki (ed.), *Akta do dziejów Króla Jana IIIgo sprawy roku 1683*, p.74.
97   *Akta grodzkie i ziemskie z czasów Rzeczypospolitej Polskiej z archiwum tak zwanego Bernardyńskiego we Lwowie, volume I* (Lwów: Drukarnia Zakładu Narodowego im. Ossolińskich, 1868), p.80

rotmistrz (12), lieutenant (5), wachmeister (2), quartermaster (2), ensign (12), two corporals (one with 13, other with 12 horses) and trumpeter (3). Pay for corporals seems to be surprisingly high, although it is impossible to understand why this should be the case. It is very likely that units that served in the army in 1683 followed a very similar organisational pattern, possibly with one more corporal due to the size of the unit.

There are some indications of how soldiers in those units would be equipped, as there are some surviving recruitment letters from the late 1660s. The men were to serve 'on good horses, [being] armoured as [winged] hussars, each with [a] brace of pistols and bandolet [long firearm]'.[98] It seems that Brulig also saw Polish *arkabuzeria* in Moravia, as he mentioned some troops marching in an orderly fashion, equipped with handguns and 'beautiful long buff-coats[99] in German style', with banners led by musicians playing kettledrums and trumpets.[100] Unfortunately there is no indication of what their tactics were, but it is probable that they fought in a similar way as hussars and *pancerni* (in two, maybe three ranks) to be able to provide fire support to other cavalry.

Light horse

Throughout the first half of seventeenth century units officially designated as 'light cavalry' were fairly rare in the Commonwealth's armies. While banners of Tatars were common, they were usually counted amongst cossack cavalry and not as separate formations. There were of course the semi-regulars of Lisowski's cossacks (*lisowczycy*), but their formation was short-lived and most of their units served abroad as mercenaries. The typical function of light cavalry, reconnaissance, was fulfilled by cossack cavalry, sometimes also supported by Zaporozhian Cossacks. It was only after the Cossack Uprising of 1648 and the high losses of in Polish army at Batoh in 1652, that a gradual rise in the number of dedicated light cavalry units can be seen. With low wages, less expensive equipment and horses, banners of such cavalry could be quickly recruited to bolster the ranks of the regular army. Two main types, based on the nominal type of soldiers recruited and their slightly different type of weaponry were Wallachian and Tatar light horse. The latter were normally raised from amongst those Tatar families that were already well settled (often for more than two centuries) in Poland and, especially in Lithuania, but also from those coming over from the Crimea, like some Tatars *mirzas* (nobles) and their retainers who fled their country due to internal conflicts. Amongst Wallachian banners were found a whole range of nationalities, from Wallachians, Moldavians, and Cossacks to Poles and Lithuanians. The main armaments of the Tatars were sabres and bows, while Wallachians would often use long firearms instead of bows. During

---

98   Zbigniew Hundert, *Między buławą a tronem*, p.232.

99   The German word he used, *colleten*, is almost the same as the Polish word for buff-coat: *kolet*.

100 Bernard Brulig, 'Pat. Bernard Brulig's Bericht über die Belagerung der Stadt Wien im Jahre 1683', p.431.

Sobieski's reign short spears were introduced, although it is probable that not all units were using them. Pistols seem to be common, especially by the end of the seventeenth century. Chainmail and *misiurka* caps would of course be used by some companions and (especially) officers but were not required by any regulations. The same is also true with *kałkan* shields. In the 1670s and 1680s serving as Wallachian troops became synonymous with light cavalry so even in official documents are found descriptions of 'Walachian-style alias leviori'[101] used as the name of the formation, indicating the type of equipment used by its soldiers.[102]

Polish light horse and dragoons. Romeyn de Hooghe, 1687 (Rijksmuseum)

The Lipka Mutiny, causing the Tatars in Polish service to change sides to join the Ottomans has already been mentioned. It is important to realise that by the time of the mutiny there were not many regular Tatar units on active service, so the majority of those who deserted to the Turks were in fact serving in private banners or were former regular troops. While a large number gradually returned and served again in Sobieski's army, these soldiers were not trusted by the rest of the army. It is no surprise that by 1683 practically all light cavalry units in Polish service were officially recruited as Wallachian, although both types started to become so similar, that they were colloquially known as light horse/cavalry. There were a fairly high number of units being raised, due to their low cost, prior to the march on Vienna. They were crucial in protecting the army during the march and became the 'eyes and ears' of Sobieski's army, as he often used them to impress allied generals by sending a single banner to capture some prisoners. The Lithuanian army retained its Tatar banners, as they did not take part in the mutiny, so the

---

101 (Latin) Or light (cavalry).
102 *Akta grodzkie i ziemskie z Archiwum Ziemskiego we Lwowie. Lauda sejmikowe halickie 1575–1697, volume XXIV* (Lwów: Towarzystwo Naukowe, 1931), p.442.

few of them that were part of the regular army took part on the march into Slovakia.

Dupont provides a basic description of the light horse, comparing them with other cavalry formations: 'the rest of the light cavalry [known] under different names, Wallachians, Tatars and Cossacks,[103] have different weaponry. Some have carbines, other bows and quivers full of arrows. All of them have pistols. Their banners are much weaker in all ways from the two other types of cavalry, but they also have excellent horses, and they are led by noble-born and experienced officers'.[104] Another of his notes states that 'Wallachians and Moldavians are tall and well-built men. They are good soldiers. In the Polish army there are many banners of their light cavalry. They are brave and stand out on each occasion. One can always find few such banners serving next to the King'.[105]

Officers of Polish cavalry. Romeyn de Hooghe, 1687 (Rijksmuseum)

After all his detailed description of hussars, *pancerni* and *petyhorcy*, Dalerac did not waste much time talking about other cavalry types. 'The rest of the Polish army consists of Companies of Valachians, Cossacks and Poles, armed like our Light Horse, with Musquetoons and Falchons, but not so uniform either in Horse or Habit. Their Standards, March, Drums, and way of drawing up, agree with the ordinary Customer of the Country. It is from [that] sort that go out on Parties, guard the Camp, and are made use of for Guards and Convoys'.[106] He also added a very interesting passage describing how Polish Tatars, prior to the 1683s campaign, were trying to assure King Jan III of their loyalty towards the Commonwealth:

I have seen Companies of Tartars amongst these, and formerly the Republic had abundance of that Nation in Pay in their Wars against the Muscovites. The King of Poland, before he went to the Relief of Vienna, had a mind to try the Pulse of the Officers of those who continued still in his Service, and all of them promised him an in violable Fidelity, not only in fighting against the Turks, but also against the Tartars, offering to leave in Poland one half of their Number as Hostages for the Loyalty of the other, who should follow his Majesty; for he had offer'd to give all of them their discharge, which they would not accept of, but served in

---

103 He means Polish cossack cavalry, not Zaporozhian Cossacks.
104 Dupont, p.83.
105 *Ibidem*, p.297.
106 Francois Paulin Dalerac, *Polish Manuscripts*, p.22.

that Expedition with extraordinary fidelity.'[107] O'Connor described light horse as 'those out of Armour (…) wear a Burka, or rough Mantle about their Necks, and have for Arms a Bow and Arrows, with a Sabre.[108]

Brulig's description of the Polish cavalry marching through Moravia mentioned what clearly seem to be units of light horse, equipped with just sabres and bows, marching without much order.[109] As a Catholic monk he is far harsher in describing Tatars marching after the main Polish army. He called them 'wild superstitious and barbaric people, [that] seems to be bad soldiers' and added that they are equipped only with daggers and poleaxes (which seems to be his word for berdiche). Instead of standards, they carried a 'horsetail on a long stick' and their officers seemed to be carrying unusual weapons.

As with other cavalry units, we can investigate the structure of light horse banners thanks to surviving muster rolls from the second part of 1670s. It is noticeable that often there was no lieutenant in the unit, as the *rotmistrz* was normally present and led his soldiers during the campaign. Also, when compared to other cavalry types, there are a very large number of retinues composed of just companions, without any retainers. With the small size of light horse banners the presence of companions as the core of the unit is emphasised.

Damian Ruszczyc's banner, 1 May 1677:[110]

Number of horses in retinue	Number of retinues of that type in banner	Additional comments
6	1 (see comments)	*Rotmistrz* retinue
2	22	
1	11	
Additional staff (not counted towards retinues)	See comments	Drummer, trumpeter, surgeon

Total: 34 retinues with 61 horses. No separate retinue for lieutenant and standard-bearer.

---

107 *Ibidem*, p.22.
108 Bernard Connor, *The history of Poland*, vol. 2, letter VI, pp 10–11.
109 Bernard Brulig, 'Pat. Bernard Brulig's Bericht über die Belagerung der Stadt Wien im Jahre 1683', p.431.
110 AGAD, ASW, dz. 85, no 114, pp.47–47v.

Stefan Bidziński's banner, 1 August 1677:[111]

Number of horses in retinue	Number of retinues of that type in banner	Additional comments
6	1 (see comments)	*Rotmistrz* retinue
3	1 (see comments)	Lieutenant's retinue
2	1 (see comments)	Standard-bearer's retinue
2	5	
1	29	
Additional staff (not counted towards retinues)	See comments	Drummer

Total: 37 retinues with 50 horses.

Stefan Nicki's banner, 1 August 1678:[112]

Number of horses in retinue	Number of retinues of that type in banner	Additional comments
5	1 (see comments)	*Rotmistrz* retinue
3	1 (see comments)	Standard-bearer's retinue
2	9	
1	14	
Additional staff (not counted towards retinues)	See comments	Drummer, surgeon

Total: 25 retinues with 40 horses. No separate retinue for lieutenant.

Andrzej Dymidecki's banner, 1 May 1678:[113]

Number of horses in retinue	Number of retinues of that type in banner	Additional comments
5	1 (see comments)	*Rotmistrz* retinue
3	1	
2	12	
1	8	
Additional staff (not counted towards retinues)	See comments	Drummer

Total: 22 retinues with 40 horses. No separate retinue for lieutenant and standard bearer.

111 AGAD, ASW, dz. 85, no 114, pp.187–187v.
112 AGAD, ASW, dz. 85, no 115, p.109.
113 AGAD, ASW, dz. 85, no 115, p.136.

As with *pancerni*, an attempt to compile the list of units (including the private ones, that later became part of regular army) raised and mustered for the campaign of 1683, is as follows:[114]

Rotmistrz	Lieutenant (if known)	Strength	Muster as of 1 August 1683
Hetman Jabłonowski	Pukaczewski or Dawidenko	150	147
Hetman Jabłonowski	Demian (Damian) Ruszczyc	80	66
Hetman Sieniawski	Probably Marcin Rykaczewski	150	No records
Andrzej Potocki		70	70
Szczęsny Potocki	Jan Marcjan Gostowski	70	73
Stanisław Herakliusz Lubomirski	Górski	80	63
Hieronim Lubomirski	Spasowski	80	No records
Franciszek Dzieduszycki	Kobielski	70	70
Stefan Bidziński	Jan Brucki	100	92
Tomasz Karczewski		60	68
Michał Zbrożek		100	90
Andrzej Sierakowski		70	70
Marcin Bogusz		90	90
Andrzej Dobraczyński		80	69
Aleksander Zaborowski (Zahorowskiego)		80	70
Stefan Nicki		100	No records
Mikołaj Zbrożek		50+50	96
Andrzej Jeżowski		100	97
Paweł Drozdowski		110	90
Jerzy Frąckiewicz		80	80
Szymon Zawisza		100	100
Jan Modzelowski		80	77
Baltazar Wilga		70	48
Aleksander Toszkowski, after him Wardyński		70	70
Tomasz Gdeszyński		60	60
Wojciech Mąkolski		70	No records
Janaki/Jonaki		80	79
Jerzy Huzdewen		70	No records
Konstanty Komar		70	67
Samuel Krzeczowski		60	60
Łukasz Dragaszeszkuł		60	60
Samuel Korycki		60	60
Kazimierz Hussakowski		70	No records
Piotr Branicki		100	No records
Mikołaj Daniłowicz		100	No records

114 Jan Wimmer, *Wiedeń 1683*, pp.225–229, Marek Wagner, *Słownik biograficzny oficerów polskich drugiej połowy XVII wieku*, volume I, *passim*, BCzart, no 2589, pp.101–102, AGAD, ASK, II, 68, *Rachunki sejmowe na sejm 1685*, pp.14v–15v.

Both Wallachian and Tatar light horse employed similar tactics on the battlefield, fighting in loose formation as skirmishers, relying on firearms and bows as their main weaponry. While banners were required to have spears as part of their equipment, it is possible that many units were not using them, relying more on hit-and-run tactics than attempting to engage the enemy head on. Light horse could provide a screen for other formations of cavalry and cooperate with infantry and dragoons in the preparation of ambushes, an example being during battle of Lesienice (also known as battle of Lwów) on 24 August 1675, where Wallachian banners engaged Tatars trying to outflank the Polish-Lithuanian army. The most crucial role was the one of the 'eyes and ears' of the army, with banners being regularly despatched for reconnaissance missions, guard and convoy duties or linking garrisons and army camps. As such light horse were very active during the 1680s and 1690s, being constantly employed during the campaigns against Turks and Tatars. Due to the low cost of raising and keeping in service such banners, and with more than enough available manpower – drawn from amongst foreigners, poorer nobility and even non-nobles – new banners could be created much quicker than those of other cavalry formations.[115] At the same time banners often disappeared from the service after even just one campaign, often with the annotation that unit was disbanded due to losses.

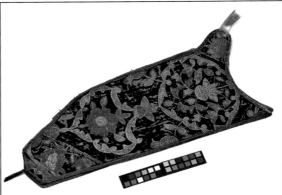

Turkish bow case from the second part of the seventeenth century. Similar types, either made locally, bought from abroad or captured during the war, were used by Poles and Lithuanians. (Wien Museum Inv.-Nr. 96514, CC BY 4.0, Foto: Birgit und Peter Kainz)

---

115 Miron Kosowski, *Chorągwie wołoskie w wojsku koronnym w II poł. XVII wieku* (Zabrze: Inforteditions, 2009), passim.

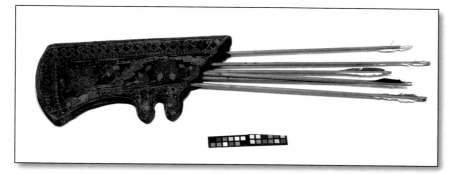

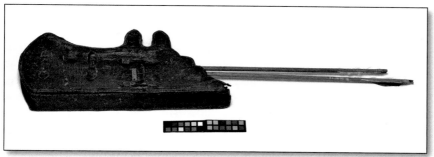

Turkish quiver from the second part of seventeenth century. Similar types, either made locally, bought from abroad or captured during the war, were used by Poles and Lithuanians. (Wien Museum Inv.-Nr. 96515, CC BY 4.0, Foto: Birgit und Peter Kainz)

Foreign infantry

The largest proportion of the infantry in the Polish army was composed of so-called foreign infantry (*piechota cudzoziemska*), sometimes also called German infantry (*piechota niemiecka*). These units were in fact composed mostly from Polish soldiers, the original name coming from the first half of the seventeenth century, when such infantry was normally recruited amongst Germans, Scots and Englishmen. The first regiment created from Poles, but equipped, dressed and trained 'in Western style' appeared in 1629, during the final stage of the war against the Swedes in Prussia. Gradually a bigger and bigger percentage of the foreign infantry was recruited locally, usually with officers and NCOs being chosen from amongst foreigners, including Swedish prisoners of war who changed sides during 'The Deluge' war of 1655–1660. Attempts to add more Polish elements to this formation can be even seen in the introduction of the first military drill for pike and shot infantry in the Polish language. It was Błażej Lipowski's *Piechotne ćwiczenie albo wojenność piesza*, published in Cracow in 1660.[116] The author seems to be connected with the previously quoted Andrzej Maksymilian Fredro, and shared his idea of introducing more Polish troops in the Western style in the Commonwealth's armies. Despite such 'Polonisation', even in 1670s and 1680s many foreigners can still be found in the ranks of the infantry, usually – as before – serving as officers and NCOs. There were two distinct and recognisable groups. One was

116 Błażej Lipowski, *Piechotne ćwiczenie albo wojenność piesza* (Kraków: Nakładem Jerzego Forstera, 1660). See also Jan Wimmer, 'Błażeja Lipowskiego pierwszy polski regulamin piechoty', *Studia i Materiały do Historii Wojskowości*, volume XX (Warszawa: Wydawnictwo Czasopisma Wojskowe, 1976), pp.335–357.

composed of those from the families already settled in the Commonwealth, either 'old' ones,[117] usually German-speaking nobles from Livonia, Courland and Prussia or 'new' ones,[118] often of Dutch, English or Scottish descent. The second, especially visible in Sobieski's army, were those that arrived in the Commonwealth as volunteers for military service or even transferred from other armies (like some Imperial and Brandenburg officers after 1683). Many Frenchmen can be found amongst this number, warmly welcomed by the royal court due to its French connections, but also Italians, Danes or German-speaking soldiers from regions like Westphalia and Mecklenburg. Remember too, that by 1683 there was also already a well-established cadre from amongst native Poles, so many native names can be seen amongst the officers, including those at the rank of colonel. Sobieski preferred specific parts of the country to raise infantry units, and in 1673 suggested that those Polish lands that are 'far away from the Silesian, Pomeranian and Prussian borders' should not be bothered with creating such formations. He was trying to focus on soldiers trained in the German, not the Hungarian style, and pointed out that 'it is nay impossible in such short time to make a [German] from a fat and unprepared Ruthenian or Masovian'.[119] At the same time he seems to have reservations towards new recently raised units, which explains why with every reduction of the army he insisted on keeping smaller regiments, that could be used as a core on which stronger units could be built in the case of war. As early as 1671 he wrote 'we have seen before on many occasions, that foreign infantry newly recruited in Poland is not fit [to fight] until three years [of service] has passed. That is why Swedes and other

Infantry or dragoons in Polish-style clothing. Romeyn de Hooghe, 1687 (Rijksmuseum)

---

117 Settled at least by the sixteenth century.

118 Normally settled during seventeenth century, they were usually former Polish or Lithuanian soldiers that decided to stay in the Commonwealth after end of their military service.

119 Franciszek Ksawery Kluczycki (ed.), *Pisma do wieku i spraw Jana Sobieskiego*, volume I, part 2 (Kraków: Akademia Umiejętności, 1881), p.1240.

orderly and smart nations place such [newly raised] regiments into fortresses [as garrisons], to first let it get used to [service]'.[120]

During Sobieski's reign infantry regiments were fairly small, between 400 and 600 portions, divided between three to five companies. Even worse, companies tended to have different strengths as well, with no attempt to create some similar, regulated structure within the army. One example, to show how complicated such an organisation could be, can be examined here. It is the regiment of Otto Ernest Rappe, which during 1680s was stationed as a garrison of Biała Cerkiew and did not take part in the relief of Vienna. The muster roll for the period 1 November 1684 and 31 January 1685 was as follows:[121]

Regimental staff with 26 portions, including 12 paid to the colonel, four to the lieutenant colonel and three to the major. After these three officers were the regimental adjutant (3 portions), regimental surgeon (2 portions) and regimental drummer (2 portions). In total just six men, so these 20 portions were in fact 'dead pay'.

The Life company with 182 portions. The captain-lieutenant and lieutenant were paid three portions each, the captains-in-arms (two of them) two portions each, and all other NCO's and privates one portion each. The company was divided into 27 files (rota) that should have had six men each but some of them were just five men strong and one had only one man. In total, company staff took 26 portions for 20 men, giving six 'dead pays'. Other staff, apart from those already mentioned officers, were four sergeants, two farriers, one under-ensign, three corporals, four drummer and two fifers.

The second company (Lieutenant colonel's) had 100 portions. The staff had 14 men, with 22 portions: lieutenant colonel (four portions), lieutenant (three), ensign (three), two sergeants, one captain-in-arms (two portions), one under-ensign, two corporals, one fourier, two drummers and two fifers (one portion). There were 13 files of men but all of them were up to strength, with six men in each. That leaves nine 'dead pays', as the lieutenant-colonel was not in fact part of the unit.

The third company (major's) had just 66 portions. The staff had 11 men with 18 portions: the major (four), lieutenant (three), ensign (two), three sergeants, fourier, captain-in-arms (two portions), under-ensign, two drummers (one portion). There were seven files of men, some of them under full strength. As the major was not in fact part of the unit, this gives us a total of eight 'dead pays'.

The fourth company was the smallest, with just 34 portions. It was led by a captain (four portions), with rest of staff being an ensign (two portions), two sergeants, a captain-in-arms (two portions) and two drummers, so seven men with 12 portions. The company had only four files, with one of them composed of four men and the rest at full strength. Due to the small size of the unit there were only five 'dead pays'.

Adding all the subunit strengths together, 'on paper' the regiment had 408 portions. The total of official 'dead pays' in the whole regiment comes to 43,

---

120 Franciszek Ksawery Kluczycki (ed.), *Pisma do wieku i spraw Jana Sobieskiego*, volume I, part 1 (Kraków: Akademia Umiejętności, 1880), p.620.

121 Wagner, *Źródła*, pp.38–47.

therefore the unit should, according to the muster, field 365 men of all ranks. The typical amount that was deducted from regiments that had 400-600 portions was 10 percent, while in case of smaller units, like regiments with 200-350 portions, the amount of such a reduction could rise to 15 percent. Of course it should not be forgotten that these are just official figures for 'dead pay' and the actual strength was further reduced by both combat and non-combat losses (especially desertion) and 'adventurous bookkeeping' when a unit's muster rolls were presented with names of soldiers no longer serving in the ranks, generating extra income that finished up in the officers' pockets. It is not surprising then that on campaign quite a few regiments had to be brigaded together to be able to deploy single battalion. Problems with understrength regiments that still had to be paid for the full 'paper strength' of the unit were very common through the whole of the seventeenth century, leading to constant complaints from nobles gathered in the local *sejmiki*. Considering that soldiers were paid from their taxes, they always had much to say about the way such money was spent. In March 1674 nobles from Halicz (part of Ruthenian Voivodship) highlighted this issue, writing that the 'Commonwealth had to spend [money] on full regiments, [while] in the field they are so small and poor, where instead of 1,200 men [in the regiment] there are only 400 men in the field (…) and even from them in the camp there are [serving] those that are worse, naked [and] hungry'.[122]

Polish infantry fighting in loose formation. Romeyn de Hooghe, 1687 (Rijksmuseum)

It appears that the late 1670s and early 1680s saw the gradual introduction of changes in the way that soldiers of the foreign infantry were equipped. The number of pikemen was reduced to 10–15 percent, with some regiments composed solely of musketeers. It is known that pikemen were definitely present in the campaign of 1683, as General Kątski mentioned them fighting

---

122 *Akta grodzkie i ziemskie z Archiwum Ziemskiego we Lwowie. Lauda sejmikowe halickie 1575–1697, volume XXIV* (Lwów: Towarzystwo Naukowe, 1931), p.376.

the Turks during Second Battle of Párkány.[123] The berdiche axe (*berdysz*) was officially introduced as part of a musketeer's equipment, used in the dual role of a musket rest and a rather fearsome hand-to-hand weapon (more about this will be covered later in this chapter). In theory all ranks should have had an additional weapon – either sabre or rapier – but it seems that in many units these were only used by officers and NCOs, while the other ranks had to rely on their bardiche axe, or a short hatchet kept on the belt. Despite the 'foreign' name, uniforms worn by the soldiers seems to be 'Polonised', with a combination of the long *żupan* garment and outer garments like the *kontusz* or *delia* worn over it. Surviving documents with bills for regiments' equipment and clothing provide rather enigmatic notes of *liberia* (which was used as a word for any type of uniform), coats (*płaszcze*), dress (*sukienka* – in this case, outer garment) and trousers. Soldiers were also provided with shoes and headgear, usually fur caps. Blue and red seems to be fairly common colours used in the uniforms of the infantry, although it is highly likely that grey and green cloth was provided as well. During Sobieski's coronation in Cracow in 1676 foreign infantry (other sources indicates it was Guard unit) can be found in the two most distinct colours associated with such units in Polish army. One regiment of six companies was wearing blue 'lined with red, having blue caps', while the second regiment (also of six companies) was in red.[124]

While there were problems with the proper clothing of Polish regiments – as some of them seemed to receive replacement uniforms during the campaign, in the vicinity of Vienna – such a situation was, rather surprisingly, used as peculiar morale booster for their German allies. When the combined armies were gathering, Lubomirski noticed that one Polish infantry regiment was very poorly clothed, as their uniforms had worn out during the march. He wanted to 'hide' those troops, suggesting to Sobieski that the regiment should march under the cover of darkness, assisting the tabor wagons. The King ordered the infantrymen to march as the first unit instead and mentioned to Lubomirski that this regiment would in fact impress all the allies. When these ragged troops were crossing the bridge, causing confusion amongst Imperial and German officers, Sobieski was to tell them: 'Gentlemen, please take a notice of this unit. It is invincible. When enlisting, each soldier needed to give his officer an oath, that as long as he is in service, he will wear a uniform taken from killed enemy. After last treaty signed [with Turks], all of them were dressed in the Turkish manner, with turbans on their heads. And in a few days, you will see them [dressed] in the same way!'[125]

A fairly critical opinion of the Polish infantry can be found in O'Connor's *The history of Poland*.[126] While in his description he mixed up Polish native infantry (including *wybraniecka*) and foreign infantry (that as we know were in fact recruited in Poland), it is interesting to see his view on this formation:

---

123 Marcin Kątski, 'Diarium Artilieriae Praefecti', Franciszek Kluczycki (ed.), *Akta do dziejów Króla Jana IIIgo*, p.607.

124 *The Manner of the Coronation of the present King of Poland*, p.4.

125 Dupont, p.191.

126 Bernard Connor, *The history of Poland*, vol. 2, letter VI, pp.11-14.

As for the Foot, they are either Poles and Lithuanians, or Foreigners, levy'd chiefly in Germany and Hungary. (…) To return to the Polish Foot, as I said before, they are either Natives or Foreigners. How the Natives are raised I shewed before. They are generally nothing but the vilest Mob, and their business is rather to serve as Pioneers than Soldiers, for the Gentry only make use of them to dig and fill up Trenches and Ditches, to undermine Walls, build Bridges, clear the Roads, to load and drive the Carriages, to keep Guard in the Camp, while the other Soldiers are absent, and, in a word, to do all manner of drudgery they shall be commanded to. These are mixt for the most part with the German hir'd Foot, who do not meet with much better treatment in the Army. (…) Among these, the word of Command is generally given in the German Tongue. They are all divided into Regiments and Companies as in other Countries, and Commanded as well by Polish and German Officers. The Soldiers are generally so ill provided for, that most of them have neither Swords nor Shooes, and when they are in Winter-Quarters, they have not above a Penny a day allowed them, besides what they can steal. Neither are their Officers much more kindlier dealt with, for they scarce fare so well in any respect, as our common Sentinels do here. (…) The Arms of all these Foot are chiefly a long hook'd Battle-Ax, and which the Poles call in their Language, Bardysz, but sometimes they have a sort of long Guns.

Gaspard de Tande also provides another description of the misery and poverty amongst the infantry in Polish armies:[127]

Infantry in Polish-style clothes by Caspar Luyken, 1698 (Rijksmuseum)

They are called foreign [infantry] because recruitment is done in German lands, drill is in German [as well] despite the fact that most soldiers and officers are Polish. They're serving in regiments of infantry or dragoons; each regiment divided into subunits [companies] as in France. It can be said that those soldiers are very poor, most of them do not have sword or shoes, [and] while stationed in towns they had to live from three szeląg that they receive each day, which is worth one French sous, also from things that they can steal from poor sellers on market. In Poland they do not have tradition to give bread to soldiers. As one can easily realise, situation of their officers is proportional to soldiers, so they are not equipped better than ordinary French soldiers.

Dalerac's description of the foreign infantry in the Polish army is in stark contrast to the wealth and splendour of

---

127 Gaspard de Tende, *Relacja historyczna o Polsce*, pp.227–228.

the hussars. We find a ragged and miserable yet very brave group, which clearly impressed the Frenchman. The famous berdiche used by the Poles is described as a very efficient weapon. He also mentioned a little about the dragoons:[128]

> That which they call the Foreign Army, hath quite another sort of Discipline, they are Regiments of Foot and Dragoons, Cloth'd and Arm'd as those of France and Germany (…). The Infantry is of all things the most pitiful, and more tatter'd than any Spaniards or Italians that ever we heard of; some of them have Caps, others Hats; some have Cloaks, others none: They are all without Swords, but carry long Battle-Axes fashioned like those that were carried before the Roman Consuls. Those I always took to be of admirable use. The Poles carry them fastened to their shoulders by a Leathern Thong, they serve them instead of Rests for their Muskets; and there's nothing in the World comparable to them for covering a Battalion, and defending them against Horse. Those miserable Fellows, all in Rags, as I have said, and more like Scullions than Soldiers, some of them with Cloaks, and others of them with a sort of Gowns of a scandalous diversity, are nevertheless incredibly stout, which in reasonable Men I should call Bravery. They resist all sorts of Inconveniencies, Nakedness, Hunger and Blows with an Heroic constancy; bear all the burden of the War, and undergo all the dangers of it, insomuch that I have seen this Infantry form the Arreir-guard in a Plain, in dangerous Retreats, when the Tartars pursued the Camp close, to cover the Polish Gens d' Arms, who retir'd before them without any scruple; I have seen those Soldiers, dying with Hunger, and quite tir'd out, lie upon the ground charging their Muskets, which they were scarce able to carry, and yet would keep firing continually. This Infantry do not indeed pride themselves in their Misery, which is so disproportionable to the splendor of the Gens d' Arms, but it's they that do the service, and are the safety of the Army, whereof the others are merely the Ornament.
>
> Tho' this Army be called Foreign, it is nevertheless compos'd of native Poles, with Officers of a Foreign Name and Model, Colonels, Lieutenant Colonels, General Majors and others. People of all Nations may be employed in this Army, whereas the Poles only are admitted into the Free Companies. There are Germans, Curlanders, French and others in the Foreign Army. The King, Queen, Princes, Generals and other Lords, have Regiments therein of both sorts. The Foot and Horse Guards, that attend the King's Person, are comprehended in this Body of the Army, as are abundance of other Free Companies of Horse, Dragoons and Heidukes, which the Generals have rais'd for their particular service, and make the Republic pay for them.

It is interesting to note that Dupont did not provide much detail on the Polish infantry and dragoons, instead stating that 'I will not talk about enlisted [foreign] troops, as both infantry and dragoons are not different from those in [the] Imperial army. All their officers are foreigners and orders are given in German'.[129] When describing the unsuccessful expedition to Bukovina in 1685, he highlighted their bravery and dedication, and said that

---

128 Francois Paulin Dalerac, *Polish Manuscripts*, pp.22–23.
129 Dupont, p.83.

they stubbornly faced much more numerous troops of janissaries and sipahi, for 10 hours fighting under constant fire from 43 Turkish cannons. He is yet another eyewitness mentioning the berdiche, describing it as a 'very sharp weapon, in shape similar to the Roman axe. It's handle was about five feet long.[130] Soldier is carrying it on his back, thanks to stripe. You both can thrust and cut with it, while [using it] double-handed. I doubt if there was more deadly weapon ever invented. In the heat of the battle soldier can behead the horse and cut off as many heads and arms as he can reach'. Additionally Dupont decided to comment on Dalerac's already quoted description of the infantry, calling it 'vile' and pointing out that '[my] Readers could see how useful those soldiers were. He [Dalerac] describes them as half-naked, frozen and hungry, [and] ragged. He claims that they lay on their bellies to load their guns (what a [stupid] position!). In other words, all that he wrote about their fighting is not worth of the discussion'.[131]

Brulig had plenty to comment on about the Polish infantry marching through Moravia, seeing both the best and the worse of them.

> One could not observe [Polish] infantry so closely, as due to big heat more of the marched [next to monastery] at night than as during the day, yet those that one could observe were fresh [looking], well equipped with sabre, musket of long flintlock, and pikes, [and] they on instruments like drums and shawms, and kept good order. On the other hand, there seem also [many] untried, tattered, tired and badly equipped people, having besides the sabre, either a musket, flintlock, or half pike, and not a few [of them instead had] morning stars, khanjar[132] or large axes, marched only with drum or shawms or just silent. Many of them looked more like gipsies as soldiers and kept rather bad or no order at all.[133]

While it is possible that some of the newly raised units were without uniforms, it is highly unlikely that they would not have had muskets. As such, many of those described as 'more like gypsies' that he had seen, could have been camp followers and not soldiers at all.

While on the subject of the berdiche, this weapon clearly impressed foreigners, as in 1672, when Werdum saw it used to great effect against the Tatars, he wrote that 'this weapon is similar to a turned scythe, with inner part [of the blade] being thick and outer part [being] sharp as butcher's knife. Polish soldiers put this piece of iron on handy snath, length of approximately four feet [circa 120cm] and, if you hit with it right, it's scary how [one] can cut off heads and hands [with it], even with small cut and in all it can harm someone in many ways. It is mostly used by infantry, but some cavalrymen take it with them on horseback as well'.[134]

---

130 Probably meant a Paris foot (*pied du roi*), which was just over 32cm, making a bardiche's handle 160cm.
131 Dupont, p.257.
132 German word used in original text is *hentzar,* so the weapon is called in Poland a *handżar.* Brulig probably meant some sort of dagger or short sword.
133 Bernard Brulig, 'Pat. Bernard Brulig's Bericht über die Belagerung der Stadt Wien im Jahre 1683', pp.431–432.
134 Ulryk Werdum, *Dziennik podróży 1670–1672. Dziennik wyprawy polowej 1671*, p.249.

Nominal commander	Officer in charge of the regiment (if known)	Strength	Muster from 1 August 1683
Royal Foot Guard of King Jan III	General-major Ernest Denhoff and Colonel Gaspar Jost Bernefour	600	597
Queen Marie Casimire	Colonel Stanisław Morstin and Lt. Colonel Gerard Tegenhoff	380	380
Grand Hetman Jabłonowski	Lt. Colonel Jakub Berens	590	580
Field Hetman Sieniawski	Lt. Colonel Aswerus Wrzospolski	590	453
Royal Prince Jakub	Colonel Jan Fryderyk Koszkiel and Lt. Colonel Otton Seswegen	590	545
Andrzej Potocki	Colonel Jan Cetner	380	380
Marcin Kątski	Colonel Henryk Henrykowski	590	590
Hieronim Lubomirski		390	343
Jan Wielopolski	Colonel Eliasz Krauze	390	390
Jan Gniński	Colonel Teodor Frank	390	311
Władysław Denhoff	Colonel Otton Fabian Felkersamb	390	399
Władysław Leszczyński	Colonel Tobiasz Knobelsdorff	380	308
Marcin Zamoyski	Colonel Wilhelm Dobszyc	380	340
General-major Ludwik de Maligny	Colonel Jan Kożuchowski	390	321
General-major Fryderyk Gröben	Lt. Colonel Jerzy Guttry	380	380
General-major Jan Wojciech Dennemark	Colonel Salomon von Sacken	380	346
General-major Eliasz Łącki	Colonel Franciszek Lanckoroński	380	290
Wacław Szczuka	Lt. Colonel Jan Weretycz	280	276
Jan Dobrogost Krasiński	Lt. Colonel Tyburcy Żórawski	300	300
Kazimierz Zamoyski	Colonel Aleksander (or Adam) Domaradzki	280	254
Jan Butler		180	179
Konstanty Wiśniowiecki		380	267
General-major Ernest Rapp		380	380
Stanisław Herakliusz Lubomirski	Lt. Colonel Stanisław Madeyski	280	280
Aleksander Cetner	Major Kurtz	280	237
Józef Lubomirski	Lt. Colonel Jan Kazimierz Nenchy (Nenchen)	280	280
Rafał Leszczyński		300	202
Michał Warszycki	Lt. Colonel Rajecki	180	175
Colonel Jan Berens		180	180
Colonel Wacław Wilhelm Dobszyc		380	346
Jan Karol von Ludinghausen Wolff		180	180
Szczęsny Potocki		380	374
Jerzy Wielhorski	Colonel Jan Samuel Chrzanowski	180	180
Stanisław Karol Łużecki	Lt. Colonel Bartłomiej Łastowiecki	180	155
Franciszek Denhoff		100	100
Garrison of Berdyczów		80	80
Total in 36 units:		**12,350**	**11,378**

Additional foreign infantry units were promised by the Polish bishops, to be paid for from their own coffers and recruited from amongst their subjects:[135]

Bishop	Unit	Strength	Notes
Jan Małachowski, Bishop of Cracow	Regiment	600	Garrison of Cracow
Konstanty Lipski, Archbishop of Lwów	Free company	100	Vienna campaign, possibly late for battle
Mikołaj Pac, Bishop of Wilno	Free company	100	Vienna campaign, possibly late for battle
Jan Opaliński, Bishop of Chełmno	Free company	100	Vienna campaign, possibly late for battle
Bonawentura Madaliński, Bishop of Włocławek	Free company	100	Vienna campaign, possibly late for battle
Stanisław Ząbski, Bishop of Przemyśl	Free company	100	Vienna campaign, possibly late for battle

In Kochowski's official account[136] 21 regiments that were present during the battle of Vienna can be identified, as he described how they were grouped into ad hoc brigades and in which Polish 'division' they were fighting:

Brigade	Regiments	Total paper strength/Muster from 1 August	Division (wing)
Ernest Denhoff	- Royal Foot Guard - Royal Prince Jakub	1190/1142	Right wing (Jabłonowski)
Stanisław Morstin	- Queen Marie Casimire - Szczuka	660/656	Right wing (Jabłonowski)
Eliasz Łącki	- Eliasz Łącki - Władysław Leszczyński	760/598	Right wing (Jabłonowski)
Fryderyk Gröben	- Fryderyk Gröben - Grand Hetman Jabłonowski - Jan Dobrogost Krasiński	1270/1260	Right wing (Jabłonowski)
Jan Butler	- Jan Butler - Marcin Kątski	770/769	Left wing (Sieniawski)
Jan Dennemark	- Jan Dennemark - Andrzej Potocki - Hieronim Lubomirski - Ludwik de Maligny	1540/1390	Left wing (Sieniawski)
Kazimierz Zamoyski	- Kazimierz Zamoyski - Marcin Zamoyski - Jan Gniński	1050/905	Left wing (Sieniawski)
Eliasz Krauze	- Jan Wielopolski - Field Hetman Sieniawski - Władysław Denhoff	1370/1242	Left wing (Sieniawski)
Total in 21 regiments:		8610/7962	

---

135 Franciszek Kluczycki (ed.), *Akta do dziejów Króla Jana IIIgo*, p.74.
136 Kochowski, *Commentarius belli adversus Turcas*, pp.33–34.

Regarding the remaining 15 units of foreign infantry, it is estimated[137] that at least six were stationed as garrisons in Poland, therefore did not take part in campaign. Rapp's regiment was in Biała Cerkiew, Cetner's in Trembowla, Szczęsny Potocki's probably in Stanisławów and the regiments of Łużecki, Wolff and Berens were in Lwów. Other regiments did join Sobieski's army after the battle of Vienna and took part in the final phase of the campaign. Some of them, alongside some Lithuanian troops, were then left as garrisons in Slovakia; for example Stanisław Karol Łużecki's unit garrisoned Sabinov, captured by Polish-Lithuanian troops on 8 December 1683.[138]

Unfortunately, as it is often the case when studying infantry in the Commonwealth's service in the seventeenth century, not much is known about the tactics employed by these formations. Diarists tend to just mention the bravery and resilience of the infantrymen but not the way in which their units were deployed and fought. Contemporary images provide us with standard pictures of blocks of pikemen, surrounded by musketeers. We know that despite lowering the proportion of pike-armed soldiers, they were still present on the battlefield, so there is at least some degree of accuracy in such a depiction.

Dragoons

As mounted infantry able to keep up with the cavalry during rapid marches and to provide fire support, dragoons quickly established themselves as a favourite of Polish and Lithuanian commanders. Since 1625 they can be seen playing an increasing role as a supporting formation for the cavalry, fighting against a vast range of enemies, from Swedes in Livonia and Prussia to Tatars on the borders of Poland. Quite often the difference between foreign infantry and dragoons was indistinguishable, if the proper conditions, that is the easy availability of horses for the unit, were met. At the same time dragoons could very quickly be 'downgraded' to infantry, when the hardships of the campaign caused them to lose their mounts, with no replacements available. Mass loss of horses during the final operations of 1673 caused six regiments of dragoons to be converted into infantry (with a decreased rate of pay, as dragoons were always better paid than infantry),[139] while, after returning from the relief of Vienna at the end of 1683 the majority of Polish dragoons were by this time on foot as well.

Dalerac did not write much about dragoons, but he did point out that they are 'Cloth'd and Arm'd as those of France and Germany, with this difference that the Dragoons are mounted on sorry Jades, miserably equipped, almost naked and all of them in different Colour'.[140] Dyakowski provides us with a completely different description of dragoons marching in the vanguard of the Polish army at the first battle of Párkány (most likely Hetman Sieniawski's

137 Jan Wimmer, *Wiedeń 1683*, p.235.
138 Marek Wagner (ed.), *Źródła*, p.18.
139 Jan Wimmer, *Wojsko polskie*, p.185.
140 Francois Paulin Dalerac, *Polish Manuscripts*, pp.22.

and Chełmski's regiments),[141] writing that they were 'beautiful and well equipped, especially with horses (as each company has horses of different colour)'.[142] Dragoons appear to have been mostly equipped with matchlock muskets, which – again during the first battle of Párkány – was their undoing, as they were not ready to shoot when surprised by the Turkish cavalry.[143] There are some sources that suggest common colours for the dragoons' uniform. During Jan III Sobieski's coronation in 1676 a dragoon regiment of 12 companies (probably a Guard unit) was dressed in 'red Cloaks'.[144] In 1678 dragoons that were part of the Polish embassy to Moscow were in 'bright red' uniforms.[145] Hetman Jabłonowski, writing about the campaign of 1689 mentioned 'blue dragoons'. Brulig saw Polish dragoons marching through Moravia and he wrote that 'most of the dragoons were equipped with pistols, muskets, and flintlocks, as well as [in] clothing in German style'. There were also those that had only sabre and muskets, and the monk noted the presence of a 'large wood axe' meaning bardiches. As with other formations, these units were also marching in good order, led by musicians, playing on drums and shawms.[146]

Regiments were fairly small, and in 1683 none of them was stronger than 600 horses, probably organised into a maximum of six companies. There are interesting details about a free company of dragoons attached to the artillery park, under the nominal command of the General of Artillery, Marcin Kątski. While surviving documents describe it in 1685, it had the same strength – 90 men – as in 1683, providing us with a good idea about its structure. The company staff had 12 men[147] while the fighting force of 78 men was divided into 13 files (rota) with six men each.[148] We can compare it with the Lithuanian privately-raised unit of Michał Kazimierz Radziwiłł, that in October 1683 was composed of 74 men.[149] The company staff had 11 men[150] and was led by a major. The fighting force of 63 men was divided into 11 files (rota), 10 of them with six men each and the final one understrength with only three men. Radziwiłł's unit was mostly used for policing and

---

141 Jan Wimmer, *Wiedeń 1683*, pp.365–369. Richard Brzezinski in his *Polish Armies 1569–1696 (2)* (London: Osprey Publishing Ltd, 1987), p.37, seems to identify the vanguard dragoon regiment as Bidziński's, probably due to the fact that this officer was in overall charge of the vanguard. His regiment did not take heavy losses during the campaign, so it is highly unlikely that it was amongst units decimated by the Turkish attack.

142 Dyakowski, p.76.

143 *Ibidem*, p.76.

144 *The Manner of the Coronation of the present King of Poland*, p.7.

145 'Dziennik Franciszka Tannera', Jan Ursyn Niemcewicz (ed.), *Zbiór pamiętników historycznych o dawnej Polszcze*, volume V (Lipsk: Bretikopf i Haertel, 1840) p.129.

146 Bernard Brulig, 'Pat. Bernard Brulig's Bericht über die Belagerung der Stadt Wien im Jahre 1683', p.431.

147 Captain, lieutenant, ensign, *wachmeister*, under-ensign, captain-in-arms, fourier, three corporals and two drummers.

148 Marek Wagner, 'Formacje dragońskie armii koronnej w czasach Jana III Sobieskiego. Lata 1667–1696', Aleksander Smoliński (ed.), *Do szarży marsz, marsz… Studia z dziejów kawalerii*, volume 5 (Toruń: Wydawnictwo Naukowe Uniwersytetu Mikołaja Kopernika, 2014), p.128.

149 AGAD, Archiwum Radziwiłłów, VII, no 229.

150 Major, lieutenant, quartermaster, ensign, *wachmeister*, under-ensign, fourier, two corporals and two drummers.

guard duties, so its structure did not have to match the proper military establishment, although it was very similar.

Despite their usefulness, dragoons made up a fairly small contingent in the Polish army, probably due to relatively large problems with recruiting and equipping units.

Nominal commander of the unit	Strength	Muster from 1 August 1683	Notes
King Jan III	600	600	Guard regiment under Franciszek Zygmunt Gałecki
King Jan III	400	355	Guard regiment under General-Major Ludwik de Maligny, Count d'Arquien. Newly raised unit.
Grand Hetman Jabłonowski	600	568	Under Colonel Jerzy Taube
Field Hetman Sieniawski	600	595	Under Colonel Fryderyk Strem
Stefan Bidziński	600	600	Under Colonel Jan Fryderyk Koszkiel
Marcjan Ścibor Chełmski	450	302	Newly raised unit. Commanded by Andrzej Chełmski
Stefan Czarniecki	400	185	Newly raised unit.
Andrzej Modrzewski	200	200	Newly raised unit.
Atanazy Miączyński	100	92	Newly raised unit.
Marcin Kątski	90	90	Free company attached to artillery park
Total in 10 units:	**4040**	**3587**	

Dragoons were very active during the whole campaign, taking heavy losses during the debacle of the first battle of Párkány. Apart from the casualties amongst the men, the loss of so many horses was crippling, so to be able to send some reinforcements to the Polish contingent in Moldavia, Sobieski had to group together all the mounted dragoons into two small regiments.[151] As with the infantry, not much is known about the tactics of dragoons. If the situation allowed, they were placed in ambush or deployed protected by anti-cavalry obstacles. The absence of the latter, combined with the retreat of the Polish cavalry, led to disaster for the dragoons during the early phase of the first battle of Párkány.

Polish-Hungarian infantry

In the second part of seventeenth century Polish-Hungarian infantry completely lost its importance and only a few units were kept as part of the regular army: one banner for each hetman and some garrison troops in Cracow and Lubowla. As already noted, hetman's units were fulfilling the role of 'military police', with the officer in charge of the Grand Hetman's banner

151 Jan Wimmer, *Wojsko polskie*, p.210, Jan Wimmer, *Wiedeń 1683*, p.414.

nominated as the Military Captain. During time of peace those units were normally located on the hetman's estate, to provide additional protection. In 1683 there were the following banners of haiduks in the regular Polish army:

Rotmistrz	Strength	Notes
Grand Hetman Jabłonowski	200	Under *rotmistrz* Jan Franciszek Gładkowski
Field Hetman Sieniawski	120	
?	100	Garrison of the Cracow castle
?	100	Garrison of Lubowla castle

It is possible to look at the structure of the hetman's banners, thanks to surviving muster rolls of the 1670s. In 1678 the Crown Grand Hetman's banner had three offices (*rotmistrz*, lieutenant, ensign) and a large music band of eight men (two drummers, one bagpiper, three musicians with shawms and two boys acting as singers).[152] Fighting men were divided into two wings, each composed of five squads, called 'tens' (*dziesiątka*), led by an NCO called '10th men' (*dziesiętnik*). Despite its name, none of unit's 'tens' had 10 men. On the right wing there were four squads of nine and one of eight men (total 44 men), while the left wing had five squads of nine men (total 45 men), for a total unit strength of 100 men.[153] It is interesting to note that there was no 'dead pay' here. In the case of larger banners, there were more 'tens' per wing, when there could also be an additional lieutenant and ensign.

Polish haiduk. Caspar Luyken, 1709 (Herzog August Bibliothek)

As will be seen in the description of Sobieski's household troops, *haiduks* seemed to be still popular as private troops, ideal as garrisons of a magnate's estates and as their private bodyguards. It is probable that not many of such units would be part of the relief army, as they would instead be kept on their owner's lands to protect them. It is possible to identify only one, of Jan Koniecpolski, that was too late to march with main army so it attached itself to the small Polish 'division' that was accompanying the Lithuanian army. Another interesting example of a unit of *haiduks* were the so-called 'Marshall's Hungarians'. A banner of 100 *haiduks* was attached to the office of Crown Grand Marshall (in 1683 it was Stanisław Herakliusz Lubomirski) and their role was to

---

152 (Pol.) *Dyszkancista*, meaning that they were boy sopranos.
153 AGAD, ASW, dz. 85, no 114, pp.44–45v.

keep order and protect the *Sejm* during its session. It is highly unlikely that they would have taken part in the campaign.

Traditionally *haiduks* in Polish service were dressed in blue, a colour normally associated with the infantry. Other colours of cloth used for their uniforms that can be found in sources from the period are green, red, white or even purple. Red seems to be used most often in units raised by high-ranking officials, as can be seen in the uniforms of the banner of Crown Grand Hetman Stanisław Potocki in 1661, and amongst guards of the Polish-Lithuanian envoys in Moscow in 1677 and with Jan Gniński in Turkey in the same year.

Zaporozhian Cossacks

By the 1680s the loyalties of the Zaporozhian Cossacks were divided between Muscovy, the Ottoman Empire and the Commonwealth. In Poland they were generally seen as good soldiers, especially useful against Turks and Tatars. As early as 1672, Sobieski mentioned in one of his letters that 'I would ask the Zaporozhian Hetman [Mykhailo Khanenko] to send us two thousand [men with] Zaporozhian firearms, as such men are the best in the defence and know [how to fight] Turks'.[154] It is not surprising that when he became King, Jan III made great efforts to keep the Cossacks in Polish service. On one hand he made many approaches to those under Muscovite rule, trying to convince them to side with Poles, while on the other he was trying whenever possible to keep as many Cossacks as he could as part of the 'registered' service supporting the Polish army.[155]

In the spring/summer of 1683, as part of the preparations for war against the Turks, the King increased recruitment amongst the Cossacks, for their involvement in the operations of the main army. Papal financial support and the King's own money was used to pay for these troops. Initially 'Zaporozhian troops' were to number 1,200 men, divided into three regiments (*pułki*),[156] each of which was then divided into four 100 men-strong sotnias. This force was quickly expanded, as there are surviving lists of the cost of recruiting 3,000 Cossacks, divided into seven regiments (two of 500 and five of 400 men), dated 7 July 1683. As well as their normal pay, officers and soldiers were also to receive cloth for uniforms:[157]

---

154 Franciszek Ksawery Kluczycki, *Pisma do wieku i spraw Jana Sobieskiego*, volume I, part 2, p.1028

155 More details about Sobieski's politics regarding Cossacks in Piotr Kroll, 'Jan III Sobieski wobec Kozaczyzny w latach 1676–1683', Dariusz Milewski (ed.), *Król Jan III Sobieski i Rzeczpospolita w latach 1674–1683* (Warszawa: Muzem Pałacu Króla Jana III w Wilanowie, 2016), pp.177–200 and Piotr Kroll, 'Hetmanat lewobrzeżny wobec Rzeczypospolitej i Prawobrzeże w dobie Ligi Świętej', Dariusz Milewski (ed.), *Jarzmo Ligi Świętej? Jan III Sobieski i Rzeczpospolita w latach 1684–1696* (Warszawa: Muzeum Pałacu Króla Jana III w Wilanowie, 2017), pp.113–136.

156 Under Semern Korsuniec, Jakub Wrona and Kalina.

157 Wagner, *Źródła*, pp.23–24.

Each of the seven colonels were to receive 11 ells (łokieć was the old Polish measurement of 0.59 m) of 'Dutch cloth' (most likely of good quality, as each ell cost 12 florins). There was also an order for fox pelts for their clothes.

Lower ranking officers – *yesauls*, general clerk, *sotniks* – were to receive 11 ells of English cloth (*falendysz*) each.

The military judge and six regimental clerks, seven regimental standard-bearers and 23 sotnia-level standard-bearers were to receive 12 ells of thick simple cloth called paklak (*pakłak*) each.

All other NCOs and the rank-and-file Cossacks were to receive eight ells of paklak (*pakłak*) each.

An interesting example of the structure of the Cossack sotnia (company) in Polish service can be found in the Polish archives, based on a unit that was in service, as part of the Royal Household troops, as early as March 1683. This 130-man unit of Jakow Potapenko (Potarenko) had a small staff of three officers: the *sotnik* himself, his second-in-command in the rank of yesaul (assawul) and a standard bearer. There were no designated musicians on the muster roll. The rest of the sotnia was divided into 12 sections led by ataman, each of between nine and 13 Cossacks.[158] Normally three to four sotnias were grouped into a regiment (*pułk*) that would number 400-500 men. Regimental staff was the colonel, his second-in-command in the rank of regimental *yesaul*, standard bearer and clerk. Additionally there was one military judge and one general clerk for whole 'Zaporozhian army'.

The newly created 'Zaporozhian army of His Royal Highness' was to be controlled by a Commissioner appointed by Sobieski, Colonel Stanisław Zygmunt Druszkiewicz. Direct recruitment of Cossacks was initially organised by Colonel Jakub Mężyński. He was supposed to gather as many troops as possible and follow the main army. He was slow in completing his mission and only managed to join the King's army in early November. In Appendix II are the dates on which Brulig noticed Cossack troops marching through Moravia. As noted earlier, seven regiments received pay and cloth, but it seems that even more were recruited, as there is information concerning 12 regiments with total strength of 3,700 men,[159] with some joining Sobieski's main army and others fighting in Podolia and Moldavia. For example Colonel Krzysztof Łączyński, who was in Polish service since the mid 1670s, received a recruitment letter for a regiment of 500 Cossacks on 20 June 1683.[160] Maksymilian Bułyh, with a regiment of 400 Cossacks, received an July order from Hetman Jabłonowski to gather his soldiers in

158 *Ibidem*, pp.21–22.
159 Zbigniew Hundert, 'Projekt organizacji i finansowania "wojska JKM i Rzptej Zaporoskiego" z 1683 roku. Przyczynek do badań nad funkcjonowaniem wojsk kozackich w strukturach sił zbrojnych Rzeczypospolitej w dobie wojny z Imperium Osmańskim 1683–1699', *Saeculum Christianum*, volume XXIII (Warszawa: Wydawnictwo Naukowe Uniwersytetu Kardynała Stefana Wyszyńskiego, 2016), p.320.
160 *Akta grodzkie i ziemskie z czasów Rzeczypospolitej Polskiej z archiwum tak zwanego bernardyńskiego we Lwowie, volume X: Spis oblat zawartych w aktach grodu i ziemstwa lwowskiego* (Lwów, 1884), p.349.

Ovruch (Owrucz) and to reach Lwów by 15 August.[161] The original seven colonels, who were to lead the Cossack regiments were: Stefan Kunicki (appointed as Cossack hetman), Bazyli Iskrzycki, Buluk Basha, Maksymilian Bułyh, Andrzej Zieleniecki, Kazimierz Stawecki and Jan Dunin Rajecki. Other colonels mentioned in contemporary sources were Apostoł, Semen Korsuniec, Jakub Worona, Jan Myśliszewski, Aleksander Barabasz, Krzysztof Łączyński, Jan Kobylan, Trofim Kochan, Kazimierz Sanecki and Zależyński – some of them taking over the command from the original officers.

Sobieski had really counted on the Cossacks' presence during the Vienna campaign, and he was unhappy that they were late to arrive. At the end of August he wrote to his wife, when talking about the delayed troops 'I do not care about anyone [from late troops] but only about those Cossacks, as I often get upset about them each day. I spent so much [money] on them and [I'm upset] to not have them [here] on time (…). Please rush those Cossacks if they will arrive [to Cracow] and send them [riding] on wagons'.[162] Only a small group, no more than 150 men led by Colonel Apostoł Paweł Szczurowski,[163] were with main army camped in Tuln. It was private unit raised by Field Hetman Sieniawski. In the meantime Mężyński, with rest of the newly-recruited men, was still in Lwów.[164] Later the King was very bitter that the main units of Cossacks were late, as 'they would be the most useful here, especially during the crossing through those mountains and forests'. He often complained in his letters to the Queen about Mężyński, so one can wonder what words were exchanged when those two finally met each other in early October. The King noticed that Mężyński employed a rather unusual ruse to stop Cossacks from deserting during the march. While he had with him the money for their pay, he did not give it to the Cossacks. Instead, he only issued them cloth for the uniforms and told them that 'over there [in Austria], once you join the King, you will receive your pay'. It prevented desertions, so a few hundred Zaporozhians reinforced the main army in the camp at Pressburg (Bratislava). Others were sent by the Queen to Upper Hungary (Slovakia) to march with the Lithuanians[165] and these finally reached the army in November.

Already in late August 1683, Stanisław Druszkiewicz was sent back by the King to replace Mężyński with responsibility for direct recruitment of the volunteers, bringing with him further Papal funds and the blessing of the Papal Nuncio in Poland. Pallavicini, in his report to Rome, mentioned that Druszkiewicz was to recruit Cosacchi d'Ukraina a fare l'irrutione contro i Tartari di Bialogrod, indicating that Cossacks were to make diversionary

---

161 Zbigniew Hundert, 'Projekt organizacji i finansowania "wojska JKM i Rzptej Zaporoskiego" z 1683 roku', p.320.

162 Antoni Zygmunt Helcel (ed.), *Listy Jana Sobieskiego do żony Marii Kazimiery*, p.376, Jan III do Marii Kazimiery, Z Heiligenbron, mil 3 od Tulmu, gdzie most budują, ultima Augusti.

163 Marek Wagner, *Słownik biograficzny oficerów polskich drugiej połowy XVII wieku, volume I*, p.257.

164 Antoni Zygmunt Helcel (ed.), *Listy Jana Sobieskiego do żony Marii Kazimiery,*, pp.381–382, Jan III do Marii Kazimiery, Za Dunajem u mostu pod Tulnem, 9 Septembra, rano o piątej.

165 *ibidem*, p.401, Jan III do Marii Kazimiery, 7 Octobris; na samemu się ruszeniu ku Parkanom, które miejsce jest na końcu mostu przeciw Strigonium, alias Gran, na tej Dunaju stronie.

raids against the Nogai Horde in Budjak.[166] Druszkiewicz wrote in his diary explaining his role as follows: 'to get cloth and money for the Cossacks, to travel on to the Ukraine and recruit them, choose their hetman, to attack [Tatar] Horde in Budjak and to pillage them as it never happened before'.[167] These operations will be discussed in more detail in Chapter 9.

While we normally associate seventeenth century Cossacks with infantry defending a well prepared tabor wagon fort, it seems that Sobieski especially valued them as light infantry, often serving in a dragoon-like role. Useful for reconnaissance and when fighting in difficult terrain, full of forests and hills, their absence was upsetting to the Polish King. Armed with firearms and sabres, they were often used to ambush Turks and Tatars, to capture badly needed prisoners. Pasek provides us with a very interesting and detailed example of such a 'small war' action, during Polish operations near Szécsény:[168]

> There was big need to capture prisoner from [garrison of] town; Cossacks were ordered to do so, promising them reward. Some of them venture into orchards [outside the town] but they were not able to capture anyone, as [defenders] were very cautious and did not leave the town. So [Cossacks] had another idea: some of them stayed in ambush in orchard, while two went closer to the town, looking at it, [walking] closer and closer. As defenders noticed that they may be in range of their guns, they started to shoot from their firearms or hookguns. One [Cossacks], even though he was not hit, fell on the ground, while the other started to seemingly taking care of him, then took off some of his clothes and run away to [Polish] camp, in such way that [defenders] could see him fleeing. One [pretending to be] killed stayed [still] lying there, well visible as he was dressed in red, [so] Turk went there to loot his body. [Defender] Came nearby, stand next to him, looking around, look towards nearby trees – no one there. So he kneeled next to Cossack and started to get off his buttons. Here Cossack grabbed him by his neck, Turk was screaming but he was already dragging him [towards Polish camp]. Other Cossacks from ambush arrived there as well (…), capturing Turk and taking him to King. Such was beautiful idea and skill of the Cossacks!

Royal Household (private) troops

While serving as Grand Hetman Jan Sobieski kept a strong private 'army', paid from his own treasury. During his reign he also tended to employ a large number of private troops, with some of them accompanying him on campaign, while others protected the court in Warsaw, royal castles and his private estates. It is necessary to make a distinction between units bearing the royal name but serving in the regular army and those being directly employed by the King. The former were composed of winged hussars, *pancerni,* foreign

---

166 Franciszek Kluczycki (ed.), *Akta do dziejów Króla Jana IIIgo',* p.306.
167 Stanisław Zygmunt Druszkiewicz, *Pamiętniki 1648–1697* (Siedlce: Wydawnictwo Akademii Podlaskiej, 2001), pp.110–111.
168 Jan Chryzostom Pasek, *Pamiętniki,* p.389.

infantry and dragoons but were paid by the national treasury, as a part of the enlisted army. The latter were the 'King's own' and as such he could do with them as he pleased and use them for his own private needs.

In the winter of 1667/1668, when Sobieski arrived in Warsaw for the royal election, he took with him all his available soldiers, as he wanted to make a show of force. In a letter to his wife from December 1667 he described them as 'all in new uniforms':[169]

> 60 guardsmen, 'dressed in blue cassocks with silver lining' (probably drabants or reiters)
> 250 dragoons
> 100 des Haydouks Hongrois (haiduk infantry)
> 100 janissaries
> 100 Tatars (light cavalry)
> 100 Wallachians (light cavalry)

Polish Janissary from the Royal Guard by Jean Le Blond (ca. 1635–1709) (Author's archive)

This last unit was still present in his service in January 1677, as they are mentioned that year – equipped with spears – as a part of the royal entourage entering Warsaw.[170] The King kept them as part of his household troops for much longer, and there are records showing that between 1683 and 1686 it was under the command of Grzegorz Habaszekuł (Grigore Habasecul). The banner was composed of pro-Polish Moldavian boyars who were allowed by Sobieski to settle in Poland after 1673.[171]

Dalerac, writing as Chevalier de Beajeu[172], described each unit of the Sobieski's household guard but he also included units that were part of the regular army, mentioning that traditionally there was regiment of infantry and regiment of cavalry, both of around 600 men each. According to him typical guard units were a company of German reiters-drabants, 'dressed and armed in the style of this [German] nation', that when accompanying the King during official events served as halberdiers. Next were the royal haiduks, composed of Hungarians but 'dressed in Polish manner', armed with muskets,

169 Antoni Zygmunt Helcel (ed.), *Listy Jana Sobieskiego do żony Marii Kazimiery* (Kraków: Biblioteka Ordynacji Myszkowskiej, 1860), p.140, Jan Sobieski do Marii Kazimiery, Żółkiew, 15 grudnia 1667 roku.
170 Biblioteka Zakładu Narodowego im. Ossolińskich we Wrocławiu, no 337, *Opisanie wjazdu Króla J. M. na Seym Walny do Warszawy*, p.52.
171 Marek Wagner, *Słownik biograficzny oficerów polskich drugiej połowy XVII wieku*, volume II (Oświęcim: Wydawnictwo Napoleon V, 2014), p.107.
172 *Pamiętniki kawalera de Beaujeu*, pp.216–220.

sabres and axes. They were divided into smaller sub-units led by what he called a sergeant (probably he means 10th man', known as *dziesiętnicy*). These NCOs were armed with halberds with a small white or red pennant under the blade.

There were more private units introduced by Sobieski and paid from his own coffers, some of whom joined the household troops after 1683 but are worth describing to paint a broader picture of his own troops, as per Dalerac's account. First was the company of janissaries, composed of Moldavians, Wallachians and 'Turkish deserters or prisoners of war, that willingly agree to their new fate'. They were dressed in green clothes, white turbans, 'Turkish shoes and other oddities'. Their weapons were muskets, war hammers [probably he means axes] and 'sabres worn on the side like hunter's knife, with blade that is not curved but straight and wide, like a cutlass'.

The second 'Turkish' company was formed from a unit of Wallachian infantrymen, that deserted 'with their officers and flags' from the garrison of Kamianets-Podilskyi in 1681 and became part of Sobieski's private troops, 'their faithful service was exemplary'. They were equipped in the same way as the first company but 'have different colour of clothes[173] and different type of caps. The latter were long, 'falling down the back of the head and brimmed with wide fur'. Unlike the first unit it was not called janissaries but *semeni*, due to its Wallachian origin.

Both companies had a Turkish-style band, very much like the original Turkish janissaries. There were 'odd drums, played on both side; oboes, flutes and some sort of brass instruments in type of flat saucers; also there is type of Jewish psalterium, which is triangle festooned with rings, on which you play with a stick'. Both units received distinctive large flags, 'one [is] blue [and] one [is] white, with King's coat of arms, figures of the eagle, lion and other writings'.

The smallest unit was composed of 30 Swiss halberdiers. While it was supposed to have been disbanded in 1681, it remained in service as guards at the Royal Castle in Warsaw. The fourth unit introduced by Sobieski was composed of Hungarians, formed from the troops of Imre Thököly, who had entered Polish service in 1687. Considering that its soldiers 'were full of hate and need of vengeance against Germans' they may seem a rather unusual choice of household troops of the Polish King, allied as he was with the Holy Roman Empire. There were 150 of these haiduks, 'dressed in Hungarian

Captain of the Janissary Royal Guard unit of King Augustus II Strong, circa 1700. Henri Bonnart (1642–1711). (National Museum, Cracow)

---

173 Sadly the actual colour was not mentioned.

style in red', their hats were adorned with feathers and their officers had eagle feathers on theirs. Their commander, dressed in hussar or Turkish deli fashion, was wearing a tiger's pelt on his back and carried 'many weapons of strange shape'. The whole unit was equipped with muskets and sabres.

Sobieski's own drabant-reiters were present in Cracow during his coronation in 1676, 'in Buff [coats] with blue Cloaks, on the backs of which were the Kings Character J. III. R. and a Crown above'.[174] In 1683 Jan III mentioned that his reiters had coats 'with his letter on them', indicating that same type of uniform was used during the Vienna campaign,[175] although he may be referring to a unit of *arkabuzeria* of the regular army and not his private one. Soldiers from the company of 100 Royal Drabants, under the command of *rotmistrz* Fegeder was part of the Polish embassy to Moscow in 1686, were dressed in elk-leather coats[176] and blue overcoats made 'from French cloth'. They were armed with swords and long firearms.[177] When accompanying the King on campaign, his guard units looked splendid, to quote Dalerac:

> The 22d of Aug. the K. after Mass, went into the Camp in a Warriors Equipage, having the Bontchouk carried before him, preceded by his Guards and Horses of War, whose Harnesses were glittering with Gold and precious Stones, and, without Exaggeration, with such a Richness, as I never saw elsewhere, or perhaps 'tis not valued but amongst those sorts of Nations, as Turks, Persians, and Muscovites, whose Pomp and Methods the Polanders imitate.[178]

Sobieski wanted to make a big impression on his allies, so it is no surprise that he did not scrimp or save on spending for the courtiers and servants assisting him on the march to Vienna. This amazing court seems large in contrast to the rather plain looking German allies and their commanders. As the King described in a letter to the Queen: 'clothes on [our] paiks[179], pages and butlers are beautiful, [they are] mounted on richly dressed mounts, [and] our tents, mine and Fanfanik's,[180] are with golden ornaments, while the third one, antechamber,[181] covered with brocade. [Germans] Do not have even a bit of silver on their horses, are dressed in simple clothes, half-German, half-Hungarian, their carriages are simple, we did not see a single page or butler so far'.[182] The Royal Guard marching through Moravia was an impressive sight,

---

174 *The Manner of the Coronation of the present King of Poland*, p.7.
175 Antoni Zygmunt Helcel (ed.), *Listy Jana Sobieskiego do żony Marii Kazimiery* (Kraków: Biblioteka Ordynacji Myszkowskiej, 1860), p.389. Jan III do Marii Kazimiery, W obozie pod wsią Szenan na gościńcu Preszowskim nad Dunajem mil trzy od Wiednia (17 Września).
176 Polish word used in the text – *kolet* – normally means buff-coat.
177 Adam Zawadzki, Aleksander Przeździecki (ed.), *Zrzódła do dziejów polskich*, volume II (Wilno: Józef Zawadzki, 1844), pp.42, 44
178 Francois Paulin Dalerac, *Polish Manuscripts*, p.83.
179 Turkish-style court servants.
180 Fanfanik was pet name for Royal Prince Jakub.
181 (Pol.) *Antykamera* – It was a room, or in this case outer part of a tent, used by servants and courtiers, leading to the main room of the tent.
182 Antoni Zygmunt Helcel (ed.), *Listy Jana Sobieskiego do żony Marii Kazimiery*, p.378, Jan III do Marii Kazimiery, A Stetelsdorf, w zamku starego Grafa Ardeka, który był Koniuszym Wielkim

Janissary from the Royal Guard unit of King Augustus II Strong, circa 1700. Henri Bonnart (1642–1711). (National Museum, Cracow)

as Brulig noted that: 'The royal bodyguard was likewise a polite, extravagant, well equipped people and was made up of Poles, Russians,[183] Pomeranians and Brandenburgers over 1,000 men strong, both with kettledrums and trumpets [with their units] as with drums and shawms [that] rode behind, and [all] kept good order.'[184]

The huge influence of the King on the army itself can be seen in the large number of units of the regular troops that were under his (and his family's) name. This so called 'Komput Guard' allowed Sobieski to directly control an important part of the military. Between 1677 and 1683, prior to the enlargement of the army due to the war with Ottomans, 13 percent of the Polish standing army was in fact units of 'Komput Guard'. There were three banners of winged hussars (under the King and the two Royal Princes), a royal banner of *pancerni*, a company of *arkabuzeria*, a strong regiment of dragoons and three regiments of foreign infantry (King's, Queen's and Royal Prince Jakub's). Interestingly, there were no regular banners of light horse or *haiduks* in the 'Komput Guard'. Additionally, including a very strong royal regiment of national cavalry (seven banners of hussars and eight banners of *pancerni*), the number of troops with strong and direct links to Sobieski rose to 24 percent. While royal influence in the Lithuanian army was far less, the King started to increase it prior to 1683, taking over – as royal banners – one banner of winged hussars and one banner of *petyhorcy* of the former Grand Lithuanian Hetman Michał Kazimierz Pac, who died in April 1682. He also created a royal regiment of national cavalry.[185]

Artillery and engineers

As mentioned earlier, the artillery corps was under the command of General of Artillery Marcin Kątski. The regular staff was not very numerous, estimated at just 160 to 180 men by the end of seventeenth century. It is important to realise that within this number were not just trained artillery crewmen but also engineers, miners and skilled artisans working for the artillery corps,

u sławnego Wallensteina, a żyje dotąd ćwierć mile od mostu pod Tulnem, 4 Septembris.

183 As there were no Muscovites in the royal guard, this statement seems a little puzzling. Possibly Brulig meant 'Ruthenians' (*Rusini*) from the territories that were part of the Commonwealth.

184 Bernard Brulig, 'Pat. Bernard Brulig's Bericht über die Belagerung der Stadt Wien im Jahre 1683', p.431.

185 Zbigniew Hundert, 'Pozycja Jana III w wojsku koronnym w latach 1674–1683', pp.142–143.

such as blacksmiths, carpenters and ironworkers. When going on campaign there was always a need to hire more specialists, especially trained gun crews and engineers.

In the early Spring of 1683 Marcin Kątski prepared a document detailing the artillery park that would be required to support the operations of the army. It is a very interesting document, clearly indicating that preparations were made with a siege of Kamianets-Podilskyi in mind. What was the thinking behind Kątski's plan?

Type of cannon	Number of cannons	Number of horses required for each cannon	Number of cannonballs required for each cannon
24-pdr	6	24	500
12-pdr	12	12	300
6-pdr (long barrelled)	8	15	200
6-pdr (short barrelled)	12	4	200
3-pdr and 2-pdr	12 (in total)	3	300
160-pdr mortar	1	10	100
60-pdr mortar	2	6	200
30-pdr mortar	2	8	200
Iron 60- and 30-pdr mortar	2	5	200

The artillery park was also to include siege equipment, with 2,400 hand grenades, numerous spades and pickaxes, six bridge pontoons and eight petards. Kątski estimated that while the park would require 1,575 horses and would need 257 men, including 50 trained artillerymen, 120 trained artillery assistants, 20 carpenters and 12 blacksmiths.[186] The total cost of such an enterprise was calculated as approximately 415,000zl. With the normal annual budget of the artillery corps in Poland at 106,000zl, it is a clear sign of how expensive Kątski's plan was. A revision of the plan of operations of the Polish army meaning that Sobieski would lead his troops to Vienna instead to Podolia, changed the composition of the artillery park taken with the relief army. All mortars and heavy cannons were left in the arsenals, and in total only 28 cannon were taken, most of them light regimental pieces and short-barrelled 6pdrs. There is an indication that some 12pdr cannon were taken as well. The artillery park taken by Kątski did not impress Dalerac, who wrote that 'the Artillery which consisted of 28 Pieces of very small size, followed the first Day for the same reason [to be concealed from Germans to not disappoint them]; for except five or six Cannon of a reasonable size, for Field-Pieces, the rest did not deserve that Name'.[187]

Kątski, in his own diary from the campaign,[188] is very terse when describing the use of Polish artillery but points out problems with moving his

186 Antoni Hniłko, 'Przygotowanie artylerji koronnej na wyprawę wiedeńską w 1683 r.', *Przegląd Historyczno-Wojskowy*, volume VI, part I (Warszawa, 1933), pp.104–107.
187 Francois Paulin Dalerac, *Polish Manuscripts*, p.83.
188 Marcin Kątski, 'Diarium Artilieriae Praefecti', Franciszek Kluczycki (ed.), *Akta do dziejów Króla Jana IIIgo*.

Marcin Kątski, Polish General of Artillery. Painting attributed to Daniel Schultz (Wikimedia Commons)

cannons on the eve of the battle. On 10 September 1683 he noted that each of the infantry brigades in Sobieski's army had two cannons attached, 'so they can try to carry them [through hills] if possible'.[189] Moving cannons through the hills was a real nightmare for the Poles and it took them the whole night of 10/11 September to safely transport them. 'Whole night without sleeping, as for each cannon and each ammunition wagon we had to practically harness all [available] horses and pull them with our hands'.[190] Relocating all the available cannon on the Polish right flank was another difficult enterprise and it took the whole day of 11 September, 'carrying them through hills, mud and impenetrable terrain, barely at dusk arriving at the bottom of Kahlenberg Hill but [we were] unable to take them there as it was impossible due to moonless night and the fact that hill and forest around it were full of different troops'. What was worse, the Poles lost their way and the whole artillery park was stuck in a burnt out town near Kahlenberg. Many soldiers wandered off and found basements full of wine, that had survived the earlier destruction, so Kątski and his officers had problems forcing them to return to the ranks and to move the cannon and ammunition wagons from there.[191] Just before dawn on 12 September Kątski ordered his soldiers to start moving the cannons uphill but the heavy wagons had to be left behind. It took the Polish crews many hours to navigate the difficult terrain, already busy with other moving troops, so only at around 1.00 p.m. had they managed to transport all the cannon onto the top of the Kahlenberg. The cannon would then be able to support the attacking troops, 'shooting non-stop from the hill'.[192] Dupont also mentioned the problems of moving the artillery into their positions and praised Kątski for his efforts. 'The Germans, after the first attempt to push the cannons uphill, decided it was impossible and left them on the plains alongside the tabor. Only Kątski, voivode of Kiev, General of Podolia and [of] Crown Artillery, took his 28 guns. They were the only cannons that the Christian army took with them during the day of the battle'.[193] He then wrote that the cannon were used to support infantry, 'shooting canister-shot, from close distance, causing panic amongst the ranks of the enemy. [The Turks] were unable to respond in kind, as their own cannons were left on the edge of vineyards'.[194] The Polish artillery was at some point so very short of cannon

189 *Ibidem*, p.589.
190 *Ibidem*, p.590.
191 *Ibidem*, p.591.
192 *Ibidem*, p.593.
193 Dupont, p.193.
194 *Ibidem*, p.195.

balls and other supplies, that the gunners had to improvise. Dalerac wrote that he later heard the French Engineer (as he always calls Dupont, without using his surname) saying that 'for want of some other thing to ram down, he made use at last of his Gloves, his Perriwig, his Cravet, and a great Pacquet of Gazets, that were in his Pocket'.[195]

Other formations.

Part of King Stephan Bathory's military reforms, initiated in 1576 when he took over the throne, was the introduction of a new type of infantry. It was supposed to be a formation conscripted from amongst the peasants from all lands: those owned by crown, nobility and the clergy. Polish nobles strongly opposed such a far-reaching idea, so the King was allowed to create the new formation based on peasants levied from crown-owned lands only. New troops were called *wybraniecka* infantry, from Polish word wybraniec, which means 'chosen'. From each 20 lans (łany)[196] one man 'who would volunteer himself, [being] amongst others braver and more eager to serve in the time of war'[197] was to be freed from any tax obligation on his lan in exchange for military service. Peasants from the other 19 lans were to take on the burden of his tax and work duties. Once every three months, a designated *rotmistrz* or lieutenant for the land was to muster and train all the troops, who should be equipped 'with good handgun, sabre, axe, in the uniform that his rotmistrz or lieutenant chosen for him, similar to those that other infantryman [in his unit] will have, [also] need to have powder and lead'.[198]

Unfortunately, despite some promising starts in its service during Bathory's wars against the Muscovites, the *wybraniecka* quickly became a marginalised force, usually relegated to garrison and engineering duties. It suffered due to problems with poor recruitment and lack of proper training; often it was raised for a campaign just as an auxiliary workforce, without proper weapons.

In the second part of the century it was usually supplemented by the military service of village's and small town's equivalents of mayors (called sołtys and wójt), who were obliged to perform military service as part of their role. These combined 'formations' serving next to the regular army rarely exceeded 1,500 men. It is also important to point out that not all lands regularly raised *wybraniecka*, deciding as an alternative to pay extra taxes. Nonetheless since the 1660s until the start of the seventeenth century such soldiers sent by the lands of central and southern Poland could be seen fighting against the Cossacks, Turks and Tatars. They played a useful role as a pioneer force, often attached to the artillery and supporting regular forces during Tatar raids. It is not surprising that *wybraniecka* were also

---

195 Dalerac, *Polish Manuscripts*, p.97.
196 Polish unit of field measurement depending on the region varied between 18 and 28 hectares.
197 'Uniwersał JKMści o wybraniu piechoty w dobrach królewskich', *Sprawy wojenne króla Stefana Batorego. Dyjaryusze, relacyje, listy i akta z lat 1576–1568* (Kraków, 1887), p.117.
198 *Ibidem*, p.118.

raised in 1683, fighting as part of the defence force in Podolia. While the exact strength of the units raised by Polish districts are unknown, an estimate in the region of 1,000 men would not be far wrong. However, it is possible to identify the officers in charge of the units and see which Polish regions provided *wybraniecka* infantry for the army in 1683.[199]

Lands/districts where infantry was organised	*Rotmistrz*
Wielkopolska	Franciszek Żychliński
Ruthenia	Andrzej Wojakowski
Cracow	Paweł Podoski
Masovia	Stanisław Zawisza
Lublin and Bełż	Franciszek Rudnicki
Podlasie	Franciszek Okolski

Wybraniecka in 1683 would be equipped in the same way as Polish-Hungarian infantry, with muskets and sabres, and also short axes. It would operate as a typical 'shot' formation, without any pikemen.

Flags and colours

When looking into the details of the flags carried by Polish and Lithuanian troops, it is difficult as none have survived. Based on existing iconography, some written sources and those items from the early post-Sobieski period that were captured by the Swedes during The Great Northern War, it is possible to at least try to reconstruct some of the most common motifs and styles.

A white eagle, normally on a red background, was one of the most common motifs. Sometimes the eagle also had incorporated in it a coat of arms – either the royal one (known as Janina) or belonging to the magnate in charge of the unit. Another often seen pattern was the Knights' Cross, usually red on a white background or white on a red background, although there is evidence of yellow, green or blue backgrounds and even a black Knights' Cross. Other religious symbols, especially of the Madonna with the Infant Jesus, could be used as well. Checks seem to be used frequently in the cavalry, for example red and white, black and red. In the infantry units we can find a Burgundian Cross/St. Andrew's Cross, in combinations of a white cross on red background or vice versa. Also in the infantry, flags with horizontal lines in alternate colours, usually three, sometimes mixed with additional emblems (i.e. the Madonna or a Burgundian Cross) was in common usage. As the most important religious symbol, the cross seems to be so prevalent that eyewitness seeing the Polish army marching through Silesia mentioned that 'all companies and units had crosses on their flags'.[200] Amongst Polish flags captured by Turks during first battle of Párkány, were some 'from red

---

199 AGAD, Archiwum Skarbu Koronnego, II, 67, pp.12–12v; Jan Wimmer, *Wieden 1683*, p.230.
200 Marcin Kopiec, *Król Sobieski na Śląsku w kościołach w drodze pod Wiedeń*, p.15.

and white material, embroidered with gold and silver, that belongs to [the] King of Poland'.[201] Such colours were a common motif in the Polish army, so there is no confirmation that any of those captured could specifically belong to units serving under King's name.

Cavalry 'of another Nation' (possibly Wallachian light horse) present at Jan Sobieski's entry into Cracow in 1676 had some black and white standards, while the others were 'sky coloured'.[202] It is possible that banners of light cavalry were using very simple (and cheaper) flags, either one or two colours, often without any additional motifs. A company of dragoons that in 1677 travelled as the guard of Jan Gniński, the Polish envoy to Turkey, had a flag 'with the picture of Holy Mary', another element used often throughout the whole period.[203]

At the beginning of 1677 the Royal Guard infantry regiment under General-Major Ernest Denhoff was composed of five companies and they all received new uniforms and flags. One standard, probably belonging to the colonel's company, was white, with a white eagle embroidered with silver thread, with a blue shield held in his claws. The remaining four flags had a blue background but different motifs. The first had 'different military symbols, like bows, quivers, arrows and others', also with a blue shield. The second was decorated with a white eagle embroidered with silver thread. On the third there was silver mounted knight with a shield in his hand, with the Lithuanian coat of arms Pogoń. The final flag also had a motif of a white eagle embroidered with silver thread but with the addition of blue shield in his claws.[204]

201 Silahdar Mehmed Aga z Fyndykły, 'Diariusz wyprawy wiedeńskiej i kronika związanych z nią wydarzeń w państwie osmańskim od 21 stycznia 1681 do 28 lutego 1684 r.', Zygmunt Abrahamowicz (ed.), *Kara Mustafa pod Wiedniem. Źródła muzułmańskie do dziejów wyprawy wiedeńskiej 1683 roku*, p.181.

202 *A True Relation of the Manner of the Coronation of the present King of Poland*, p.4.

203 Franciszek Pułaski (ed.), *Źródła do poselstwa Jana Gnińskiego wojewody chełmińskiego do Turcyi w latach 1677–1678* (Warszawa: Druk Rubieszewskiego i Wrotnowskiego, 1907), p.3.

204 Biblioteka Zakładu Narodowego im. Ossolińskich we Wrocławiu, no 337, *Opisanie wjazdu Króla J. M. na Seym Walny do Warszawy*, p.52.

6

Lubomirski's corps in Imperial service

In 1682 the Imperial envoy to Poland, Hans Christoph Zierowsky, began negotiations with King Jan III Sobieski for the raising of a cavalry corps, directly onto the Imperial payroll. Polish cavalry, with its experience in fighting against the Turks and Tatars, would be a great reinforcement for the Duke of Lorraine's army. Despite the very vocal opposition of many nobles, who were arguing during the *Sejm* that such recruitment would drain available manpower prior to raising the Polish army, Sobieski agreed, and on 1 February 1683 both parties signed a contract to raise just over 2,800 cavalry and dragoons. Hieronim Augustyn Lubomirski (1647–1706) was nominated as commander of this the auxiliary corps, and he received the Austrian rank of *Feldmarschallleutnant*. He was an experienced soldier, previously fighting under Sobieski's command against the Turks and Tatars. Interestingly enough, in the late 1670s he was part of pro-French faction that raised troops to support Hungarian *kuruc* rebels led by Imre Thököly who were fighting against Imperial rule in Royal Hungary. By 1682 he switched his political allegiance and supported Sobieski's alliance with Austria. Lubomirski's corps was to be composed of:

- His own cuirassier regiment, under Colonel Jan (Johann) Butler – 817 horses
- A cuirassier regiment under Colonel Jan Kazimierz (Johann Casimir) Tedtwin – 817 horses
- A dragoon regiment under Colonel Kazimierz (Casimir) Königsegg – 817 horses
- Four banners (companies) of Polish *pancerni* cavalry (called in German *Pantzer Reiter*), under *rotmistrz* Marcin Bielicki, Remigian Grocholski, Andrzej Kreuz and Władysław Mroczek.

There is some evidence that there were at least two more banners of *pancerni*, under Modrzejowski and Józef Dymiszewicz, but these officers could have been in charge of the cuirassiers companies or serving alongside Lubomirski as volunteers. Imperial sources seem to confirm only 400 *pancerni* were employed, with 100 horses per banner being the standard size of such units in the Polish army. Grocholski was the most experienced amongst their officers, serving in the Polish army as a companion since 1649,[1] so he was nominated as a colonel in charge of all *pancerni* banners.

Both cuirassier regiments were to be organised as per Imperial regulations, with 10 companies. Regimental staff was to consist of the colonel, lieutenant colonel, major, quartermaster, auditor, chaplain, clerk (regimental secretary), supply officer, adjutant, wagon master, regimental armourer and the provost with his men (between two and four), so up to 17 men. Each company would have 11 men on the staff (*primaplana*): rittmeister, lieutenant, cornet (ensign), sergeant, quartermaster, company clerk, barber (surgeon), trumpeter, saddler, blacksmith and armourer. The rank and file of each company was composed of 3 corporals and 66 privates, divided into three corporalships. The dragoon regiment had a very similar structure and was also divided into 10 companies. The regimental staff was almost the same as the cuirassiers, lacking just the regimental armourer. Each company's *primaplana* was led by a captain (instead of rittmeister), the ensign was called a *fendrich,* a drummer replaced the trumpeter and there was no armourer. Each company had a strength of three corporals and 67 privates.[2] The exact structure of the *pancerni* banners is unknown, but it is certain that it followed the normal organisation of such units in the Polish army, described in earlier chapters.

Hieronim Augustyn Lubomirski. Painter unknown (Wikimedia Commons)

While initial correspondence about the raising of the corps mentioned that the two main regiments would be 'of lighter horse' (*leichter Reutterey*), they were equipped as Imperial cuirassiers, with helmets, breast and backplate, sword, a brace of pistols and carbine. Polish sources called them *arkabuzeria*, so the same word as used for Polish reiters, showing that they were indeed the equivalent of Imperial horse. *Pancerni* used the standard equipment of such units of that time: chainmail, a *misiurka* helmet, wicker *kałkan* shields, sabres, pistols, bows and carbines. Eyewitnesses also mention spears (*dzidy*) being used during the battle of Bratislava (Pressburg) in July 1683,[3] so it would appear that at least some of the *pancerni* were using them. Dragoons were again most likely equipped the same as their Imperial counterparts, with muskets and swords.

To entice soldiers to serve in Imperial army, they were to receive very good initial payments,

---

1 Marek Wagner, *Słownik biograficzny oficerów polskich drugiej połowy XVII wieku,* volume I, p.109.

2 Franciszek Kluczycki (ed.), *Akta do dziejów Króla Jana IIIgo',* pp.136–140.

3 Franciszek Kluczycki (ed.), *Akta do dziejów Króla Jana IIIgo',* p.206, 'Relacya potrzeby z Turkami y Węgrami pod Prezburgiem, 28 Julii 1683,

While this Western-type horseman was drawn in 1654, his equipment and weapons are a good representation of how Lubomirski's cuirassiers would have looked like. Theodorus von Kessel (Rijksemuseum)

so called 'recruitment money'. In cuirassier units corporals and privates received 40 reichstalers (rthl) each, in the dragoon regiment (also for corporals and privates) 30rthl. each, and *pancerni* 60rthl each (including officers). Officers and NCOs in both cuirassiers and dragoons were not due any recruitment payment. Additionally Imperial commissioners were to issue flags for cuirassiers and dragoons (but not for *pancerni*) that would cost a total of 800rthl. Raising the three regiments and the four banners of Polish cavalry cost a total of 101,000rthl or 151,500 florins and it did not include any additional payments for weapons, equipment and horses, as soldiers had to buy these for themselves, from their first payment. Pay for each quarter (three months) of service, which included the only pay for the *primaplana's* staff in all three regiments, all corporals and privates of those regiments and all *pancerni* was estimated as 50,625 florins, or about 33,000rthl.[4]

Units were recruited in areas near the border with Silesia, so it is probable that many of the soldiers would be in fact Imperial subjects. Jan Chryzostom Pasek sarcastically commented on the quality of the recruits joining Lubomirski's troops, saying that many of them were not nobles: 'and they had recruited some rabble: valets became *rotmistrz* and lieutenants; a servant arriving on foot, he was given a horse and he is now companion'.[5] Desertion was rife, as many soldiers took the advanced pay and promptly left the ranks. Additionally, the newly raised units were pillaging off the local population, leading to many official complaints. King Jan III issued orders to capture all deserters, as he wanted to protect other areas of the country from marauding soldiers. Lubomirski finally managed to bring back order and discipline, offering amnesty to those who had left the ranks. This amnesty brought back a whole company from Tedtwin's regiment, indicating that desertion was on a large scale and included whole units![6] At the end of June 1683, after mustering in front of Imperial Commissioner Christoph Wenzel, the corps left Poland, to join the Imperial army in Moravia. Problems with desertion and the absence of further pay from Imperial envoys meant that the units never achieved their planned size, and it is estimated that only around 2,000 soldiers went to Moravia, with Lubomirski's regiment being

4   Franciszek Kluczycki (ed.), *Akta do dziejów Króla Jana IIIgo'*, pp.42–43, 'Entwurf Der Werbegelder…'.
5   Jan Chryzostom Pasek, *Pamiętniki*, p.375.
6   Kazimierz Konarski, *Polska przed odsieczą wiedeńską 1683 roku*, p.155.

the most under strength, with only 400 cuirassiers. In his memoire of the campaign Hermann von Baden estimated the strength of Lubomirski's corps at 2,700 men but most likely he was referring to its 'paper strength'.[7]

At the beginning of July, Tedtwin's cuirassiers were part of the vanguard of Polish troops ambushed by 500 *kuruc* near Bytča and took heavy losses, with 40 killed and many wounded, also losing many horses.[8] After that, the regiment supported Imperial cuirassiers and dragoons defending the island Tabor on the Danube the against Turks. Here the unit lost its Major, Greben, who according to Lubomirski's own words, 'died with incomparable bravery, in front of the whole army killing three Turks'.[9] Königsegg's dragoons entered the combat next, and in mid-July 1683 the regiment was sent as part of Johann Heinrich Graf von Dünewald's division[10] to protect Krems from Tatars and to attack Turkish supply lines. The rest of Lubomirski's troops were at that point part of the main field army led by the Duke of Lorraine. Here they played an essential part in battle of Bratislava (Pressburg) on 29 July 1683. Polish *pancerni* and cuirassiers fought as the vanguard of the Imperial army in battle against Hungarian *kuruc* supported by Turkish *sipahi*. It was first major victory of the Imperial army in this war, raising the morale of the troops and allowing them to forget about their earlier defeat at Petronell. The *Pancerni* and their commanding officer, Colonel Grocholski, were especially praised for their actions during the battle.[11] The Duke of Lorraine wrote to the King and mentioned that 'Prince Lubomirski and his Polish Officers and Soldiers alone, most prudently, valiantly, and with the natural Vigor of the renowned Polish Nation'.[12] Allied losses were very small, and an anonymous Polish soldier mentioned in his account only one companion and two retainers

Kuruc fighting with Imperial cuirassier. Fragment of map from period (Wikimedia Commons)

---

7   Franciszek Kluczycki (ed.), *Akta do dziejów Króla Jana IIIgo*, p.629, Mémoire Badois.
8   *Das Kriegsjahr 1683*, p.68.
9   Franciszek Kluczycki (ed.), *Akta do dziejów Króla Jana IIIgo'*, p.184.
10 Dünewald's own cuirassier regiment, and the Croat regiments of Lodron and Kery.
11 'Relacya potrzeby z Turkami y Węgrami pod Prezburgiem…', p.208.
12 Dupont, p.143, letter from Imperial camp at Marcheck, 31 July 1683.

were killed.[13] The Turks and Hungarians allegedly lost between 600 and 1,000 killed and many prisoners. Their camp was captured but Lubomirski ordered it to be burned. Servants (*czeladź*) of the Polish cavalry were pillaging it and he was concerned that enemy may return and surprise the army while it was ransacking the camp. Despite the fire, Imperial troops managed to capture 1,200 to 1,500 wagons full of loot and a few thousand sheep. The epilogue of the battle was gruesome as only the few most important prisoners were kept alive for future ransom, while the rest were killed.

Further actions of Lubomirski's troops concentrated on fighting against Hungarian *kuruc* raids in Moravia, where again Grocholski seemed to excel in leading the Polish cavalry in the actions of this 'small war'. The Hungarian cavalry was beaten and forced to retreat, giving the Imperial army time for some respite.[14] In early August the Duke of Lorraine, writing again to Sobieski, described a fight where a small unit of Poles was sent against 400 *kuruc*. Once they met the enemy, Lubomirski's troops realised that they were facing a much stronger force of up to 4,000 Hungarians. This realisation did not stop the Polish cavalrymen however, as they 'charged with such energy and bravery, that they forced them [the enemy] to retreat, saved all the Austrian prisoners, recaptured the whole loot, killed three hundred enemies and captured a few hundreds of Hungarian horses and ten standards'. When Lorraine arrived with a relief force, expecting to have to help his Polish allies, he instead found them victorious and returning to the Imperial camp. He wrote that 'their strength and courage was so unyielding that they lost no more than twenty dead and wounded'.[15] Previously quoted anonymous soldiers from Lubomirski's command described the *kuruc* group as numbering 3,500 men, so slightly weaker than the numbers mentioned by Lorraine. He also wrote that Colonel Grocholski had 1,000 Poles, which is a fairly strong force. According to him, the defeated Hungarian rebels lost up to 700 killed, and additionally a few high ranking officers were captured by the Poles.[16] Dalerac praised the actions of Lubomirski and his troops, as the former 'led on his Men with extraordinary Vigor, and obtained an entire Victory, without giving the Enemy time to rally'.[17] The Frenchman paid the Polish officers many compliments, describing them as 'certainly one of the bravest Men of his Age, being all Fire, and having all the vigour that can be desired for a brisk Expedition; he despises Danger, is without Fear, a good Partisan, a Lover of War, but especially of Battles, desires always to be charging the Enemy, as all brave Men do, who are not answerable for the Event of an Action'.[18] Polish troops also played a role in the Imperial victory at Bisamberg, where on 24 August Lorraine defeated a Turkish and Tatar force of Abaza Kör Hüseyin Pasha. The Duke wrote that 'once again they showed the bravery of the Polish soldier in this fight'.[19] Another anonymous account, written by a Polish

---

13   'Relacya potrzeby z Turkami y Węgrami pod Prezburgiem…', p.210.
14   *Ibidem*, p.210.
15   Dupont, pp.154–156, letter from Imperial camp, 7 August 1683.
16   'Relacya potrzeby z Turkami y Węgrami pod Prezburgiem…', p.210.
17   Francois Paulin Dalerac, *Polish Manuscripts*, p.73.
18   *Ibidem*, p.73.
19   Dupont, pp.171–172, letter from Imperial camp at Korneuburg, 26 August 1683.

soldier, provides us with some more details of the Polish involvement in this battle.[20] Lorraine had under his command 10,000 Imperial cuirassiers and dragoons, supported by 2,000 Poles. The latter were deployed as the centre of the allied force. Turkish cavalry managed to break through Lubomirski's regiment but were then stopped by the fire of Imperial and Polish dragoons from the second line and counter charged by Grocholski's *pancerni*. It seems that yet again these Polish cavalrymen, armed with spears, proved their worth, forcing the *sipahi* to retreat. The Imperial wings also managed to stop and push back the Turkish and Tatar cavalry, forcing the whole army of Abaza Kör Hüseyin Pasha to quickly retreat. Lorraine ordered Lubomirski to chase after Pasha's forces, killing many Turkish horsemen when they tried to swim across the Danube. The Duke's army captured 25 flags and a few hundred horses. The Turks lost between 1,000 and 1,200 killed or captured. Abaza Kör Hüseyin Pasha, already wounded during the fighting, was one of those drowned during the retreat. Polish accounts mention fairly low losses: the *pancerni* had one companion and 12 retainers killed, while the Polish cuirassiers had over a dozen killed.

Battle of Vienna. By Sobieski's court painter, Martino Altomonte (Author's archive)

The Auxiliary Corps fought at the battle of Vienna, taking part in relief of the city. Lubomirski's soldiers were part of the left flank of the allied army, alongside the Imperial troops. Here they were supported by Saxon soldiers and some Poles from Sobieski's army: three banners of winged hussars and six banners of *pancerni*. In the fierce struggle for the fortified village Kahlenbergerdörfl, Polish and Saxon dragoons (from the Reuss regiment) took heavy losses when fighting against the Turkish infantry and cavalry.

---

20   Unfortunately it was not possible to access the original manuscript from the Scientific Library of the PAAS and the PAS in Cracow, therefore the description is provided after Jan Wimmer, *Wiedeń 1683*, pp, 265–267.

Colonel Kazimierz Königsegg was killed, his skull split by Turkish sabre, even though he had a horseshoe in his hat as added protection.[21] Reinforced by more units, the dragoons managed to retake the village. During the final phase of the battle, Lubomirski's cavalry and the attached Polish units of hussars and *pancerni* led the attack on Ober-Döbling and then the northern part of the Turkish main camp.

Soon after the battle there were some changes in the command structure of Lubomirski's corps. Jan Kazimierz Tedtwin took over the late Colonel Königsegg's dragoon regiment and the unit served in the Imperial army until 1700, albeit under a few different colonels.[22] There is no information about which officer took command of Tedtwin's cuirassiers, although it is possible that both cuirassier regiments were merged into one, under command of Lubomirski and Butler. Official records tell of only one such regiment in service post-1683[23] but it seems that Alphons von Wrede made a mistake, of identifying – due to the change of commanding officer – Tedtwin's cuirassiers as dragoons.[24] The Polish units took part in the second battle of Párkány, where they were deployed on the right wing of the allied armies. Lubomirski was in charge of this sector of the battleline, where his corps was supported by cavalry and infantry from the regular Polish army. After this victory he went with the main Imperial army in further operations against the Turks and finished the campaign in winter quarters in Spiš. Officially the cuirassiers and *pancerni* were disbanded in 1685, but it has not been possible to find any information about their service in 1684 and 1685, prior to their disbandment.

While the size and role of Lubomirski's auxiliary corps was a not main factor in the Imperial military effort in 1683, it is important to remember the positive effect brought about by the presence of Polish cavalry supporting their Imperial counterparts, as was shown at Bratislava and Bisamberg. It is also interesting to note that, while raised and paid for from the Emperor's treasury, the provision of 2,000 men under the command of Lubomirski can be counted as yet another part of the wide range of military support provided by the Commonwealth against the Ottomans.

---

21 Francois Paulin Dalerac, *Polish Manuscripts*, p.93.
22 Alphons von Wrede, *Geschichte der K. Und K. Wehrmacht*, volume III, part 2 (Wien: W. Seidel und Sohn, 1901), p.650.
23 *Ibidem*, p.552.
24 *Ibidem*, p.648.

7

The Campaign of 1683

The concentration and march of the Polish army

Since April 1683 regular Polish troops had been gathering in a large camp near Trembowla, where in late May they were joined by Hetmans Jabłonowski and Sieniawski. As many of them had spent the winter in areas far away from Podolia, they needed time to return to the field, especially as many of the companions were away from units, visiting their homes. Unfortunately, on 1 July 1683 a fire broke out in the camp, causing many losses amongst horses and equipment, which set the preparations of the troops back. Newly raised units were initially ordered to gather near Lwów but later this was changed to Łobzów near Kraków. As Sobieski received more urgent messages from Austria, asking him to lead the relief force and reinforce the Imperialists, he ordered Hetman Sieniawski to take a large part of the cavalry from the regular

King Jan III Sobieski with Royal Prince Jakub. Portrait by Jan Tricius (Wikimedia Commons)

army and to march from Trembowla to Kraków. Sieniawski received the King's order around 10 July and after gathering more troops, on 18 July he led them towards Kraków. A few days later Hetman Jabłonowski, leading infantry, dragoons and artillery, also left the camp at Trembowla.

Sobieski arrived at Łobzów on 29 July and shortly afterwards, on 2 August, Sieniawski and his cavalry, after marching almost 600km in two weeks, entered the camp. Jabłonowski and the rest of the regular troops arrived there six days later. More and more of newly raised troops joined, but many were still forming and equipping and were not ready to march towards Vienna. Some troops had to stay in Poland to defend against Ottoman and Tatar raids, and others were delayed and joined the main army later, either during the march through Silesia and Moravia or even after the relief of Vienna, during the follow-up campaign in Slovakia. The preparations and march of the Lithuanian troops will be described in Chapter 8.

Soon after the arrival of Jabłonowski's troops the first Polish 'division' started its journey towards Vienna. Sieniawski was in command of the vanguard, composed of *pancerni*, light horse and one or two regiments of dragoons. He led roughly 6,000 to 7,000 men, leaving Łobzów on 11 August. Jabłonowski left camp on 13 August, leading the main army, including hussars, infantry and the artillery park. The King, accompanied by the Queen, Royal Prince Jakub and many courtiers followed them on 15 August. It seems that at the start of the journey to Austria morale in the army was high and that Jan III lead by example, 'going there like for certain victory, taking with him historians and aretologists so they can write and praise virtue of the King and Polish Nation'.[1] Pasek mentions that on the day of the royal departure from Kraków he heard Sobieski saying 'I pray to God that I will meet them [Turks] there; so [soon] it will be easy to get Turkish horses in Poland'.[2] As is seen in Brulig's account, the remaining Polish troops, in both small and large groups, were rushing to join the army, marching through Moravia as late as the end of September. This was especially the case where the Cossacks were concerned, as it took time to organise and prepare their units, causing a delay in their arrival.

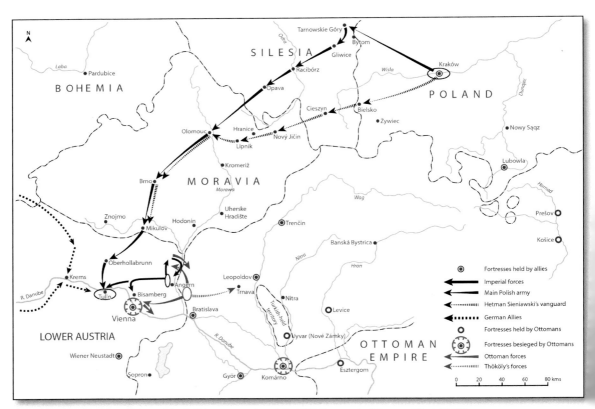

Route of the Polish troops to Austria in 1683. [Source: Jan Wimmer, *Wiedeń 1683*]

---

1   Jan Chryzostom Pasek, *Pamiętniki*, p.375.
2   *Ibidem*, p.375.

Sieniawski's group marched through Eastern Moravia, to protect the main army against any Ottoman or *kuruc* attack. His route went through Cieszyn (Teschen), Nový Jičín (Neutitschein), Hranice (Weißkrchen) and Lipník nad Bečvou (Leipnik), where his troops arrived on 20 August. While he was supposed to wait there for new orders from Sobieski, he disobeyed him and, after receiving more and more alarming letters from Duke Charles of Lorraine, decided to march through Olomouc and Brunn to Mikulov. Again, Brulig's account (Appendix II) states that on 24 August his troops marched through Rajhradice, 13km south of Brno and around 120km from Vienna. It appears that such an independent move of his Field Hetman really alarmed King Jan III, who was worried that Sieniawski might be convinced by Duke Charles and Lubomirski to join the Imperial armies and engage the Ottomans prematurely. That explains why the Polish monarch decided to go ahead of the main army and, as we will see below, rush to stop his commander from committing to doing anything rash. Sieniawski, it seems, realised that he may have advanced too far ahead of the main army so did not leave Mikulov, and waited with his troops for the arrival of the King. Overall, the whole march from the army camp near Kraków to Mikulov in Moravia took the Hetman's soldiers 15 days, during which they covered around 330km.

Ottoman army besieging Vienna. Romeyn de Hooghe, 1684 (Rijksmuseum)

Date of arrival	Name and location of the place	Notes
17 August	Lipowiec, Poland	
18 August	Mysłowice, Poland	
19 August	Bytom, Poland	
20 August	Tarnowskie Góry, Poland	Stayed there for two days. Queen Marie Casimire left him there and returned to Cracow.
22 August	Gliwice, Silesia	From here the King travelled faster ahead of main army with some cavalry and dragoons.
23 August	Ruda, Silesia	
24 August	Piotrowice, Silesia	
25 August	Dvorce (Hoff), Moravia	
26 August	Olomouc, Moravia	
27 August	Vyškov, Moravia	King and his troops camped in tents.
28 August	Kowalowice, Moravia	
29 August	Modřice, Moravia	
30 August	Mikulov, Moravia	
31 August	Oberhollabrunn, Austria	The King's group joined Sieniawski's group here.

The King initially marched alongside the main army, but as mentioned earlier, to rein in Sieniawski, he decided to quickly ride ahead of Jabłonowski's forces and to catch up with his Sieniawski's troops. When he left on 22 August, the King took with him '20 and some' banners of light horse and a few hundred dragoons.[3] According to Royal Prince Jakub, each banner of hussars in main army had to detach six companions (it is almost certain that this was with their retinues) and also join the King's bodyguards,[4] while Dalerac wrote that there were 20 hussars from each banner and that they were without lances.[5] Depending on the source, this group had 2,000 (Dupont), 3,000 (Royal Prince Jakub) or 4,000 men (Dalerac). Dupont also wrote that the King ordered soldiers to leave their baggage wagons with the main army and that even royal servants 'had only necessary things for him and his son'. He also added that while there was a six-horse carriage that accompanied the group, that neither Jan III nor Royal Prince Jakub used it until they arrived at the Danube.[6] The King initially forced a fast daily pace, 'of eight to nine German miles'[7] although later, when he was informed that the Hetman had stopped at Mikulov and was not going to move from there, he slowed the speed of his forced march. During this leg of the journey Sobieski was updated daily about the current situation on the main front, thanks to letters sent by the Duke of Lorraine and Sieniawski. Lorraine's letters to the King can be found in Appendix VII, as they give a very interesting insight into the relationship

---

3   Antoni Zygmunt Helcel (ed.), *Listy Jana Sobieskiego do żony Marii Kazimiery*, pp.372–373, Jan III do Marii Kazimiery, W Opawie, d. 25 Sierpnia o pierwszej z południa.

4   Jakub Ludwik Sobieski, *Dyaryusz wyprawy wiedeńskliej w 1683 r.*, p.7

5   Francois Paulin Dalerac, *Polish Manuscripts*, p.84. Considering the size of the retinues (usually two or three horses strong), those 20 hussars mentioned by him could be companions and retainers counted together.

6   Dupont, p.183.

7   *Ibidem*, p.185. German mile was approx. 7.5km.

Plate A
A1. King Jan III Sobieski; A2. Crown Grand Hetman Stanisław Jan Jabłonowski
(Illustration by Sergey Shamenkov © Helion & Company 2021)
See Colour Plate Commentaries for further information.

Plate B
B1. General of Artillery Marcin Kątski; B2. *Rotmistrz* **of** *pancerni*
(Illustration by Sergey Shamenkov © Helion & Company 2021)
See Colour Plate Commentaries for further information.

Plate C
C1. Hussar companion; C2. _Pancerny/petyhorzec_
(Illustration by Sergey Shamenkov © Helion & Company 2021)
See Colour Plate Commentaries for further information.

Plate D
D1. Light horseman; D2. *Arkabuzer*/reiter
(Illustration by Sergey Shamenkov © Helion & Company 2021)
See Colour Plate Commentaries for further information.

Plate E
E1. Musketeer of foreign infantry; E2. Dragoon
(Illustration by Sergey Shamenkov © Helion & Company 2021)
See Colour Plate Commentaries for further information.

Plate F
F1. Haiduk; F2. Royal Guard Janissary
(Illustration by Sergey Shamenkov © Helion & Company 2021)
See Colour Plate Commentaries for further information.

Plate G
G1. Cossack; G2. Polish Tatar
(Illustration by Sergey Shamenkov © Helion & Company 2021)
See Colour Plate Commentaries for further information.

Plate H
H1. Artilleryman; H2. Cavalry servant (*czeladź*)
(Illustration by Sergey Shamenkov © Helion & Company 2021)
See Colour Plate Commentaries for further information.

between the two commanders of the allied armies. Finally, on 30 August, Jan III met with Sieniawski and a day later he visited his troops and had his first meeting with Duke Charles. Sobieski described the clothes of Charles V Duke of Lorraine, commander in chief of the Imperial army when allies met for the first time:

> His clothes are grey, without anything [ornaments] only the buttons are golden, fairly new; he had no feathers on his hat. His boots were [initially] yellow two or three months ago, [now] they have cork heels. His horse is good, with an old saddle, [horse] tack simple, made from strap, very bad and old (…) He had a blond wig but a rather poor one, it looks like he do not care about his appearance.

The Polish monarch quickly warmed to the Imperial commander, writing to the Queen that 'we had good discussion about any topic. He is modest, does not talk much, seems like good natured man, and he had good understanding of the art of warfare and is eager for it'. The King mentioned that the Duke was not used to drink, so during dinner he mostly drank Mosel wine with plenty of water. Once he felt more comfortable in the company of the Poles, he moved on to much stronger Hungarian wines and despite the warnings of Imperial diplomats, he apparently enjoyed a little too much of it. He became very friendly with his Polish allies, learning Polish words like 'father', 'son' (for King's son Jakub] and 'my brothers'. This first meeting started on a very good note, although one can only imagine the poor shape that the Duke was in the next morning.[8]

The main army, with all the artillery and a large baggage train, marched at a much slower pace. Brulig records that they passed Rajhradice on 30 August. It seems that by 2 September they had arrived at the agreed concentration place at Oberhollabrunn, where they were met by soldiers from Sobieski's and Sieniawski's groups. As mentioned earlier, a steady stream of delayed units was marching through Moravia into Austria throughout the whole of September.

One of the crucial elements in the march of the Polish army through Silesia and Moravia was keeping good discipline amongst soldiers and their servants. Imperial officials, knowing the structure of the Polish army, realised

Carolus v. Dei Gratia Lotharingiæ. Barri etc. Dux.

Charles V, Duke of Lorraine. Artist unknown (Wikimedia Commons)

---

8   Antoni Zygmunt Helcel (ed.), *Listy Jana Sobieskiego do żony Marii Kazimiery*, p.375, Jan III do Marii Kazimiery, Z Heiligenbron, mil 3 od Tulmu, gdzie most budją, ultima Augusti.

that Sobieski's army would be accompanied by large numbers of servants and camp followers, that in their search for food and forage could devastate territory they passed through on the march. Therefore they prepared very well, setting up a chain of magazines throughout Silesia and those parts of Moravia as yet untouched by the war. According to Mikołaj Dyakowski such supply points were set up every four miles.[9] He was very positively surprised how well prepared were these places. 'In each magazine there was a shed full bread, fresh from the oven, herds of cattle and sheep, heaps of hay, barrels of beer and next to each shed [a] few thousands carts, each with five or six horses, ready carry those supplies [for the soldiers].[10] In advance, each magazine received a register of supplies and units that were to receive them. Dyakowski mentions in which order these provisions were issued to the Poles: 'first [for] the Royal Court, then the Hetman's court, after them the Royal Regiment, Hetman's regiment, regiments of other nobles, for the vanguard [troops], for infantry and similar types'.[11] In fact there were so many supplies, mostly likely prepared for a larger number of troops, that during the initial phases of the march soldiers were only able to take half of the contents of the magazines. The situation worsened once the army reached the area near Brunn, where the territory had already been ravaged due to *kuruc* incursions. Brulig had the opportunity to see how Polish soldiers and their servants behaved in such situations, where there were not enough supplies. He mentions that due to lack of food the Poles started to pillage the areas along their march, even approaching Brulig's own monastery. Interestingly, he added that soldiers 'never acted violently, as one could always calm them down with good word, some bread or beer'.[12] It seems that servants 'that normally [were] staying with the baggage train' were the worst, as they 'throw stones into windows, trying to get inside, often breaking gates as they wanted to plunder basements and barns with wheat'.[13] Brulig praised the Polish officers leading the marching units, as, when begged to by the monks, they always stopped and punished marauding servants with the *bastinado*[14]

Silesia's long-term connection to Poland, meant that Sobieski's army could count on a very warm welcome, with celebrations and greetings all the way along the route of the march. Dalerac mentions that there was 'extraordinary concourse of the Nobility of Silesia, who flocked thither to see this famous King, from whom the Deliverance of the Empire was expected'.[15] He even went so far as to write that 'no Monarch ever received so much respectful Homage from People of a Foreign Dominion, as the King of Poland received from the Emperor's Subjects'.[16] Dupont also noted how well the Poles were received in Racibórz in Upper Silesia, and Olomouc in Moravia, with 'people from both towns and surrounding villages gathering from everywhere to see

---

9   Dyakowski probably meant a Polish mile, which in the seventeenth century was 7.1km.

10   Mikołaj Dyakowski, p.44.

11   *Ibidem*, p.44.

12   Brulig, pp.427–428.

13   *Ibidem*, p.430.

14   Painful foot or back whipping.

15   Francois Paulin Dalerac, *Polish Manuscripts*, p.82.

16   *Ibidem*, p.84.

the one [Jan III Sobieski] in which they placed their hopes of saving their freedom, lives and belongings. They repeated it on and on with their hails'.[17] The initial part of the journey ran so smoothly that the King wrote in a letter to the Queen that 'people here are extremely good and [they] bless us; the country is very merry'.[18] As the army marched further into Moravia, the situation was not so good, and Sobieski complained that 'everything here is expensive and [people] do not want to sell us anything'.[19] Despite the King's and Dupony's comments, the Moravians were not so happy to see yet another army marching through their territory, especially in areas already ravaged by the war. What is more, the Bohemian *Hofkanzlei* (Court Chancellery) issued a decree to people in Moravia, ordering them to sell provisions in exchange for Polish currency.[20] It was not a very popular move, as Polish coins contained a lower percentage of silver and, because of this were of lower value.

Despite such good marching conditions, the army was still suffering due to desertion, especially amongst the infantry, retainers and servants of the cavalry. Officers complained to Sobieski, who wrote in one of his regular letters to the Queen 'by God, by God! They need to be captured, especially around Częstochowa'.[21] It could indicate that desertion was especially rife amongst the delayed units, marching behind the main army. Bands of marauders could also be dangerous for both the local population and messengers travelling between Poland and the main army. In early September the general postmaster complained to Sobieski that two of his men were killed 'for their horses' by 'those that are marching on the back [of the army]'.[22]

Emperor Leopold I. Pieter
Schenk the Elder, 1670–1713
(Rijksmuseum)

---

17 Dupont, p.186.

18 Antoni Zygmunt Helcel (ed.), *Listy Jana Sobieskiego do żony Marii Kazimiery*, p.373, Jan III do Marii Kazimiery, W Opawie, d. 25 Sierpnia o pierwszej z południa.

19 *Ibidem*, p.374, Jan III do Marii Kazimiery, W Prostkowie, 2 mili za Ołomuńcem ku Nikielszpurkowi, dn. 27 Augusti 1683.

20 *Akta do dziejów Króla Jana IIIgo*, pp.227–228, 'De moneta Regni Poloniae a militibus Polonis durante eorum per fines Imperii itinere acceptanda'.

21 Antoni Zygmunt Helcel (ed.), *Listy Jana Sobieskiego do żony Marii Kazimiery*, p.376, Jan III do Marii Kazimiery, Z Heligenbron, mil 3 od Tulmu, gdzie most budują, ultima Augusti.

22 *Ibidem*, p.380, Jan III do Marii Kazimiery, Za Dunajem u mostu pod Tulnem, 9 Septembra, rano o piątej.

Turkish besiegers vs Imperial defenders of Vienna. Romeyn de Hooghe, 1684 (Rijksmuseum)

Towards the battle

As the situation of the defenders of Vienna was getting more desperate with each day, the only possible action of the joint allied armies had to be the direct relief of the city. Both Sobieski and Duke Charles wanted to engage the Ottomans near Vienna so there was no doubt that any plan agreed had to include a pitched battle against the besiegers. At the meeting of the Imperial and allied German generals (without Sobieski and Elector Johann George III), which took place on 3 September, they prepared a 13-resolution plan of action. It was then submitted, in French, to the Polish and Saxon monarchs, meeting with their approval. The points were as follows:[23]

1. The relief operation should take place between the Danube and the Wien rivers. All other places (of attack) needed too much time and there is not enough food and forage there. Moving operations away from the Danube would surrender too much of the country to the enemy.

---

23   Johann Georg von Rauchbar, *Leben und Thaten des Fürsten Georg Friedrich von Waldech (1620–1692)* (Arolsen: Speyer, 1872), pp.261–263.

2. Due to the absence of the Emperor, overall command will be in hands of the King of Poland, but all (allied) generals will be in command of their (respective) troops.

3. All troops will approach the bridges on Sunday (5 September), so they can cross on Monday (6 Sept.) or Tuesday (7 Sept.) at the latest, and they will all receive their forage and bread.

4. Imperial and Polish troops will cross (the Danube) in Tulln, and the Saxon troops in Krems, to join with those that are already on the other (right) bank of the river to see if they can reach the bridge to Trasmaur again.

5. Troops should cross and meet on Monday (6 Sept.).

6. It is highly unlikely that the enemy will attack the allied forces through the Vienna Woods or during the crossing. But (to protect against it), Polish forces will cross between Monday and Tuesday and join with the allies on the right bank (of the Danube) to support them while the main Imperial army crosses (after them).

7. Regarding supplies (delivered via the river), each allied army will detach officers that will (be in charge of) picking up the supplies of bread and oats to last for eight days, that will be then placed in a supply store in Tulln.

8. Protection of the bridges and supply depots. The one in Tulln is protected on one side by the town and on the other by a palisade, while the security of the bridge and supply depot in Krems is ensured thanks to the town in front of it, manned by townsfolk and supported by some soldiers.

9. Further supplies will be delivered in boats via river.

10. Regarding the plan of the attack (against the Ottomans), details of the cooperation between the allied armies, including signals, watchwords and patrols: it is postponed until the allies have a better knowledge of the situation and better communications. In general it is agreed that the main body will be composed of a mix of infantry and cavalry, with further infantry protecting the flanks, and ensuring that there were enough reserves.

Prince Georg Friedrich of Waldeck. Matthijs van Marebeek, between 1670 and 1699 (Rijksmuseum)

11. Territories on the left side (of the Danube) will be protected by a detachment of 2,000 (Imperial) cavalry, that will be (later) supported by 4,000 Polish soldiers, that are currently delayed, and then by the Lithuanian army which will march from Silesia.

12. The reserve force will protect the allied army in case of enemy attack via the Vienna Woods.

13. In the case of the victory of the allied armies, it is important to use this success wisely, either by following the (fleeing) enemy or by attacking Neuhäusel (Uyvar).

Sobieski was planning to group the majority of the Polish cavalry – especially the hussars – on one wing, believing that they would play a decisive role in the coming battle. As such he opposed the idea of the German commanders, who wanted to deploy Polish troops on both wings of the allied army. The King had drawn up his own battle plan, in which he presented his ideas for the troop deployment. Dupont[24] published Sobieski's orders with the description of his plan:

The centre of our battle line will be made of Imperial troops, supported by Court Marshal's [Hieronim Augustyn Lubomirski] regiment of cavalry[25] and four or five hussar banners; in exchange from them we will receive units of [Imperial] dragoons or some other German units. This corps will be under command of [Charles V] Duke of Lorraine.

The right wing will be composed of Polish troops, led by Crown Grand Hetman Jabłonowski and other Polish commanders.

On the left wing there will be troops of the Electors of Bavaria and Saxony, also supported by a few banners of hussars and other Polish cavalry, for which we will receive some dragoons or infantry.

Cannons will be divided in this way, that if Electors who do not have enough of them, [some] will be provided by Duke of Lorraine. This wing will be led by the Electors.

Troops from the German Circle will be deployed with the left wing alongside the Danube, orientated slightly to the right, with two main missions: firstly to harass the enemy and convince him that he will be attacked from this wing, secondly to move strong reinforcements into the town [Vienna] in case we are not be able to defeat the enemy in the way we plan. This corps will be under command of Duke von Waldeck.

In the first line [of the army] we will deploy infantry with cannons, behind them a line of cavalry. If those two lines should mix up, there would be plenty of problems crossing all the ravines, forests and hills; once we enter the plain field, cavalry will be deployed between battalions of infantry, that will be set up in proper order, we will do it especially for the [Polish] hussars that will strike first. If we would deploy the whole army in only three lines, it would cover more than one and half of German miles,[26] which would not be beneficial for us, [additionally] we would have to cross the river Wienfluss, which should be on right of [battle line]. That is why we want to deploy in four lines, where the fourth will be our reserve corps.

For the better protection against the first charge of the Turkish cavalry (which is always very rapid) our infantry could use *chevaux de frise,* but very light, so they can be easily carried and with each stop placed in the front of battalions.

I would like to ask all generals to ensure that, once their troops leave the hills and enter the plains, they take their right place in the battle line, as per this plan.

---

24 Dupont, op. cit. pp.188–189.
25 Composed of up to six *pancerni* banners.
26 The King was referring to a so-called 'Imperial' mile (*Reichsmeile*), which is the equivalent of 7.5km.

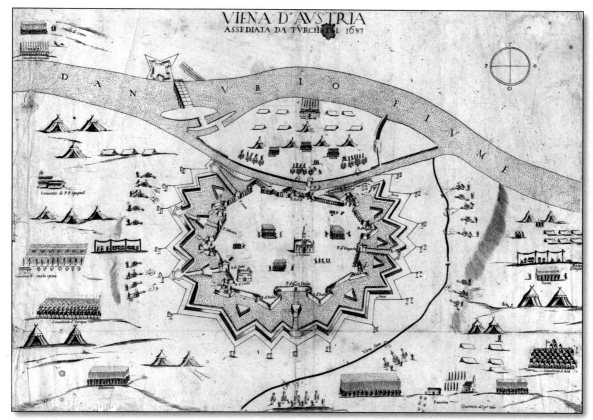

Vienna besieged by Turks.
Plate by unknown author.
(Wien Museum Inv.-Nr. 8675,
CC0)

This plan was modified, probably during the night of 3/4 September and the final placement of the troops, that commanders agreed to, was as follows:

The left wing, composed of the Imperial army under Duke Lorraine, the Saxon corps under Elector Johann George III and the Polish auxiliary corps under Lubomirski. As this part of the army was to break through to Vienna, it was additionally supported by contingent of Polish cavalry detached from Sobieski's army. There were three banners of hussars (the units of Jan Gniński, Samuel Prażmowski and Jan Cetner)[27] and one regiment of *pancerni* (maximum of six banners), where the nominal colonel was Hieronim Lubomirski (leading the auxiliary corps), but actual command was in the hands of the lieutenant of his *pancerni* banner, Stanisław Świeżawski.

In centre there were the Bavarian army and allied German Circle contingents,[28] supported by a large group of Imperial cavalry (eight regiments of cuirassiers, two of dragoons and one of Croats). All these allied troops were under the command of Georg Friedrich von Waldeck, with the Bavarian troops led by Elector Maximilian II Emanuel

---

27 'Relatio a comitiss anni 1683 biennalium gestorum et laborum exercitus…', p.844. All three of them were nominal commanders of the units, during the campaigns banners were led by their lieutenants.

28 Mostly Franconian, with some troops from Brunswick (Hanover) and Württemberg.

Elector of Saxony, Johann Georg III. Leonhard Heckenauer, between 1690 and 1697 (Rijksmuseum)

Elector of Bavaria, Maximilian II Emanuel. Martin Bernigeroth, late seventeenth/early eighteenth century (Rijksmuseum)

The Polish army received the honour of deploying on the right wing of the allied force, and it was divided into three 'divisions'. It is not known where the private units of volunteers were deployed. They attached themselves to regiments of cavalry, based on the links between officers and the owners of the private troops (i.e. a noble who was *rotmistrz* of the regular banner could have his private banner serving alongside the regiment he was part of):

The right wing was under the command of Grand Hetman Jabłonowski. He had six regiments of cavalry (Hetman Jabłonowski, Konstanty Wiśniowiecki, Stefan Bidziński, Rafał Leszczyński, Michał Zbrożek, Atanazy Miączyński) and his own company of *arkabuzeria*. There were six banners of hussars present[29] but it is not known how many of the 26 banners of *pancerni* were present. Jan Wimmer estimated their number as between 20 and 22, with 13 named in sources.[30] Some Wallachian light horse were assigned here as well, at least 10 banners. All six regiments of dragoons (Guard under Franciszek Gałecki, Guard under Ludwik de Maligny, Hetman Jabłonowski, Hetman Sieniawski, Stefan Bidziński, Marcjan Ścibor Chełmski) and the Hetman's Hungarian infantry banner were also attached to this wing. Finally, as mentioned already in Chapter 5, there were four brigades of foreign infantry (Ernest Denhoff, Stanisław Morstin, Eliasz Łącki and Fryderyk Gröben), with a total of nine regiments. The allies supplied added support to this

---

29   There should have been eight, but one was late, and one was detached to support the Imperialists.
30   Jan Wimmer, *Wiedeń 1683*, p.325.

part of the Polish army, attaching to it four battalions of infantry (one each: Imperial, Bavarian, Saxon and Franconian).

The centre, under the direct command of the King, was composed of the Royal cavalry regiment, which on paper was the strongest regiment in the army, with 11 banners of hussars and 10 banners of *pancerni*. In fact one banner of hussars was not present at Vienna and two others were detached to fight in support of Imperial forces, and it is also not known if all *pancerni* banners were present. The royal *arkabuzeria*, janissaries and Hungarian infantry were posted in this part of the battle line. Other private Household units, if any remained, were placed here as well.

The left wing was under Field Hetman Sieniawski. There were three regiments of cavalry (Hetman Sieniawski, Andrzej Potocki and Szczęsny Potocki), and it is most likely that the two remaining regiments were deployed here as well (Tomasz Karczewski and Mikołaj Radecki). There were seven banners of hussars and up to 23 banners of *pancerni,* with estimates of 16–18 present.[31] The Wallachian banners were deployed here, again with at least 10 banners supporting the main cavalry formations. Finally there were four brigades of foreign infantry (Jan Butler, Jan Dennemark, Kazimierz Zamoyski and Eliasz Krauze), with a total of 12 regiments of foot. The Hetman's units of *arkabuzeria* and Hungarian infantry were also part of this wing.

One of the main problems now met by the allied army was the weather, with heavy rain falling in the area since 1 September and slowing the construction of the two pontoon bridges near Tulln. Imperial soldiers and local peasants worked in very difficult conditions, trying to prepare ways for the allies to cross the Danube. Muddy roads were yet another problem, delaying the large Polish tabor wagons and slowing the march of the troops. On 5 September the vanguard of Polish troops approached the bridges and next morning, thanks to the rain stopping, the first soldiers started to move across to the other bank. Sobieski, Jabłonowski and Sieniawski led the way, aided by courtiers and other officers. A group of allied generals also joined the Polish commanders, reviewing the marching troops. The Polish army (without its tabor) crossed first and by the morning of 7 September the Imperial soldiers followed. The Polish tabor marched after them, but it took until 9 September to cross the river. The crossing was very difficult, as the bridges kept breaking and many wagons had to cross 'via fords through the arms of Danube, as there is no other river with such strong current in the whole world'.[32] A few Imperial units were either posted on the left bank to protect the bridges or were sent towards Moravia to meet the delayed Polish troops marching as quickly as they could to join the main army. Bavarian, Franconian and Saxon troops arrived from Krems, and all the allied soldiers set up a large camp around Tulln. The concentration of troops was completed by 8 September, with between 65,000 and 76,400 soldiers from all allied contingents preparing for the battle.

---

31 *ibidem*, p.327.
32 Antoni Zygmunt Helcel (ed.), *Listy Jana Sobieskiego do żony Marii Kazimiery*, p.383, Jan III do Marii Kazimiery, Z gór Kalenberg nazwanych, na których klasztor Kamedułów teraz spalony, nad obozem Tureckim, 12 Septembris o trzeciej przede dniem.

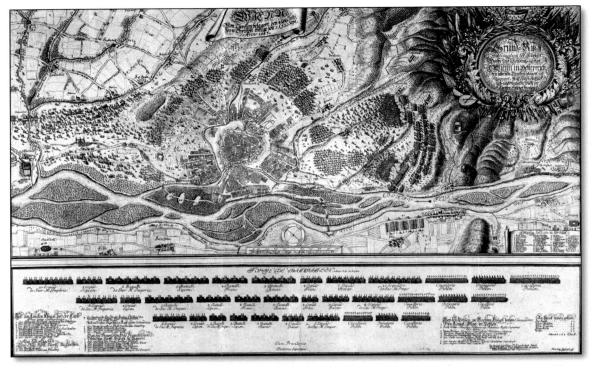

Relief of Vienna and order of battle of the allied army. Moritz (Mauritius) Bodenehr (copper engraver) and Daniel Suttinger (drawer), 1688 (Wien Museum Inv.-Nr. 57188, CC0)

Throughout 8 and 9 September units moved across into position, deploying as per the plan agreed on 4 September. Each of the three main corps of the allied force totalled just over 22,000 men, with the left (Imperial-Saxon-Polish) having the strongest contingent of infantry, while right (Polish) had the strongest concentration of the cavalry, led by most of the hussar banners. The Imperialists and Poles also sent some cavalry forward on reconnaissance missions, checking roads and skirmishing with any Turks and Tatars they encountered. Dyakowski mentions that the Imperial allies were truly surprised at the size of the forces sent by Sobieski for these reconnaissance missions. The officers in command were Damian Szumlański, *rotmistrz* of the *pancerni* banner, while Roman Ruszczyc was lieutenant in command of Damian Ruszczyc's Wallachian banner. The King sent them each 'with one hundred good horses from the vanguard' and ordered them to return with prisoners within 24 hours. Ruszczyc brought back 13 Turks, taken without any losses amongst Poles. Szumlański had less luck, and as his group was returning to the allied camp it was ambushed by Turkish forces and took some losses. The Poles still managed to capture seven janissaries but the *rotmistrz* was severely wounded in the stomach and it proved mortal as he died in camp four days later.[33]

During the night of 8/9 September the whole army remained awake, as due to some incidents on the left wing commanders and soldiers were under the impression that Turks might have been starting to counterattack. After a sleepless night, the vanguard of the army began to move towards the Vienna

---

33   Dyakowski, pp.47–48.

Woods. The troops were moving very slowly through muddy terrain, with the Poles not starting their march until the early afternoon. By the end of the day the allies finally reached the edge of the Vienna Woods, getting ready to begin to march through them. The task awaiting the soldiers was not an easy one. The armies had to cross difficult terrain, with thick forests, countless hills (the highest being 542 metres) and few proper roads, blocked in many places by barricades made from felled trees. The many paths leading through the hills and woods were narrow and, due to a week of near constant rain, difficult to move along. Depending on where they began their move some soldiers had to march between 10 and 20km, fully expecting attacks from the Turks and Tatars along the way.

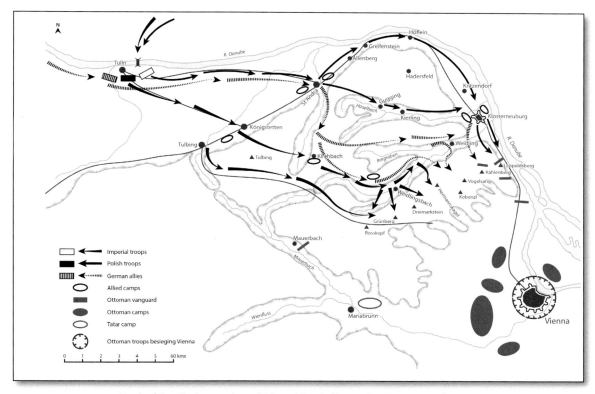

March of the allied troops through Vienna Woods. [Source: Jan Wimmer, *Wiedeń 1683*]

From here the movements of the Polish wing will be the focus of this narrative, witnessing their ordeal during the passage of the Vienna Woods and their preparations for the battle. Sobieski's soldiers spent the night of 9/10 September in the area between Tulbing and Königstetten, where every house had been burnt to the ground by Tatars. On the morning of 10 September the Polish army received provisions from their supply wagons, after which majority of the tabor was moved to Greiffenstein to wait for further orders. A smaller tabor with additional supplies of food stayed with the army. As already mentioned in Chapter 5 the artillery was divided, with the heavier cannons marching with the Imperial troops on left flank of the whole allied army, while smaller guns and their ammunition wagons were attached to the Polish infantry brigades. Dalerac noted that the Imperialists sent a few of the Emperor's huntsmen, who knew the area very well, to act as guides for the Poles and lead 'the Army through the least difficult ways, and over the easiest Hills, though this Mountainous Country is everywhere bad for a March'.[34] Jan Dobrogost Krasiński wrote about how difficult it was for the Polish army to journey through the Vienna Woods, as soldiers had to march through 'impassable chasms and woods, paths known only to the [wild] animals'. He also pointed out the lack of proper supplies, as the army 'had to spend three nights in great discomfort, people having only bread to eat, while horses fed on oak leaves'.[35] Considering how important a role the Polish cavalry was to play in the allied battle plan, the damage done to its fighting capacities while marching to the battle can be imagined. On 12 September Sobieski wrote to the Queen admitting that the terrain was very difficult, as the army had to climb through mountains and 'starting from Friday [10 September] neither we nor our horses had chance to eat or sleep'.[36] Despite the hardships, the soldiers were in good spirits, especially once they had set eyes on the massive Turkish camp and had a chance to think about the riches waiting for them there. The biggest concern was for

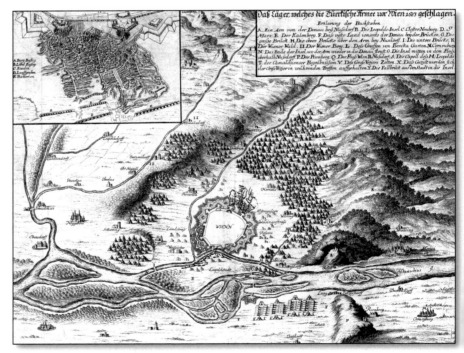

Turkish siege of Vienna in 1683. Published in Frankfurt in 1691 (National Library, Warsaw)

34 Dalerac, *Polish Manuscripts*, pp.86–87.

35 'Relatia seu descriptia wojny pod Wiedniem, pod Strygoniem i dalszej kampaniej A. 1683', Otton Laskowski (ed.), *Przegląd Historyczno-Wojskowy*, volume II, part 1 (Warszawa: Główna Księgarnia Wojskowa, 1930), p.164.

36 Antoni Zygmunt Helcel (ed.), *Listy Jana Sobieskiego do żony Marii Kazimiery*, p.383, Jan III do Marii Kazimiery, Z gór Kalenberg nazwanych, na których klasztor Kamedułów teraz spalony, nad obozem Tureckim, 12 Septembris o trzeciej przede dniem.

the state of their mounts, as the horses did not receive any provisions and had to be fed with tree leaves, so the King referred to the same problem as Krasiński.[37] Even descending from the hills was not an easy task, so the Polish cavalry had to march on foot, carefully leading their horses, before they were able to mount and prepare them for the forthcoming battle.[38] Lack of supplies affected even the King and the other commanders, who shared the ordeals of the marching army. According to Dalerac 'this March was very tiresome to the whole Army, for besides the great heat of the Season, they wanted Water, Provisions, Tents, &c. the Equipages staying behind in the Bottom: And the King as well as Generals had only Muleteers to follow them; so that His Majesty was forced one Day to eat nothing but Bread, and drink only Water that was in the Flagons of the Bavarian Soldiery, which they carried at their Sides.'[39] Marcin Kątski's diary, quoted in the earlier section describing the artillery, makes reference how difficult it was to move even the light cannons accompanying the Polish army.

Facing the Poles was the left flank of the Ottoman army (both Turks and Tatars) and some from the centre of their line.[40] The extreme left flank, on the right bank of Als stream, was held by Tatars, who were able to threaten Jabłonowski's force. Sources vary on the size of this force, with an estimated 10,000 Tatars being present but only 2,000 or 3,000 making a few weak attempts to engage the Poles. The Turkish left flank was led by Abaza Sari Hussein Pasha and was composed of his own troops from Damascus and a large contingent from Rumelia. They were mostly *sipahi* supported by some provincial soldiers, perhaps some light artillery as well, in total no more than 15,000 men. The centre of the Ottoman line, under the command of Grand Vizier Kara Mustafa himself, was composed of his own household troops (infantry and cavalry), up to 2,000 janissaries, Guard *sipahi* (up to 3,000) and *silahdars* (up to 3,000), with approximately 30 cannon. A Turkish diarist present on this part of the battlefield estimated the overall strength of these troops as between 3,000 and 4,000 infantry and 5,000 to 6,000 cavalry.[41]

Grand Vizier Kara Mustafa. Jacob Gole, late seventeenth/ early eighteenth (Rijksmuseum)

37   *Ibidem*, p.384.
38   Dalerac, *Polish Manuscripts*, p.97.
39   *Ibidem*, p.88.
40   Andrzej Witkowski, *Czerwone sztandary Osmanów. Wojna roku 1683 opisana na nowo* (Warszawa: Muzeum Pałacu Króla Jana III w Wilanowie, 2016), pp.373–376.
41   Dżebedżi Hasan Esiri, 'Wspomnienia i refleksje o wyprawie wiedeńskiej', Zygmunt Abrahamowicz (ed.), *Kara Mustafa pod Wiedniem. Źródła muzułmańskie do dziejów wyprawy wiedeńskiej 1683 roku*, p.225,

The Tatars could, if used aggressively, disturb the Pole's march, and there is a very interesting anecdote about this from Dalerac. The Frenchman wrote about an unusual encounter between Polish infantry and a small group of Tatars. 'But that which happened to a Colume of Polish Foot will certainly appear to be very odd. A Tartar Officer commanding a Party of about 30 Horse, happened in his March to fall into a Closs-Valley, and finding the said Body of Poles there, he came up to General de Henoff,[42] who was at their Head, not to fire upon him, but coolly to ask him News, as if they had been Friends; and when he was told, That they were Part of the Polish Army, which was advancing under the command of the King in Person, he answered jeeringly, That he knew very well that Prince Lubomirski had brought some Polish Troops to the succour of the Germans: After which he rode off with his Troop without General de Henoff's thinking fit to attack him, or perhaps he could not do it in that hollow Way, or that the Tartars kept himself at some distance from him.'[43] It is clear that the Tatars were not at all eager to engage the Polish army, contrary to the Vizier's orders. There were some small-scale skirmishes between Cossacks and dragoons and Tatars while the army was on the final part of their march, but it was nothing that would seriously affect the Poles.

According to Dupont, a map that King Jan III had received from the Imperialists gave him the incorrect impression of what was to be the battlefield. The right wing, where the Poles massed their cavalry, was supposed to be open terrain, ideal for cavalry. The French engineer sent by Sobieski for a quick reconnaissance mission noted that the map lacked some important details, like the forests, ravines and hills that were now visible in front of the Polish troops. In a letter to the Queen, written at 3.00 a.m. on 12 September, the King wrote that despite the promises of the Imperial generals, the terrain where the Polish army was due to attack was very difficult, and it would be another two days until the allied armies would be able to engage the Turks. 'Now we need to change whole battleline and manner of warfare, and fight in the way of grand Maurice [de Orange] and [Ambrogio] Spinola'.[44] Sobieski was in contact with the other allied commanders, as Lorraine, both Electors and Waldeck sent 'a few good cavaliers' to act as liaison officers and aides-de-camp, allowing for a constant exchange of messages.[45] Despite the King's worries that the allied army were not ready to engage the Ottoman force in such difficult terrain, there was no way to avoid the battle. At around 5.00 a.m. the Turkish counterattack struck at the allied left wing. The Battle of Kahlenbergh started.[46]

---

42   Ernest Denhoff, leading Foot Guard.

43   Dalerac, *Polish Manuscripts*, p.87.

44   Antoni Zygmunt Helcel (ed.), *Listy Jana Sobieskiego do żony Marii Kazimiery*, p.384, Jan III do Marii Kazimiery, Z gór Kalenberg nazwanych, na których klasztor Kamedułów teraz spalony, nad obozem Tureckim, 12 Septembris o trzeciej przede dniem.

45   *Ibidem*, p.383, Dalerac, *Polish Manuscripts*, p.92.

46   In the following part, the focus will be mostly on the actions of the Polish army, but providing brief information about the movements of the rest of the allied forces. It should still allow the reader to imagine the overall picture of the battle and its events, but at the same time present a more in-depth description of the Sobieski and his soldiers.

The Relief of Vienna (the Battle of the Kahlenberg), 12 September 1683

King Jan III leading allied armies in relief of Vienna in 1683. Pandolfo Reschi or his workshop, end of seventeenth/beginning of eighteenth century (Zamek Królewski w Warszawie)

The Turkish force of Ibrahim Pasha, composed of *sipahi* and janissaries, attacked the Imperial infantry who were busy building a fortification for the field battery at the foot of the Kahlenberg mountain. Lorraine, who at that time was resting in the burned-out Chapel of St. Joseph on the Kahlenberg, reacted quickly by sending more Imperial infantry under Charles Eugène de Croÿ. They managed to push back the Turks and held the line, supported by Saxon infantry and two regiments of dismounted Imperial dragoons. Around 6.00 a.m. when the morning mist disappeared, Lorraine was finally able to see the strong forces deployed on the Ottoman right wing and centre awaiting the allied attack. He then rode to meet Sobieski and the rest of the allied commanders in an impromptu council of war on the Kahlenberg. It was decided that the allied army would begin the attack. Lorraine was to advance with the left wing, while Sobieski issued orders to Waldeck to start moving troops forward in the centre. The King then attended Holy Mass consecrated by the Capuchin friar Marco d'Aviano, a close confidant of Leopold I and a special Papal envoy to the Emperor. In his sermon the friar encouraged the Christian soldiers to defeat the enemies of the faith and during communion spoke directly to the Polish king, highlighting 'how important it is to risk one's life for the glory of the Lord, whose Body he just took from his hands'.[47] It was very significant moment for Sobieski, who without a doubt saw himself as a Soldier of Christ, now facing the enemies of his faith. Initially he stayed close to the left wing, observing the Imperial, Saxon and Polish troops as their attack developed. He and Royal Prince Jakub breakfasted there as well, while since 6.00 a.m. the first Polish troops of the right wing were slowly moving through the difficult terrain towards the Turks. The King stayed on the left wing until around 10.00 a.m. witnessing the slow progress of Lorraine's troops and the heavy fighting with the Turks. Waldeck's centre was moving even slower, with the Franconian troops not

---

47   Dupont, pp.194–195.

supporting their Imperial and Saxon allies, leading to a short-lived crisis in the face of a Turkish counterattack. Luckily, the Hanoverian Colonel Pallandt used his own initiative and decided to support the Saxons, and his guard battalion, despite heavy losses (including the colonel himself) managed to fill the gap in the line. Lorraine had to pause his attack, waiting for the second and third line of his wing and the full complement of Waldeck's troops. The allied troops then had to withstand a series of fierce counterattacks by the Ottomans, trying to prevent them for capturing Nussdorf, Heiligenstadt and the line of the Nesselbach stream. Imperial and Saxon infantry and dragoons, despite being protected by *chevaux de frise,* were hard pressed by these attacks and Lorraine had to support them with his cuirassiers. Finally by 1.00 p.m. the Turks were pushed back, and the left wing was able to halt and consolidate its position, awaiting the movement of the remaining parts of the allied armies. Waldeck and his soldiers in the centre faced a much weaker defence, mostly confined to skirmishing with Turkish infantry amongst the vineyards on the hills of Kobenzl and Pfaffenberg. By 1.00 p.m. this part of the allied army also stopped, after connecting with flanking force of Saxons from the left wing.

As mentioned elsewhere, the first Polish units left the improvised camp as early as 6:00 a.m., struggling through the hills and forests, while the infantry was helping drag Kątski's cannon into position. In an earlier chapter we saw how much effort was put into transporting the artillery over the Kahlenberg.

Battle of Vienna. Published in Rome by Giovanni Giacomo De Rossi (National Library, Warsaw)

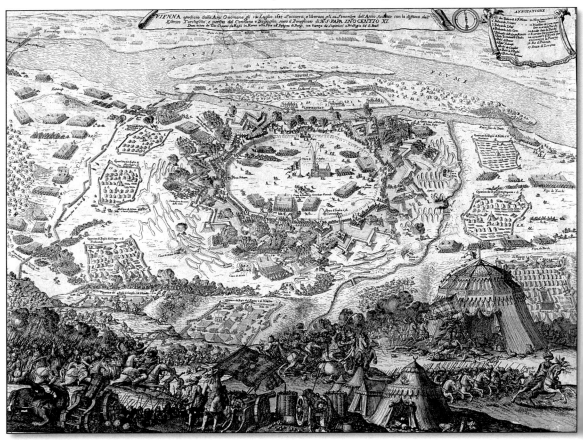

As the cavalry had to march dismounted, leading their mounts downhill, it again fell on the infantry to enter the fight first. Brigades from Hetman Sieniawski's 'division' (the Polish left wing) were engaged against janissaries, defending ravines near Krottenbach stream. Dupont wrote that 'one unit [brigade] was attacking the hill, while a second [brigade] was fighting in the ravine. As soon as the Turks were forced out from there, they returned to the hills and had to be dislodged from there'.[48] Regimental cannons provided invaluable support, while the infantry often had to exchange their muskets for bardiches and engage the Turks in hand-to-hand combat. Additionally two brigades of Polish infantry were sent against the Turkish position at Pötzleinsdorf, where janissaries managed to initially push back the Imperial dragoons from their position in the centre of the allied line. Kątski mentions that 'many Germans were killed there, both officers and privates'.[49] Polish infantry, probably supported by the reserve of Imperial cuirassiers from the centre,[50] managed to finally dislodge the Ottoman units from their position after heavy fighting. The Polish officers were leading from the front, as can be seen from the example of Lt. Colonel Aswerus Wrzospolski, commanding officer of Hetman Sieniawski's infantry regiment. He was mortally wounded leading his troops, and died on 23 September.

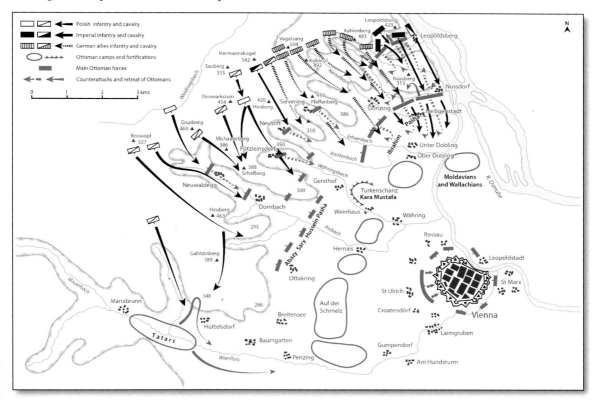

Battle of Vienna – actions between 5 am and 2 pm. [Source: Jan Wimmer, *Wiedeń 1683*]

48 Dupont, p.195.
49 Marcin Kątski, 'Diarium Artilieriae Praefecti', Franciszek Kluczycki (ed.), *Akta do dziejów Króla Jana IIIgo sprawy roku 1683*, p.593.
50 Dyakowski, p.64.

At approximately 2:00 p.m. Sieniawski's soldiers, including hussars and *pancerni,* finally captured Michaelerberg and linked up with the Imperial and German troops of the centre. The Polish centre 'division' was following Sieniawski's, as Sobieski was hoping to deploy a large contingent of his lance-armed cavalry here to break through the Turkish lines. At the same time Jabłonowski and his right wing 'division' was also busy, engaging the Ottoman left wing. The Grand Hetman's infantry brigades were engaged in heavy fighting pushing through ravines near Neuwaldegg and Dornbach, paying a steep price for their victory, 'many men were killed, and many were shot [wounded] but [Turks] could not stop eagerly attacking infantry'.[51] At the same time dragoons captured Heuberg and Gallitzbinger. On the latter hill they faced the Tatars, who made a few half-hearted attacks against the Poles. Jabłonowski protected his flank by detaching the cavalry regiment of Rafał Leszczyński, who with a few banners of *pancerni* and Wallachian light horse quickly discouraged the Tatars from further attacks.

Jan III Sobieski leading the Polish cavalry at Vienna in 1683. Romeyn de Hooghe, 1684 (Rijksmuseum)

It was nearing 4:00 p.m. when the Poles finally started to form up in a proper battle line, with squadrons of hussars and *pancerni* moving to the front, supported on the flanks by infantry. Sieniawski deployed mostly near Pötzleinsdorf, with the large Royal cavalry regiment on Schafberg and Jabłonowski near Dornbach. The Polish cavalry was facing a large Turkish force, by now reinforced by further troops moved from their right wing. There were masses of cavalry, mostly *sipahi,* deployed near the village of Gersthof and Shalfberg hill, while most of the infantry was deployed around the *Türkenschanz,* where Kara Mustafa, protected by his household troops and Levantine infantry, was in command. Both sides seemed to realise that this was the crucial point in the battle and that whoever was victorious on this part of the field, would triumph in the whole battle. Sobieski and his officers were not sure if they could throw their cavalry forward to immediately charge the Turks, as they did not know exactly what terrain features could affect the masses of charging cavalry. As

51   Marcin Kątski, 'Diarium Artilieriae Praefecti', Franciszek Kluczycki (ed.), *Akta do dziejów Króla Jana IIIgo sprawy roku 1683,* p.593.

such, both Hetman Sieniawski and King Jan III decided independently to send out strong reconnaissance forces to scout the battlefield.

The Hetman despatched a 'few banners of hussars and *pancerni*',[52] in the form of two squadrons of cavalry, so two banners of hussars and four of *pancerni* in total.[53] One was part of Andrzej Potocki's regiment, while the other was Szczęsny Potocki's regiment. The units were led by Stanisław Potocki, son of Andrzej Potocki (who stayed in Poland in charge of the defence of the country). The Poles charged under heavy fire past small hills and vineyards occupied by janissaries, after which they clashed with the massed ranks of *sipahi*. No surprise perhaps that this charge ended in a costly defeat. Many soldiers, including Stanisław Potocki and at least one lieutenant, were killed,[54] and Dalerac wrote that young Potocki 'notwithstanding his coat of Mail, was shot through the Body with a Musket shot', indicating that officer died by the hands of the Turkish infantry.[55] Dyakowski presented a different version of the death of the *rotmistrz,* claiming that his head 'despite having *misiurka* helmet' was chopped off by a Turkish cavalryman.[56] The broken banners, chased by Turkish cavalry, retreated under covering fire from Bavarian infantry. Sieniawski counterattacked with a new group of his own troops, under Marek Matczyński, composed probably of the Hetman's own regiment and the remaining banners from both of Potocki's regiments. Polish cavalry again had to move through difficult terrain, over ditches and through vines, under the fire of the janissaries and Turkish cannon. While they managed to break the first line of the Ottoman cavalry, they were facing large reserves of *sipahi* and were being outflanked by them, and this Polish attack also faltered and was forced to retreat. Thanks to the fire support of Kątski's artillery, Polish infantry brigades and one battalion of Franconian infantry, the cavalry managed to withdraw safely. Under orders from Sobieski, Sachsen-Lauenburg sent Imperial cuirassiers and dragoons to counterattack. They managed to stop the Turks, who retreated towards Gersthof.

While Sieniawski's hussars and *pancerni* were unsuccessfully fighting with the janissaries and *sipahi*, the King despatched his own unit to scout battlefield conditions in front of the Polish centre. He chose to give this task to the hussar banner of Royal Prince Aleksander, under the

Colonel of His Royal Highness' regiment *karacena* armour. During the battle of Vienna he served as lieutenant (in charge) of Royal Prince Aleksander Sobieski's banner of winged hussars. It was his unit that led the probing attack against the Turks at Vienna, testing if the ground could sustain a proper charge of the allied cavalry. Despite taking severe losses, the banner managed to successfully charge and withdraw, confirming to King Jan III that a full cavalry attack was possible. Painter unknown. (National Museum, Cracow)

52   *Ibidem*, p.594.
53   Radosław Sikora, *Husaria pod Wiedniem*, pp.207, 213.
54   'Relatio a comitiss anni 1683 biennalium gestorum et laborum exercitus…', p.845.
55   Dalerac, *Polish Manuscripts*, p.96.
56   Dyakowski, p.63.

command of Lieutenant Zygmunt Zbierzchowski. According to Dyakowski, the King ordered Zbierzchowski to charge towards the hill where Kara Mustafa had his *sejwen*.[57] The unit was to attack on its own, to test the ground and, if it faced a Turkish counterattack, it was to withdraw. The hussars were accompanied by one of royal courtiers, Andrzej Modrzewski, who decided to join the fight. He did not take his *pancerni* banner with him, instead quickly moving to the front of Zbierzchowski's hussars, when the unit was slowly moving through ditch. His rashness was to be his doom, as he was quickly overwhelmed by Turkish horsemen, Modrzewski was killed before the hussars managed to arrive by his side. Zbierzchowski's banner avenged his death, striking the first line of Ottoman cavalry.[58] Unfortunately the impact of the charge was quickly lost, and hussars were engaged by Turkish infantry, while *sipahi* who had fled from the charging Poles re-engaged, outflanking them. Hasan Esiri, who took part in the battle, gives a vivid description of the fight between the Polish hussars and Kara Mustafa's elite Levantine infantry:[59]

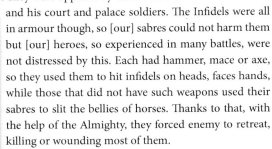

Mikołaj Wybranowski in *karacena* armour. During the battle of Vienna he served as a companion in Royal Prince Aleksander Sobieski's banner of winged hussars. He was one of the soldiers that captured the standard identified by the Poles as 'flag of the Prophet', later sent by Sobieski to the Sanctuary in Loreto. Painter unknown. (National Museum, Cracow)

> First unit of the enemies, wearing heavy armour, attacked the troops of His Gracious Serdar [Vizier]. They were opposed by the Serdar's own levend soldiers, and his court and palace soldiers. The Infidels were all in armour though, so [our] sabres could not harm them but [our] heroes, so experienced in many battles, were not distressed by this. Each had hammer, mace or axe, so they used them to hit infidels on heads, faces hands, while those that did not have such weapons used their sabres to slit the bellies of horses. Thanks to that, with the help of the Almighty, they forced enemy to retreat, killing or wounding most of them.

Another interesting account of this attack was penned by Wojciech Stanisław Chróściński (1665–1722?). During the relief of Vienna he was the courtier of Andrzej Modrzewski, while between 1685 and 1697 he was serving as royal secretary, in charge of Jan III's chancellery. In 1684 he wrote about this event in the relief of Vienna, focusing on the death of his then master, Modrzewski. Chróściński. He was marching with the main Polish army from Tulln, overseeing his master's wagons carrying provisions. He did not take part in the main battle, as he had to stay with the tabor because Polish commanders were afraid of the possibility of a diversionary attack by the Tatars. At

---

57   A type of sun cover, a tent without walls.

58   'Relatio a comitiss anni 1683 biennalium gestorum et laborum exercitus…', p.845.

59   Dżebedżi Hasan Esiri, 'Wspomnienia i refleksje o wyprawie wiedeńskiej', Zygmunt Abrahamowicz (ed.), *Kara Mustafa pod Wiedniem. Źródła muzułmańskie do dziejów wyprawy wiedeńskiej 1683 roku*, pp.226–227.

some point he left them under the care of Lieutenant Kiełtyg (from the Royal Guard) and at noon returned to the Polish lines, as he wanted to accompany Modrzewski. He did not witness the death of his master and only at dawn the following day he was able to find his body on the battlefield. Chróściński talked to some eyewitnesses of different stages of the fight as in his account he wrote a very detailed description of the charge of the Polish cavalry. Modrzewski, nominal *rotmistrz* of *pancerni* banner, did not fight leading his own soldiers, despite them 'asking him to not leave them'. Instead he stayed with Sobieski's entourage and joined the hussar banner of Royal Prince Aleksander during their costly charge. The hot-headed noble got separated from the unit, when the hussars got stuck in a ravine. Because of that he suddenly faced a group of Turks (possibly *sipahi*) and had to fight with them on his own. Chróściński mentions that Modrzewski discharged both pistols, used a spear to kill another Turk and then with sabre in hand charged the rest of the enemy. Sadly, he did not stand a chance against overwhelming odds and after taking many wounds he was killed. '[Took] javelin under his left eye, that went straight through his face, and on right side under jaw few spears [...], struck with mace in his breast, [they] massively slashed his left hand, right shoulder and his thighs, then throw him down one the ground. Victorious Turks took his chainmail, *misiurka* helmet and sabre but, despite three attempts, did not manage to cut off his head, as arriving hussars forced them to retreat. His body was so mutilated that when Chróściński and his servants found him after the battle, they could only recognise him thanks to elk-leather coat that Chróściński bought for his master in Cracow. It seems that pillaging troops had been there before him, as Modrzewski was missing many personal items, but his body was covered with a dragoon's coat. Even

Allied army attacking the Turkish camp during the battle of Vienna in 1683. Justus van den Nijpoort, 1694 (Rijksmuseum)

WIENN.

worse, when transporting the body on a spare horse, the Poles were almost killed by Imperial soldiers 'who thought that we were carrying some loot'. Chróściński spoke to some Imperial officers in Latin and calmed down the situation.[60]

Meanwhile the badly mauled banner of hussars managed to break off contact with the enemy and return to Polish lines. Zbierzchowski survived the fight, and made his way to where the King was stationed with his entourage and told him 'I fulfilled Your Highness' order'. Recalling those words, Dyakowski mentioned that Royal Prince Aleksander's banner had 19 companions and 36 retainers killed during the charge.[61] Jan III lowered those estimates in his letter to the Queen, dated 10 October 1683, where he wrote that banner had 12 companions killed at Vienna, four more at first battle of Párkány and one more at second battle of Párkány. Additionally by 10 October, the unit had lost 33 retainers killed.[62] Considering that the unit had 'paper strength' of 200 horses and that in August 1683 mustered only 149 horses (so 130–135 men), we can see how high a price was paid for this reconnaissance. Nonetheless the mission was a success, as Sobieski now knew that it would be possible to use the massed formations of allied

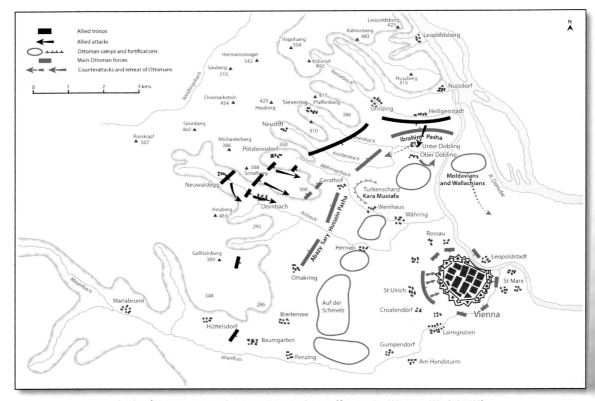

Battle of Vienna – actions between 2 pm and 4 pm. [Source: Jan Wimmer, *Wiedeń 1683*]

60   'Nieznana relacja o batalii wiedeńskiej 1683 roku', pp.37–39.
61   Dyakowski, p.61.
62   Antoni Zygmunt Helcel (ed.), *Listy Jana Sobieskiego do żony Marii Kazimiery*, p.406, Jan III do Marii Kazimiery, Przeciwko Strigonium pod Parkanem, 10 Octobris rano.

cavalry to charge the Ottoman positions. Jan Dobrogost Krasiński, fighting on the right wing, who was not a witness to this fighting, criticised sending hussars on such small scale attacks, where they had to face very difficult terrain and janissaries.[63] Johann George Anhalt in his letter to the Elector of Brandenburg, mentioned the reconnaissance missions of Polish cavalry, describing how two banners of hussars struck through the Turkish line but were forced to retreat after their lances were broken. He added that further hussar banners then charged into the fray, causing much damage and forcing the Turks to 'retreat in great confusion'.[64]

It seems that around this time (4.00 p.m.) Abaza Sary Hussein Pasha, ordered the unfurling of a huge standard in the middle of his troops to raise the morale of the left wing of the Ottoman army. The Poles, mistaking it for the standard of the Prophet, focused the attention of their artillery on this new target. The battle was now at the crucial phase, with the Polish army getting ready to throw its whole might against the Turks. Lorraine took advantage of the weakened Ottoman

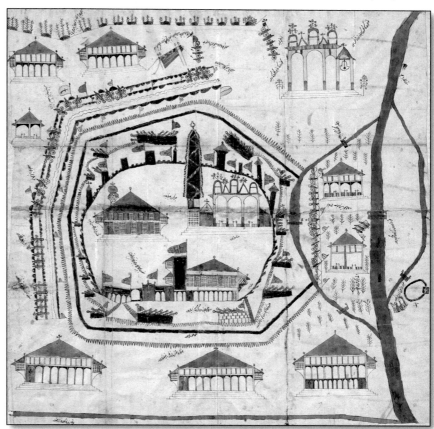

Ottoman plan of the siege works around Vienna in 1683. (Wien Museum Inv.-Nr. 52816/1, CC0)

right wing by sending many soldiers towards the centre and the left wing, and he ordered his troops to renew the attack. He was not sure if the Saxons would be willing to take part as well but old general Johan Rudiger von Goltz quickly put his mind to rest by saying the 'enemy seems to be frightened, so I think we should follow them and pursue the victory, striking while the iron is still hot. Myself, I am a crooked old man and I wish for tonight evening to rest in a nice quarter in Vienna'.[65] The attack commenced and within an hour Imperial, Saxon and Polish troops broke through the Turkish

---

63   'Relatia seu descriptia wojny pod Wiedniem, pod Strygoniem i dalszej kampaniej A. 1683', p.164.

64   Franciszek Kluczycki (ed.), *Akta do dziejów Króla Jana IIIgo*, p.383, Relation Joannis-Georgii Principis d'Anhalt, ad Electorem Brandenburgiae.

65   Jan Wimmer, *Wiedeń 1683*, p.334.

right wing. At this point Lorraine ordered his troops to change direction. No longer were they to march alongside the Danube towards Vienna, but instead they turned right and pushed through the northern part of the Ottoman camp. In the first line Lubomirski led his auxiliary corps and attached Polish hussars and *pancerni,* with rest of the allied horse following them into the camp. At the same time Bavarian and Franconian infantry from the centre also moved towards the Ottoman lines, engaging the defenders of *Türkenschanz.*

If until now Sobieski had any notions of keeping his troops under control and waiting until the next day for the decisive battle, he quickly abandoned them and decided to call for a full on attack. Allied soldiers from the centre and right wings were eager to fight and the reconnaissance mission of hussars, although costly, proved that a cavalry charge would be possible. There were still one-and-half to two hours of sunlight remaining, so conditions were favourable. He sent messengers to the commanders of the allied centre and both Polish wings: all those formations were to attack. The King led his own regiment in the initial stage, when the hussars and *pancerni* were slowly moving down from Schafberg. Many paintings commissioned after the battle show Jan III with his *karacena* armour and helmet, commanding troops with sabre in hand. The reality was completely different. Kochowski gives a detailed description of the King's appearance. He was wearing a white silk *żupan* with a dark blue *kontusz* outer garment over it. On his head he had a fur hat called *kołpak,* with a heron's feather attached to it.[66] Royal Prince Jakub was at his father's side, both accompanied by an entourage of soldiers, messengers and courtiers, including a standard-bearer with the royal tug (*buńczuk*). Sobieski stopped in the vicinity of the Ottoman positions, while his soldiers continued with their charge. One by one, mixed squadrons of hussars and *pancerni* were speeding towards enemy. One or two squadrons of cavalry (up to two banners of hussars and four of *pancerni*) were moved during this part of the fight from Jabłonowski's wing into the centre, to support the attack.[67] Here they joined three squadrons from the Royal regiment and together those 12 to 15 banners (including four to five units of hussars) led the charge. Not all units from the Royal regiment took part in the fight though, as the King's and Royal Prince Jakub's hussar banners, with attached *pancerni,* were kept in reserve.[68] The royal *arkabuzeria* were engaged in this fighting as well, as its commander, Jan Górzyński, died in the battle. At the same time further units of cavalry moved from their positions and attacked the Turks. Hetman Sieniawski send out his soldiers and, unless he had kept any reserves, had thrown into the fight seven mixed squadrons of hussars and *pancerni,* with some additional *pancerni* and light horse as support. From the centre of the allied army Sachsen-Lauenburg was leading thousands of German cavalry, made up of Imperial, Bavarian and Franconian regiments. The left wing troops, with Lubomirski's soldiers and attached Polish units at the front, were already engaged, fighting in the Turkish camp. The right wing attack under

---

66   Kochowski, p.30.
67   Radosław Sikora, *Husaria pod Wiedniem*, p.233.
68   Jakub Ludwik Sobieski, *Dyaryusz wyprawy wiedeńskliej w 1683 r.*, p.12.

Jabłonowski was initially spearheaded by infantry, who were to open the way for the cavalry to charge. The Hetman especially praised Ernest Denhoff and Eliasz Łącki, leading two of his brigades. Dragoons, fighting dismounted, were in the middle of the fray as well, led by the 'old' regiment of Guard under Franciszek Gałecki.[69] After detaching some cavalry to the Polish centre, the remaining units, including four banners of hussars, were to play an important role in defeating the left wing of the Ottoman army. *Rotmistrz* Krasiński, leading his hussars as part of this 'division', mentions that Jabłonowski's troops stopped several Turkish counterattacks and that it was the Hetman's soldiers that captured the large flag mistaken for the standard of the Prophet. In the final stage of the fight, supported by reserve Imperial cavalry that were in the centre of the battle line, soldiers from the right wing broke through the Turkish army and reached the camp, then pursued their opponents, stopping just one mile short of Vienna itself.[70] Kątski wrote about the Turkish counterattacks in this part of the battlefield that 'almost the whole [Ottoman] might alongside the Vizier himself turned against the [Polish] right wing but they were greeted here with great order and resolution, so they were, thanks to [Polish] reserves, pushed back towards the woods, straight into the camp, where [already] the left [Polish] wing made its entry.'[71] According to Dalerac the brunt of the fight was born by the infantry, dragoons and hussars, who 'bore the Fire, and engaged the Enemy'.[72]

Jan III Sobieski leading Polish troops at Vienna. Jan Wyck, 1698. (Photo: Birgit and Peter Kainz, Wien Museum Inv.-Nr. 31604, CC BY 4.0)

69   'Relatio a comitiss anni 1683 biennalium gestorum et laborum exercitus…', p.845.
70   'Relatia seu descriptia wojny pod Wiedniem, pod Strygoniem i dalszej kampaniej A. 1683', p.164.
71   Marcin Kątski, 'Diarium Artilieriae Praefecti', Franciszek Kluczycki (ed.), *Akta do dziejów Króla Jana IIIgo sprawy roku 1683*, p.595.
72   Dalerac, *Polish Manuscripts*, p.100.

The Polish attack was led by the heroic banner of Royal Prince Alexander, badly bloodied in the earlier reconnaissance mission. Now, they continued the fight, striking against the place where earlier Sobieski had seen the Vizier's tent. 'While many of them were killed, they managed to break Turkish ranks and force Vizier to flee'.[73] Despite heavy fire from janissaries, Polish cavalry did not falter and thrust into the Turkish *sipahi*. Lance-armed hussars, with the support of *pancerni* 'fighting with sabres in their hands'[74] routed the Ottoman cavalry and rode into the Turkish camp hot on their heels. Kara Mustafa's Levantines and units of janissaries were desperately defending field fortifications, but they were now facing allied infantry, with Bavarian and Franconian regiments, from one side and Sieniawski's brigades, supported by Kątski's artillery, from the other. Outnumbered and outgunned, the Turkish infantry was also forced to retreat. They tried another stand in the middle of the camp, where Kara Mustafa's household troops bought him some time to save the actual standard of the Prophet and run away with army pay chest. It was about 6:00 p.m. when it became clear that the Turkish army was in full retreat and was abandoning the camp and siege works. Vienna was saved and the allied army was victorious!

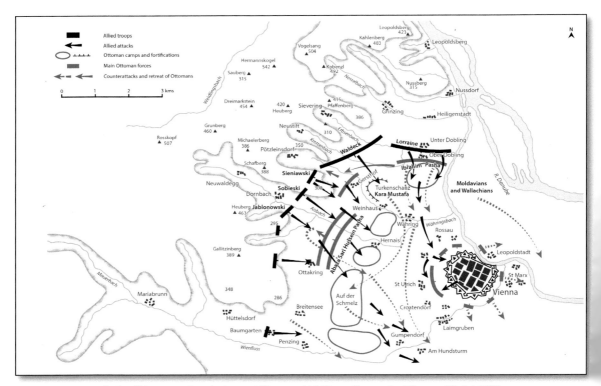

Battle of Vienna – actions between 4.00 pm and 10.00 pm. [Source: Jan Wimmer, *Wiedeń 1683*]

73   Jakub Ludwik Sobieski, *Dyaryusz wyprawy wiedeńskliej w 1683 r.*, p.12.
74   Which can suggest that many banners did not receive their spears on time.

After the battle

NAMIOT TURECKI Z POD CHOCIMIA

Turkish tent captured during the battle of Khotyn (Chocim) in 1673. From the collection of the Podhorce Castle, photo from 1880 by Edward Trzemeski (National Museum, Warsaw)

The Ottoman army was far from being completely beaten and managed to retreat in an orderly fashion – especially the cavalry units. Sobieski ordered his army to stay ready, in case 'the Enemy rallying behind the Camp, should renew the Fight, and so rob them of such a cheap Victory'.[75] Polish soldiers were, under penalty of death, ordered to stay with their units the whole night, and the King himself was to spend the night under a tree, using a saddle as a pillow, ready at short notice to lead his troops.[76] Against such strict orders, many soldiers still ventured into the camp and during the night, under the light of candles, grabbed what they could from the Turkish tents. Servants and marauders were there as well, so fighting between the looters were common. A high ranking official sent some troops to protect the most important spoils of battle and guard them from marauding soldiers. Sobieski wrote that the official in charge of the Royal Kitchen,[77] Franciszek Zygmunt Gałecki, was taking care of the prizes that no one else was interested in. 'His biggest booty was in oxen (…). He took them [all] and even next day was buying them [from the other] for thaler each, he [also] gathered all kinds of copper and brass dishes, that were left in the camp even four days after the battle'. The people of Vienna also took part in looting, competing with Gałecki's servants

---

75   Dalerac, *Polish Manuscripts*, p.99.
76   *Ibidem*, p.100.
77   His Polish title was *kuchmistrz wielki koronny* (*magister culinae Regni*), which translates as the Master of the Royal Kitchen in English. He oversaw the kitchen, its staff and supplies, and he also aided the King during feasts and announced all dishes as they were served.

for kitchen dishes, also taking poorer quality tents, that where of no interest to the soldiers.[78] Krasiński mentions that soldiers had to 'spend the whole night in the saddle', as there was still the danger that the retreating Ottoman army may counterattack. This is another indicator that despite the success on the battlefield, it was not such an overwhelming victory, and that the main Turkish army was withdrawing in reasonable order.[79] Barker claims that Sobieski 'forbade all but the lightest pursuit'[80] but such a statement is incorrect and unfair when compared with Polish sources. Kątski mentions that Polish cavalry banners were chasing the retreating Turks for the whole night.[81] Dupont explained that the pursuing troops 'due to darkness, poor knowledge of the local terrain and horses' fatigue did not go too far. But they did kill many marauders'.[82] Dyakowski described the pursuing troops as 2,000 cavalry under Atanazy Miączyński, who were following the Turks so vigorously that their arms were dead tired from slashing with their sabres at the fleeing enemies.[83] While it is easy to criticise the lack of a longer pursuit and blame Sobieski for not using a larger group of cavalry, it is necessary to understand factors behind such a decision by the King. From among all the allied cavalry, only the Polish troops (and the Imperial Croats) were suitable for such a pursuit; *pancerni*, Wallachians and Tatars were ideal for chasing after a retreating enemy. The entire ordeal of marching through the Vienna Woods, followed by the intense battle, took a heavy toll on the endurance of both men and horses. Lack of food for people and provisions for their mounts was yet another factor, and it should not be forgotten that the horses had to be fed with leaves during the march through the hills and woods. Sending in piecemeal small groups of cavalry, in the face of a still strong Ottoman army,

Turkish tents captured by the Polish army at Vienna in 1683. A set of six drawings, made by Martino Altomonte after he arrived in Poland in 1684. He saw the 'Turkish camp' set up near Żółkiew, a town owned by Sobieski. It was a special show prepared by the Polish King for his guests, including the Papal nuncio and Venetian ambassador (Author's archive)

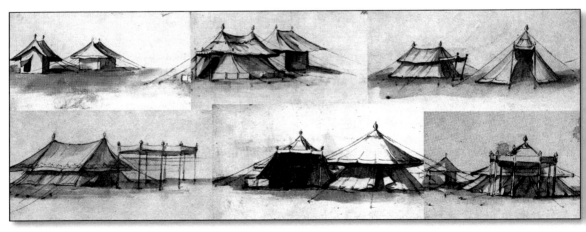

78   Antoni Zygmunt Helcel (ed.), *Listy Jana Sobieskiego do żony Marii Kazimiery*, p.402, Jan III do Marii Kazimiery, 7 Octobris; na samem się ruszeniu, ku Parkanom które miejsce jest na końcu mostu przeciw Strigonium, alias Gran, na tej Dunaju stronie.
79   'Relatia seu descriptia wojny pod Wiedniem, pod Strygoniem i dalszej kampaniej A. 1683', p.165.
80   Thomas Barker, *Double Eagle and Crescent*, p.333.
81   Marcin Kątski, 'Diarium Artilieriae Praefecti', Franciszek Kluczycki (ed.), *Akta do dziejów Króla Jana IIIgo sprawy roku 1683*, p.595.
82   Dupont, p.197.
83   Dyakowski, p.68.

could quickly lead to disaster and affect both the situation and the morale of the recently victorious allies. Remember too that the soldiers were less than willing to abandon the captured Turkish camp, with its riches beyond the imagination now in the hands of Polish troops.

Amongst the captured prizes was the Vizier's own 'War-Horse which was barded with Steel-Armour, damask'd with Gold, and quilted with Crimson Velvet'. One of Kara Mustafa's servants brought it to Sobieski, when the Polish King entered the Turkish camp. 'A young Turk of a comely aspect presented him with the Grand Visiers Horse, very fit indeed for the Parade of a Publick Entry; but for no other use by reason of the weight of its Armour. Another Turk came with great haste, and one of the Grand Visiers stirrups in his hand to present to his Polish Majesty, which he sent to the Queen to be laid at the feet of the Miraculous Crucifix of the Cathedral of Cracow'.[84] More of the captured servants were also eager to please their new master, directing them towards the Vizier's tents and belongings. Sobieski sent with them a unit of dragoons, to protect them and previously looted treasures from marauders.[85] While writing a post-battle letter to the Queen, the King even signed it 'from Vizier's tents' and he described many trophies captured during the fight. Amongst them were all the Vizier's standards, usually carried in front of the Ottoman official. The large standard captured during the battle found by Sobieski was incorrectly identified as the 'standard of the Prophet' and his envoys Abbot Jan Kazimierz Denhoff and Secretary Tommaso Talenti were to deliver it, along with the King's letter, to Pope Innocent XI in Rome. The entire personal baggage train of Kara Mustafa became the spoils of war of the Polish monarch and Sobieski joked with the Queen, writing 'you would not be able to say [to me], my soul, like those Tatar women who tell their husbands when they return without loot "you are not brave warrior, as you are returning without the spoils of war", as one that [is able to] capture, [clearly] had to fight at the front'. He then mentioned the Vizier's horse and a few bow quivers[86] decorated with rubies and sapphires, worth a few thousand ducats.[87] The King added a brief passage about loot captured by his soldiers, mentioning that they laid their hands on many golden sabres and other military equipment.[88] Surprising for him was that the Poles also managed to liberate many diamond-studded belts and girdles. He was not sure what they were for, as Turkish soldiers did not wear them, so he guessed that they were to be used 'for the ladies of Vienna, which they expect to capture and dress with those'. The King added that the diamonds were thin and small but the whole jewellery work was beautiful and valuable.[89]

---

84 Dalerac, *Polish Manuscripts*, pp.97–99.
85 *Ibidem*, p.99.
86 The word he is using, *sajdak*, would normally show a set composed of quiver for the bow itself and a separate quiver for arrows.
87 The Polish term used in the letter is *czerwony złoty* (red złoty), meaning gold coin, often called florin or ducat.
88 Antoni Zygmunt Helcel (ed.), *Listy Jana Sobieskiego do żony Marii Kazimiery*, p.385, Jan III do Marii Kazimiery, W namiotach Wezyrskich, 13 Septembra w nocy.
89 *Ibidem*, p.398, Jan III do Marii Kazimiery, Na insule Szutt, między Preszburkiem a Komorą pod San Peter. 28 Septembra.

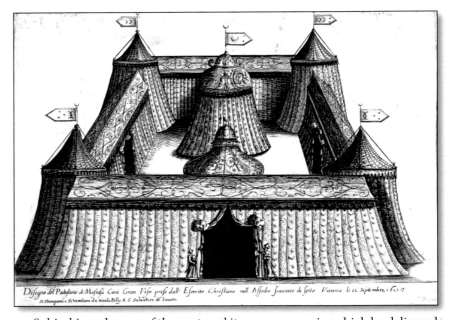

Sobieski used some of the captured items as souvenirs which he delivered to allied monarchs and generals. On 16 September, as a farewell gift, he sent Johann George III of Saxony two horses, two Turkish standards, four prisoners, two beautiful porcelain items (small dishes) and an ornamental curtain for his wife. Saxon Field Marshall Joachim von Goltz received a Turkish sabre 'covered in gold'. One of the Vizier's standards was sent with Polish envoys to Emperor Leopold I but was stolen 'due to the carelessness' of the standard-bearer Jaskulski, when the Poles were waiting in an empty garden for the Austrian monarch. Therefore Sobieski had to send another one, while commenting 'but I still have two more'.[90] Additionally the Emperor received two beautiful Turkish horses, that he had previously asked for. They had 'very rich saddles, decorated with rubies and sapphires, while the horse tack was covered with diamonds'.[91] A few days after the battle, Jan III presented the Bavarian Elector Maximilian II Emanuel with a nice collection of captured prizes. Dalerac mentioned 'three very fine Turkish Horses, two Standards, and some Jewels fit for a Lady's wear; with a design that the Elector should send them into France, to his Sister the Dauphiness [Maria Anna Victoria of Bavaria, wife of Louis, Dauphin of France]', also 'Bontchouk of the Bassa of Egypt, adorn'd at the Top with an Hair Lace of diverse Colours, with a Tuft of Horse-Tail round the gilded Crest, which was the Summit of this Bountchouk; which the Turks call Touk'.[92] It seems that the gifts were well received and both monarchs liked each other. Just as well, as in 1694, two years after death of his wife, Maria Antonia of Austria, Maximilian II was to marry Theresa Kunegunda Sobieska, Jan III's daughter. Another horse was

90   *Ibidem*, p.388, Jan III do Marii Kazimiery, W obozie pod wsią Szenan na gościńcu Preszowskim nad Dunajem mil trzy od Wiednia (17go Września).

91   *Ibidem*, p.393, Jan III do Marii Kazimiery, Mila od Preszburku, 19 Septembris.

92   Dalerac, *Polish Manuscripts*, p.106.

sent out to the old friend of the King, Johan Georg von Anhalt. Sobieski grumpily commented on his own generosity, saying that 'if he will continue to give away horses at this rate, he will end up returning to Poland riding on an ox or a camel'.[93]

Losses

The Ottomans lost their whole camp but what about their manpower losses? It is very hard to calculate an exact figure, with the numbers varying between 10,000 and 20,000 killed, with the highest losses amongst the infantry. Those numbers include some of the prisoners killed in the camp and few hundred soldiers that stayed in the trenches around Vienna and died after the battle. Another few thousand, especially the wounded, were taken prisoner. What is worthy of note is that none of the high-ranking Ottoman officials and officers were killed during the fight.

Estimates of the allied losses presents us with a figure of 1,500 killed and wounded, with up to half of those numbers being amongst the Poles.[94] Primary sources tend to give rather sketchy details. Dalerac wrote that the whole allied army lost only 600 men,[95] while Dupont did not know the number of losses, but did write an interesting passage about it. 'As I left [to Poland] next day at dawn, I never knew the exact number of the dead. I know only that losses on the side of Christians were not high. The worst were amongst the Polish cavalry, especially hussars, [especially] if you compare it to their overall strength. One banner [of hussars] had 22 killed from the first line. All of them were nobles. We also lost some infantry and dragoons'.[96] The King, in his letters to the Queen, does not give detailed information about Polish losses, mentioning only that they were 'not little', although it seems that Dupont was to tell Marie Casimire directly about most famous officers who fell; Modrzewski and Potocki. Dyakowski, except for the already mentioned overestimate of the losses of Royal Prince Alexander's hussar banner, does not provide any further information. Francis Taaffe focused on Imperial losses, writing 'I must add, that never a Victory of so great Importance, cost so little blood. There were no Officers kill'd on our side but the Brother of the Prince de Crouy,[97] the Count de Trautmanstorf, Major, the Count de Batzi, Captain of Dragoons, and some people of quality amongst the Poles, who stood the shock of a very rude Encounter, with a Transcendent Bravery'.[98] In the earlier description of the battle two passages from Kątski's diary are mentioned,

93   Antoni Zygmunt Helcel (ed.), *Listy Jana Sobieskiego do żony Marii Kazimiery*, p.392, Jan III do Marii Kazimiery, W obozie pod wsią Szenan na gościńcu Preszowskim nad Dunajem mil trzy od Wiednia (17go Września).
94   Thomas Barker, *Double Eagle and Crescent*, p.338, Jan Wimmer, *Wiedeń 1683*, pp.339–340.
95   Dalerac, *Polish Manuscripts*, p.100.
96   Dupont, p.199.
97   Maurice de Croy, brother of Imperial general Charles Eugen de Croy.
98   *Count Taaffe's letters from the Imperial camp to his brother the Earl of Carlingford here in London giving an account of the most considerable actions, both before, and at, the raising of the siege at Vienna, together with several remarkable passages afterward, in the victorious campagne against*

where he wrote about the losses of the Polish infantry in the early stage of the fight and then amongst cavalry on their reconnaissance mission, he does not provided any further information. Amongst the Polish officers who it is known were killed were: Stanisław Potocki (*rotmistrz* of *pancerni* banner and lieutenant of his father's hussar banner), Andrzej Modrzewski (*rotmistrz* of *pancerni* banner and Court Treasurer), Jan Górzyński (commander of Royal *arkabuzeria*) and Stanisław Opaliński (*rotmistrz* of *pancerni* banner).[99] Additionally some were mortally wounded and died later, we know about Bogusław Zbąski (*rotmistrz* of a private *pancerni* banner, who died two days after the battle)[100] and Aswerus Wrzospolski (Lt. Colonel of Hetman Sieniawski's infantry regiment, who died on 23 September).[101]

Turkish prisoners and spoils of war in front of Leopold I. Author unknown (Wien Museum Inv.-Nr. 19746, CC0)

Publicising the victory

The relief of Vienna and the victory over the Ottoman army was at once used by both the Imperial and Polish propaganda machines to praise their own monarchs, highlight the bravery and skill of their armies and add fuel to the fire of the anti-Ottoman coalition. Engravings, medals and pamphlets were produced and sent all over Europe, and court painters were employed to produce massive battle scenes, some of which are reproduced in this book. Accounts of officers and other eyewitnesses were translated and published within a year in many European cities, from Vienna to Paris and London.

---

the Turks in Hungary: with an addition of two other letters from a young English nobleman, a volunteer in the imperial army. (London: printed for T.B, 1684), pp.17–18.

99 BCzart, number 2755, p.99, Kochowski, p.35, Dupont, p.198.

100 Kochowski, p.35.

101 Dupont, p.198.

Triumph of King Jan III and Emperor Leopold I. Giuseppe Maria Mitelli, 1683 (National Museum, Warsaw)

Of course the propaganda was set up with a slightly different emphasis in each country. The Imperialists praised Leopold I, always showing him as a triumphant commander, with allied generals usually just flanking him or depicted in the background. What is interesting is that sometimes such scenes of the triumphal victory omit the Duke of Lorraine, despite him being Imperial commander-in-chief. Polish propaganda of course focused on Jan III as saviour of Christendom, usually presented as a triumphant monarch, reminiscent of ancient Roman emperors. Already mentioned is the famous letter sent to Pope Innocent XI, opening with *Venimus, vidimus, Deus vicit!* 'We came, we saw, God conquered', as a bold statement of the victory over the 'enemies of the Cross'.[102] Sobieski was highly focused on showing his – and the Polish army's – role in the battle in the proper light. He recommended that the Queen use his post-battle letter to her as a broadsheet.[103] 'This letter is the best gazette, from which [you] can issued world-wide gazette, writing that *que c'est la lettre du Roi* à la Reine'.[104] After his return to Poland, he ordered many paintings and medals, which were to highlight his status as a victorious King and general.

102 Augustin Sauer, *Rom und Wien in Jahre 1683*, p.59.
103 Antoni Zygmunt Helcel (ed.), *Listy Jana Sobieskiego do żony Marii Kazimiery*, p.387, Jan III do Marii Kazimiery, W namiotach Wezyrskich, 13 Septembera w nocy.
104 Letter from the King to the Queen.

Typical Imperial propaganda broadsheet, presenting Leopold I as a victorious commander at Vienna in 1683. Next to him are the allied generals but what is interesting is the absence of The Duke of Lorraine. Engraving by Johann Azelt (Wien Museum Inv.-Nr. 163639, CC0)

Disagreements between the allies

Count Ernst Rüdiger von Starhemberg. Pieter Schenk the Elder (Wikimedia Commons)

Immediately after the relief of Vienna the military and political alliance gathered to save the city started to slowly erode. A political clash between Emperor Leopold I and King Jan III was unavoidable. Leopold I was still wary of the dynastic plans of the Polish monarch (who was looking to carve out a Hungarian throne for his son) while Sobieski, full of pride and expecting to be shown respect for Polish involvement in the relief, was easily hurt by any disrespect shown towards him and his soldiers.

The first sight of such problems appear on 13 September, when the King, along with Lorraine and the Bavarian and Saxon Electors, was visiting the Turkish siege works. Von Starhembergh was eager to show them the captured positions and equipment but tried to make excuses when the King wanted to enter the city. Blocked gates did not stop Sobieski who just followed the Imperial general through the same small gate that he initially used to meet the commanders of the relief force. The Polish monarch, aided by Royal Prince Jakub, Hetman Jabłonowski, Hetman Sieniawski and few other high-ranking officers, took part in Holy Mass in the Augustinian Church, after which he visited the Loreto Chapel in the same church. The King led the gathered soldiers and citizens in singing *Te Deum laudamus,* to celebrate the victory over the Turks. Then he took part in a dinner hosted by von Starhembergh, where, as already mentioned when describing hussars' attire, Imperial officers were confused by odd choices in Polish dress. After that he visited St. Stephen's Cathedral, and he then returned to camp. While many citizens of Vienna crowded enthusiastically around the Polish monarch, trying to kiss his hands, feet or clothes, he noted that not many of them shouted *Vivat*, as 'they were careful of their Officers and Elders (…) as it was frowned upon [to celebrate with the Poles]'.[105] On 14 September, when the Emperor arrived in Vienna, Sobieski hoped to meet him, as he was looking to discuss with him the plans of the marriage between Royal Prince Jakub and Maria Antonia of Austria, which could support the case of a Hungarian-based throne for Jakub. Of course Leopold I was not interested in losing Hungary to the Poles, especially now, when Vienna was saved, and the Turks forced to retreat. Additionally, he was irritated that Jan III was the first monarch to enter Vienna, stealing this moment of glory from the Emperor. As such he answered

Jan III Sobieski after the triumph at Vienna in 1683. Author unknown (Wien Museum Inv.-Nr. 19746, CC0)

via a letter, telling Sobieski that they could discuss all those matters in private, once they met. Jan III took that as another slight, so he did not even take part in the official entry of Leopold I into Vienna, sending as his envoy Vice-Chancellor Krzysztof Jan Gniński. Officially the Polish King was simply too busy to attend, as he was moving his army to a new camp, in Schwechat, south-east of Vienna.

Both monarchs finally met the next day, on 15 September, where Leopold I, with a large entourage of his officers and courtiers arrived to see the muster of the Polish army. The meeting started well, with the Emperor's long speech in Latin, where he thanked the Poles for arriving to save the city and highlighted the crucial role of Jan III and his army in the battle. Sobieski answered in Latin also, with polite thanks for such praise. Here is where the real problem started. Jan III introduced his son Jakub to the Emperor, but Leopold did not raise his hat when replying to the Polish Prince's bow. It clearly upset Sobieski, who wrote to the Queen 'at this moment I almost get stiff'. Royal Prince Jakub mentioned in his diary 'I do not know, what was the reason of him not returning my bow. If it was due to long feathers [from the hat] falling down his arms and blocking his view or he was afraid that his wild horse, who he had to keep still with both hands, will carry him away, if he will raise one hand to the hat to return my bow: Austrian still argue about it and this

105 Antoni Zygmunt Helcel (ed.), *Listy Jana Sobieskiego do żony Marii Kazimiery*, p.386, Jan III do Marii Kazimiery, W namiotach Wezyrskich, 13 Septembera w nocy, Jakub Ludwik Sobieski, *Dyaryusz wyprawy wiedeńskliej* w 1683 r., p.14, Dupont, p.201.

dispute is yet not resolved'. What was worse, the Emperor did not raise his hat when introduced to high-ranking Polish officers and courtiers. Dalerac described the scene as follows:[106]

> [Sobieski] presented the Young Prince his Son to him, adding, That he had brought him along with him to teach him how he ought to succour his Allies; He likewise presented to him the two Generals of the Crown, who saluted the Emperor without alighting. Lastly, seeing that this Prince [Emperor Leopold] was stiff and mute, without returning a word of Answer, or showing any token of Honour, not so much as saluting the Young Prince, the King left him very bluntly, and said, *Without doubt, Brother, you, have a mind to take a view of my Army; there are my Generals whom I have order'd to show it your Majesty.* With that he turn'd his Head from him, and march'd away; and the Emperor with the same indifference that he had heard this Discource, suffer'd him to depart; whilst he for his part went to visit the Lines.

For Sobieski, it was a clear affront and a definite answer towards his enquiry about a marriage between Jakub and Maria Antonia of Austria. He also felt that the Emperor was being churlish and did not want to show any gratitude towards the Poles. It seems that the Polish rank-and-file were even more upset than their King, as during the muster '[soldiers] loudly complained that for such hard work and losses [during the relief] they could be at least awarded by a [raised] hat'. [107] According to Dyakowski, Field Hetman Sieniawski managed to find the way to force the Emperor to honour some of his troops. When meeting both monarchs, he took off his hat and bowed towards Sobieski, after which he put hat back on and only saluted with his *buława* mace towards the Emperor. When the monarchs and officers were passing the mustered troops, cavalry banners from Royal and Grand Hetman's regiments saluted them with their flags. When they reached the Field Hetman's regiment, none of the standard-bearers moved. Confused, the Emperor asked why that was the case and was told that the soldiers were upset, as he had not raised his hat to their Hetman. Hearing that, Leopold was very surprised, and he did honour the remaining troops, even Tatars and Wallachian light horse, by raising his hat.[108] Unfortunately none of the other sources support Dyakowski's anecdote, and General Kątski in his diary even pointed out that soldiers 'were a bit upset with Austrian pride, as the Emperor did not raise his hat to anyone beside the King'.[109]

The whole affair is of course still a matter of controversy. Barker pointed out it could be just a misunderstanding on the grounds of Leopold being prevented by court etiquette to show a more open attitude towards the Poles,

---

106 Dalerac, *Polish Manuscripts*, pp.108–109.
107 Antoni Zygmunt Helcel (ed.), *Listy Jana Sobieskiego do żony Marii Kazimiery,* pp.388–389, Jan III do Marii Kazimiery, W obozie pod wsią Szenau na gościńcu Przeszowskim nad Dunajem mil trzy od Wiednia (17go Września), Jakub Ludwik Sobieski, *Dyaryusz wyprawy wiedeńskliej w 1683 r.,* pp.14–15.
108 Dyakowski, pp.71–73.
109 Marcin Kątski, 'Diarium Artilieriae Praefecti', Franciszek Kluczycki (ed.), *Akta do dziejów Króla Jana IIIgo sprawy roku 1683*, p.597.

Meeting between Leopold I and Jan III. Here, unlike in the real event, we can see the Emperor is taking off his hat in greeting. Author unknown. (Wien Museum Inv.-Nr. 110506, CC0)

who were used to rather different behaviour from their own monarch.[110] The change of Leopold's attitude towards the Poles was at least partially the direct effect of the inner politics of the Habsburg court, as the council of ministers was able to convince the Emperor that Sobieski's plans regarding Jakub and Hungary were serious enough and that it could negatively affect the situation within the Empire. The fact that the Polish army took the lion's share of the loot from the Turkish camp also had to play some role, as from that point many changes in the attitude of Imperial soldiers and citizens towards Poles begin to appear. Despite initially showing their gratitude, now, just days after the battle, the situation quickly changed for the worse. Sobieski, in his letter to the Queen dated 17 September, not only described the whole event with Leopold and Jakub but also listed many insults and problems facing him and his army. Imperial envoys left the Polish army, and the Spanish envoy to the Imperal court, Carlo Emanuele d'Este, Marchese di Borgomanero, suddenly cancelled his planned personal audience with Jan III. Promised food, to be paid for from Papal money, was not delivered. Many Polish wounded and sick, 'and there are many of them', were lying on dung, without proper help. Even though the King wanted to pay for boats to take them to Pressburg, not even one was offered. The Poles were refused permission to bury Polish dead in church graveyards, instead being offered ruined graveyards outside the city, which were already full of Turkish dead. More and more Polish soldiers were attacked and robbed by Imperial soldiers who were 'looting our baggage train and stealing our horses that were left behind [before crossing Vienna Woods]'. Even a few of the royal guardsmen, protecting captured Turkish cannons, were assaulted and robbed, losing their clothes and horses.[111] It seems that a few days after the

110 Thomas Barker, *Double Eagle and Crescent*, p.343.
111 Antoni Zygmunt Helcel (ed.), *Listy Jana Sobieskiego do żony Marii Kazimiery*, p.389, Jan III do Marii Kazimiery, W obozie pod wsią Szenau na gościńcu Przeszowskim nad Dunajem mil trzy

whole disagreement, the Emperor made some attempts to fix his relations with the Poles. He offered two horses from his own stables to Sobieski,[112] while Jabłonowski and Sieniawski were gifted 3,000 ducats each and Royal Prince Jakub a 'sword set with Diamonds, of about a thousand Pistols[113] value'.[114]

Medal commemorating two victories against Turks besieging Vienna: in 1529 and in 1683. Made by Johann Kittel in 1683. (Wien Museum Inv.-Nr. 37942, CC BY 4.0)

Changes in the post-battle situation also affected the other allied armies. The Saxons were first to leave, with Elector Johann George III unhappy due to the lack of Imperial finance to support him. His troops left the allied camp on 15 September. The German Circle allies were another contingent that was not keen on continuing operations. Waldeck was seriously ill, and he left for Klosterneuburg to recover, while another Franconian commander, the Margrave of Bayreuth, was strongly objecting to any further actions, categorically claiming that 'his troops cannot [without further orders] move forward'. They were both awaiting orders from their countries and until then were unwilling to commit their soldiers to a further campaign. The Bavarians were in a very poor state. Maximilian II Emanuel wrote to Lorraine on 27 September that 'his cavalry cannot continue campaigning this year (…) while from my infantry there are only 5,000 left in rank and even those are getting more unwell with each day'.[115] He also wanted to have independent command, leading a Bavarian-Imperial corps against the Turks, otherwise he was planning to leave as well. Lorraine managed to convince him to stay, with the Bavarian Elector offered overall command of the remaining Circle troops, alongside his own army. Due to the poor shape of the Bavarians corps, the main brunt of the following campaign lay in the hands of the Imperial and Polish armies.

The remaining allied commanders and Imperial court officials were now discussing the plans for furthering the campaign. Many Imperialists wanted to march to Upper Hungary (Slovakia), to end the *kuruc* threat and gain possession of good winter quarters. There were two main strategic targets that were considered: Esztergom (called Gran in German and Ostrzyhom in Polish) or Nové Zámky. Sobieski wanted to attack Buda, location of the new main camp and gathering place of the Ottoman army. Lorraine wanted to march towards Esztergom. It seems that the Imperialists were by now more wary of Sobieski's political agenda, as Imre Thököly was sending his own envoys directly to the Polish King, hoping that he would mediate between

---

od Wiednia (17go Września),
112 *Ibidem*, p.392.
113 *Pistole* was French name for golden coin.
114 Dalerac, *Polish Manuscripts*, p.109.
115 Dupont, p.213.

the rebels and the Emperor. Added to Jan III's musings about a possible Hungarian throne for his son, it led to a strained political situation. On 16 and 17 September, during another meeting of the commanders, where Sobieski was not present, it was decided that the plan to attack Buda was too risky and that instead allied forces would march towards Estrzegom.

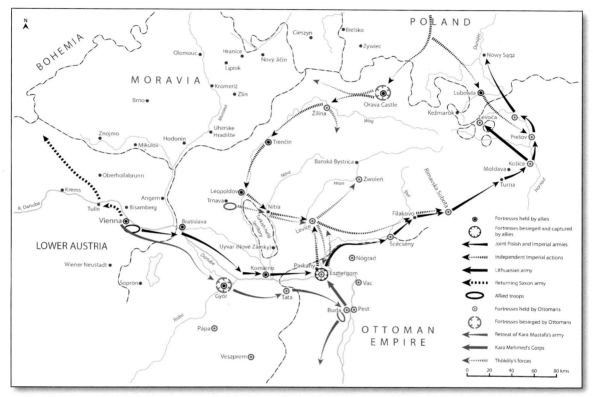

Further campaigns in Hungary and Slovakia, mid-September to mid-December 1683. [Source: Jan Wimmer, *Wiedeń 1683*]

The first battle of Párkány, 7 October 1683

Most of the Polish commanders, happy with the outcome of the battle and relief of besieged Vienna, wanted to finish the campaign there and then, and take their troops and return home to Poland. It appears that many nobles, especially those who joined the army with their private units as volunteers, did in fact leave and took their troops back to Poland. This was a great cause of concern to Jan III, who wrote to the Queen 'many of our men want to leave and it will be difficult to keep them here. Some are leaving with rich loot, other because their horses are starving (we captured lots of food for men in the enemy camp) or have enough of the war or have some business and things to take care of [in Poland].[116] The Queen even recommended that

116 Antoni Zygmunt Helcel (ed.), *Listy Jana Sobieskiego do żony Marii Kazimiery*, p.391, Jan III do Marii Kazimiery, W obozie pod wsią Szenau na gościńcu Przeszowskim nad Dunajem mil trzy

her husband return to Poland, seeing that Vienna was saved and that the main goal of the campaign was achieved. The final decision about the fate of the army was in the hands of Sobieski and 'the King hearkened neither to these Advices, nor to the repeated Instances of the Queen: He was for completing the Business, and thereby to lay the Empire under stronger Obligations to him'.[117] The Polish army left their camp on 19 September, and it seems that, in eyes of the rest of the allies, it was a surprising move. While Lorraine gathered his troops and followed the Poles, the rest of the gathered contingents remained near Vienna, for now.

Ottoman standard captured during the relief of Vienna in 1683. (Wien Museum Inv.-Nr. 240466, CC0)

The Polish army was marching along the right bank of Danube, travelling slowly as it was now accompanied by the baggage train left behind prior to the battle. Logistics started to fail, as supplies promised by the Imperialists did not arrive. An interesting observation from Dalerac talks about the misery of Sobieski's army: 'Besides this, the Poles thought they were at the far-end of the World, and long'd for their Beer, their Colworts,[118] and their Cacha,[119] without which they fancy'd they could not live'.[120] Soldiers were marching in baking heat, through destroyed and territory laid waste, among the dead bodies of the local population killed by Tatars, and with many of the Ottoman soldiers killed at Vienna thrown into the Danube. It is no surprise that dysentery quickly spread amongst soldiers and servants alike. On 20 September Kątski mentions that 'due to [drinking] water and [eating] fruits but most of all due to the stench, sicknesses started to attack the troops and because of this many men already died'.[121] The army had to

---

od Wiednia (17go Września),

117 Dalerac, *Polish Manuscripts*, p.101.
118 In this context most likely cabbage.
119 (Polish) *Kasza* meaning groats.
120 Dalerac, *Polish Manuscripts*, p.137.
121 Marcin Kątski, 'Diarium Artilieriae Praefecti', Franciszek Kluczycki (ed.), *Akta do dziejów Króla Jana IIIgo sprawy roku 1683*, pp.598–599.

camp near Pressburg (Bratislava) for three days, waiting for the bridge to be built. By the end of September sickness had decimated the ranks. As the King wrote in a letter to the Queen dated 28 September: 'We came into country ravaged by war, although we find here plenty of forage for horses; it is of no matter though, as almost half of the army is sick due to plague. This fever, known as the Hungarian one, [causes] bloody dysentery, also vomiting, nausea and delirium. [So many] Nobles and high-ranking commanders are laying sick in Pressburg, where we had to leave them and many of them already died; what is worse, this sickness even comes back to those that were already cured. Now companions, soldiers and servants are starting to die'.[122] It seems that officers were especially badly affected, with many of them sick and dying. It badly affected the readiness of the army and caused a problem with the proper command of the troops. When Jan III and Jabłonowski went to inspect the defences of Győr,[123] there was no high-ranking officer that could replace them in their absence as a temporary commander. Szczęsny Potocki, who survived the fever, wrote to the King 'I'm better now but, as I'm laying between dead, as both companions and servant are dying around me, it is worrying me'.[124] *Rotmistrz* Krasiński also described the poor state of the Polish army at that time, mentioning losses due to sickness, 'from the change of the air and from Vienna infection'. The army lost many horses, as can be imagined as the ordeal of marching through the Vienna Woods, followed by an intense battle took its toll. He also complained about losses amongst servants (*czeladź*) of the Polish cavalry, that lost 'few hundred on its first foray to Turkish Hungary', with added losses due to a combination of sickness and desertion also affecting this non-combatant, yet essential, part of the army.[125] Vice-Chancellor Krzysztof Jan Gniński, wrote to the Queen on 5 October, and mentions the very poor state of the Polish army. 'They completely stopped delivering food for the men, because of it we are so weak, that our infantrymen are falling like sheaves [under the sickle]; almost all officers are ill [and] companions are dying'.[126] Dupont adds that 'our stay at the banks of the Danube costs us lives of more soldiers, that [were] lost during both battles. The Poles were painfully affected by the same thing as one of the armies of Charlemagne, the story of which I read in my youth, as it recounted that it died to the man due to dysentery caused by drinking water from the river. We suffered from it [here], in a short period of time losing many men and horses'.[127]

---

122 Antoni Zygmunt Helcel (ed.), *Listy Jana Sobieskiego do żony Marii Kazimiery*, p.396. Jan III do Marii Kazimiery, Na insule Szutt, między Preszburkiem a Komorą pod San Peter. 28 Septembra.

123 Called Jawaryn in Polish and Raab in German.

124 Antoni Zygmunt Helcel (ed.), *Listy Jana Sobieskiego do żony Marii Kazimiery*, p.397. Jan III do Marii Kazimiery, Na insule Szutt, między Preszburkiem a Komorą pod San Peter. 28 Septembra.

125 'Relatia seu descriptia wojny pod Wiedniem, pod Strygoniem i dalszej kampaniej A. 1683', p.165.

126 Franciszek Kluczycki (ed.), *Akta do dziejów Króla Jana IIIgo*, p.440. Literae Vice Cancellari Gniński, ad Reginam, quibus nuntios de Rege refert, et de nonnullis rebus gerendis consulit.

127 Dupont, p.227.

At the beginning of October allied troops started to slowly gather near Komárno. It is worth noting that it was at this time that Dupont returned from Poland with letters from the Queen and he re-joined the army. Both the Polish and Imperial armies suffered due to sickness, so they were waiting for reinforcements. Some of the delayed Polish units, which had not taken part in the relief of Vienna, finally managed to catch up with Sobieski's army. Amongst them were a few newly raised infantry regiments and some cavalry. Lorraine's army was reinforced by some Croat cavalry and some severely depleted infantry regiments from the garrison of Vienna. Allied commanders did not have much information about the Turkish army, and they were considering a pause in operations, to allow for more of the delayed units to arrive: Bavarians, a Brandenburg contingent and further Polish troops. After some deliberations it was decided that the joint armies would march towards Esztergom, hoping to capture this fortress and cut off another crucial location – Nové Zámky – and *kuruc*-held territories. There was even hope that after Esztergom, allies could move towards Pest. After receiving new orders the armies started to slowly move across two bridges on the Danube and the Wag, with Polish cavalry and dragoons leading the way, followed by Imperial cavalry, and the combined infantry and artillery. On 6 October the Polish vanguard was 20km from Párkány and, contrary to the previously agree plan of action, Sobieski decided to re-rout his troops and on the morning of 7 October to march towards this small fortress. From captured prisoners he knew that Párkány is held only by few hundred janissaries and was hoping to surprise them and capture the bridge intact on the Danube in that location, opening a new route for the attack against Esztergom. The fortifications of Párkány were composed of a *palanka, a* wooden palisade and two rows of stockades with a ditch in the ground outside the palisade. As can be imagined, Lorraine was not happy with such a sudden change of plans, especially as his cavalry had set up the camp and was to rest through the whole 7 October. Despite this, he gathered his troops and marched after the Poles, with Lubomirski's cavalry and dragoons as his vanguard. To make matters worse, the allies did not have proper intelligence on their enemy. During a reconnaissance mission near Párkány some Polish cavalrymen were surprised at night by Turks, while camping in an abandoned village or small town. One officer and 20 or 30 of his men were killed and their heads were cut off and left as a horrific memento in plain sight of the marching Polish army. How badly this sight affected the morale of soldiers can be imagined, already struggling as they were due to sickness and a lack of provisions.[128]

Because of these problems, the allied commanders did not know that Turks had sent a large part of their available troops to the vicinity of the town. Kara Mustafa, hoping to stop the attack against Esztergom, despatched Kara Mehmed Pasha with large force of cavalry from seven eyalets (Rumelia, Eger, Buda, Silistria-Ochakiv, Bosnia, Karaman and Sivas) to protect Párkány.[129] Kara Mehmed did not look for a pitched battle, as he did not have support of infantry and cavalry. Instead he was hoping for a diversionary attack, to

---

128 Dalerac, *Polish Manuscripts*, p.136, Dupont, p.218.
129 Andrzej Witkowicz, *Czerwone sztandary Osmanów*, pp.424–425.

harass the marching enemy forces, using his provincial cavalry. There are different estimates of the size of the force he had under his command, and the majority of researched tend to agree to 12,000–15,000 men, with no more than 7,000 taking part in first battle. The Turks also had advantage of the terrain, as a few small hills near Párkány allowed them to hide most of their soldiers.

The rash decision of Jan III to divert his troops towards Párkány was just the first of the mistakes that were to lead to disaster. The Polish army marched in a very long and loose column, with soldiers and their commanders not expecting much resistance. It should be remembered that all banners and companies were well below their normal strength, as many men died or were left behind due to sickness. The vanguard was led by the experienced Stefan Bidziński, who had some cavalry (*pancerni* and light horse) and two dragoon regiments, with a total of 1,000 to 1,200 men. Further units of cavalry (including hussars) and dragoons, 4,000 to 5,000 men in total, were marching after them, led by Grand Hetman Jabłonowski and accompanied by the King and Royal Prince Jakub. General Kątski was in charge of the infantry and artillery, marching further down the road, with two more regiments of Polish cavalry closing on the long column of march of the army. Hurrying after them was Lorraine with the Imperial cavalry. One of the Turkish chronicles mentioned that '12,000 elite, dressed in blue, cavalry and infantry' were marching towards Párkány.[130]

Siege and relief of Vienna in 1683. Giuseppe Longhi, 1683. (Wien Museum Inv.-Nr. 8676, CC0)

---

130 Silahdar Mehmed Aga z Fyndykły, 'Diariusz wyprawy wiedeńskiej i kronika związanych z nią wydarzeń w państwie osmańskim od 21 stycznia 1681 do 28 lutego 1684 r', p.180.

The Polish vanguard was ordered to gather all available boats on the Danube, to be used by Cossacks to get onto the opposite bank of the river. The King's plan was to capture Párkány in case the fortress and bridge were abandoned by the Turks or, in the case of meeting a defensive force, to stop and wait for the Imperial army and artillery.[131] Despite Sobieski's orders to stop one mile from Párkány and wait for rest of the army, Bidziński led his soldiers into a quick attack against the few hundred Turkish cavalrymen that were seen near the fortress. His *pancerni* and light horse quickly caught up with *sipahi*, broke them and forced them to retreat. There is no evidence that sending this group of horsemen was a ruse leading the Poles into an ambush, but it is known that the fleeing *sipahi* hid behind a hill and Bidziński's pursuing soldiers suddenly met thousands of fresh Ottoman troops. The Polish commander quickly ordered a retreat, especially as his flank was by then under fire from the garrison of Párkány. Kara Mehmed quickly took the initiative and threw his cavalry after the fleeing Poles. In the meantime Hetman Jabłonowski, accompanied by some of his cavalry, arrived where two dragoon regiments from the vanguard were milling around in confusion. They were not prepared to face the enemy, as the matches of their muskets were not lit, and they did not have any anti-cavalry obstacles that they could use. To add to the ensuing chaos, Jabłonowski ordered the dragoons to dismount and only some of the soldiers had done so. The Hetman then led his cavalry against the charging *sipahi* but both his and Bidziński's troops were outnumbered and forced to retreat. What was worse, this retreat left the dragoons on their own and they were quickly and mercilessly cut down by the Turkish cavalry. The Polish command completely failed at this stage, with officers caught by surprise and unable to organise a proper defence. Sadly it was the dragoons, now abandoned by the vanguard cavalry, that had to pay the steep price for the mistakes made in the opening phase of the combat. According to Dalerac, Jabłonowski's regiment managed to remount and attempted to flee but the Royal dragoons (de Maligny's regiment) did not have time to get to their horses and it was them that took heavy losses. After the campaign the overall strength of the latter regiment was lowered by 85 men, supporting Dalerac's observation about heavy losses.

Light cavalry officer or companion. Caspar Luyken, 1709 (Herzog August Bibliothek)

Sobieski quickly realised what a dangerous situation his troops were in. He despatched messengers to Lorraine, Kątski and the remaining Polish cavalry to hurry and join his forces. With his remaining troops, mostly cavalry, he set up

---

131 Antoni Zygmunt Helcel (ed.), *Listy Jana Sobieskiego do żony Marii Kazimiery*, p.403, Jan III do Marii Kazimiery, 8 Octobris, milę od Grana.

a new battle line. Jabłonowski and his retreating troops were to take right wing, the centre was held by Marcin Zamoyski and the left wing by Szczęsny Potocki. The whole line was hastily prepared, at some points held only by one banner and without enough support troops. The King estimated his available troops as 5,000 men, 'as some were killed [during relief of Vienna], died [from sickness], were [still] sick and the largest number stayed with the baggage train, with their oxen, cattle, sheep and loot'.[132] Hetman Jabłonowski urged the King to flee the battle, seeing the poor condition of the troops and the confusion amongst the ranks. Jan III would not hear of this and remained near the centre of the battleline. The brunt of the fighting fell on Jabłonowski's troops, and they managed to hold on and pushed back two Turkish attacks. A third attack ended with a feigned flight and in the heat of the moment the Hetman's banners chased after *sipahi*. The Ottoman cavalry suddenly stopped and counterattacked. Some units managed to outflank the Polish right wing and attacked the rear of the battleline. Sobieski pulled a few hussar banners together and ordered them to counterattack to protect Jabłonowski's wing. One of them was Władysław Denhoff's unit, a 'beautiful and well-equipped banner', that was woefully unprepared to face the enemy, as none of the companions and retainers had their guns ready. It came as no surprise then that the 'Turks swatted them like flies'.[133] Seeing the sudden move of the best of its cavalry, and thinking that even hussars were fleeing, unengaged troops from centre and left flank broke their ranks and started to run from the battlefield in panic. Soon after Jabłonowski's soldiers followed and whole Polish army was in retreat. Fleeing soldiers were throwing their flags, drums and the hussars their lances to the ground. Many men lost their horses and were trampled by the crowd or killed by Turks.

The King fled with just small group of men: Crown Equerry Marek Matczyński, Crown Venator[134] Atanazy Miączyński, Lieutenants Czerkas and Piekarski, an unknown companion from the Royal hussar banner and another unknown companion from one of the Royal Princes' hussar banners. Sobieski was struggling, and due to his obesity he quickly became exhausted during the flight. Courtiers were trying to encourage other soldiers to protect the King but in answer only heard from them 'to get lost'.[135] The situation became extremely dangerous, as Turkish horsemen were fast approaching. Suddenly the stranded monarch and his entourage were met by another fleeing Polish soldier, one of the reiters (or officially – *arkabuzer*) from the royal squadron. Matczyński begged him to stay, saying 'reiter, you are from the royal regiment, hold your horse and protect us, you will receive great fame and reward, if you do not flee'. It will never be known if the soldier decided to stay due to sense of duty or the promise of the reward, nonetheless he aided the fleeing monarch. When the first of the pursuing Turks, *sipahi* armed with spears, neared the Polish group, Matczyński yet again asked

---

132 Antoni Zygmunt Helcel (ed.), *Listy Jana Sobieskiego do żony Marii Kazimiery*, p.403, Jan III do Marii Kazimiery, 8 Octobris, milę od Grana.
133 Mikołaj Dyakowski, p.76.
134 He oversaw the organising of royal hunts.
135 Original Polish idiom *jechał cię pies z nim* does not allow for a direct translation.

the reiter for help, telling him 'show some mercy, turn around [and face] the Turk!'. The guardsman did turn against the *sipahi*, killing one with his pistol. He then managed to defeat another Ottoman horseman, who had charged him with sabre in hand. Sadly he was then attacked by a larger group of *sipahi*, yet the reiter did not waver, and in a suicidal last stand bought the King and his entourage enough time to flee to safety. The Poles heard two more shots from his pistols and then the brave man was killed by his attackers.[136] Despite some attempts to find the name of his saviour, Sobieski was unable to identify the reiter and the soldier remained anonymous. It is possible that the guard squadron took heavy losses and there was no chance to find out which of the killed it was who saved the king. Sobieski did write to the Queen, saying that the soldier was 'worth at least, to say prayer to God for his soul' and he was well remembered in writings from the period.

Polish cavalry in combat with Turks. From painting by Franz (Frans) Geffels, 1683–1694. (Photo: Birgit and Peter Kainz, Wien Museum Inv.-Nr. 40132, CC BY 4.0)

In his account describing the first battle of Párkány, *rotmistrz* Krasiński wrote that Polish soldiers were not aware of the Turkish force in the vicinity, and the army was ill prepared, lacked proper reconnaissance and was marching without proper order. It was caught at a complete disadvantage, having around 6,000 men against 15,000 Turks. Krasiński wrote about the chaos in the ranks, the massacre of the dragoons and the contradictory orders from some high-ranking commanders. Of course he praised those serving under Grand Hetman Jabłonowski, especially Colonel Rafał Leszczyński and himself.[137] He also mentions that Władysław Denhoff, Voivode of Pomerania, died during the battle.[138] Krasiński omitted the fact however, that by the next

---

136 Dyakowski, pp.78–80, Antoni Zygmunt Helcel (ed.), *Listy Jana Sobieskiego do żony Marii Kazimiery*, p.404, Jan III do Marii Kazimiery, 8 Octobris, milę od Grana.

137 His account was written as an anonymous work, so he could pretend not be connected to such gallant officer.

138 'Relatia seu descriptia wojny pod Wiedniem, pod Strygoniem i dalszej kampaniej A. 1683', pp.165–166.

day he was already asking King Jan III for the office vacated by Denhoff's demise. He was refused, as Sobieski had promised it to Jan Gniński the Younger, so it is no surprise that the whole account of the campaign of 1683 written by Krasiński is full of often poorly concealed criticism of the King. Another Polish diarist wrote of Denhoff's death, 'being obese, he was not able to run away anymore; he dismounted and, on his knees, gave himself unto God when the Turks arrived, and there they killed him on the spot, along with his loyal servant, who did not want to run away and preferred to die alongside his master'.[139] When describing the defeat, Kątski, who did not take part in the fight, focused only on the officers, mentioning Denhoff, lieutenants of hussars Kalinowski and Siemianowski, and also wrote rather enigmatically about 'others'. He highlighted the losses amongst the dragoons, '[who] were hurt the most, amongst them many officers [were] killed'.[140] Dupont mentioned the loss of 300 men, including 200 dismounted dragoons, whose heads were cut off by the Turks.[141] Pasek seems to grossly exaggerate the losses inflicted on the Polish army, as can be expected from a second-hand account. Nonetheless it is interesting to see his description of the battle. He mentions the severe defeat of the vanguard under Stefan Bidziński, where Bidziński's own dragoon regiment was supposed to 'be wiped out; while other dragoons marching with the vanguard, lost many [men]'. In all this part of the army 'lost more than 2,000 men; many young officers and nobles, many of Bidziński's kinsmen amongst them'. Pasek also wrote that Denhoff was a 'man very obese', and was killed, alongside Lieutenant Siemianowski and many companions. 'Flags, lance, drums were all abandoned'.[142] According to Dalerac, Denhoff was wounded by a musket shot despite the 'Waistcoat he had on, quilted with Taffata Cotton, 1,000 or 1,200 times double, which he had prefer'd before Armour, that could not be fitted to his fat corps'. Seven or eight of his servants tried to lift him from the ground into the saddle but without luck. He ordered them to flee and soon after was caught and beheaded by the Turks. Dalerac also wrote of Sobieski's ordeal, mentioning that his 'Arms and Thighs were mortify'd and bruis'd, by the justling of Horses and Arms, and by the Blows he accidentally receiv'd from those that rush'd by him with all the violence imaginable'.[143] Francis Taaffe, serving in the Imperial army as colonel of a cuirassier regiment, estimated Polish losses as 'around one thousand killed, most of the dragoons, who having alighted from their horses in a plain were abandoned by the horse [cavalry] , and so cut in pieces by the enemy'.[144] Royal Prince Jakub did not give any information about losses in his diary although he mentioned fleeing from the battle once the Polish lines were broken. He was quickly separated from the King and

---

139 Stanisław Wierzbowski, *Konnotata wypadków w domu i kraju zaszłych od 1634 do 1689* (Lipsk: Księgarnia Zagraniczna, 1858), p.196.

140 Marcin Kątski, 'Diarium Artilieriae Praefecti', p.604.

141 Dupont, p.220.

142 Jan Chryzostom Pasek, *Pamiętniki*, p.383.

143 Dalerac, *Polish Manuscripts*, pp.143–145.

144 Franciszek Kluczycki (ed.), *Akta do dziejów Króla Jana IIIgo*, p.462, Francis Taaffe to Earl of Carlingford, from the camp near Barrakan facing Gran, 10 October 1683.

had to flee on his own, looking for safety amongst the Imperial cavalry.[145] Jan III himself, writing to the Queen the day after the battle, mentioned the state of the battlefield, littered with dead bodies and abandoned armour, lances, drums and flags.[146] Imperial envoy Hans Christoph Zierowsky wrote of 2,000 Polish dead, and that Denhoff died in battle.[147] On the Ottoman side, Silahdar Mehmed Aga wrote how valiantly the Turkish cavalrymen charged the enemy, 'striking them like a hurricane'. The number of losses amongst the allied army are a huge exaggeration however, as according to his chronicle the 'enemies of the Faith' lost 8,000 killed, including all infantry present at the battlefield. He also mentions that remnants of the defeated army were chased for two hours, until they reached their own camp.[148] Another Turkish chronicle goes even further, claiming that there were 10,000 killed 'or even more'.[149] Defterdar Sary Mehmed Pasha gave similarly high figures, as according to him there were 24,000 Polish soldiers present,[150] with 10,000 of them killed during the battle.[151]

There are many estimates of the total Polish losses, including those already mentioned above, taken from Turkish sources. Average numbers given by modern historians vary between 1,000 and 2,000 killed, with Jan Wimmer lowering it to 500, based on an analysis of post-campaign muster rolls, which in this case seems to be conservative in number. To

Camel captured in the Turkish camp during relief of Vienna. Author unknown. (Wien Museum Inv.-Nr. 31577, CC0)

Le present Camel a este' pris sur les Turcs deuant Vienne par H.B. en 1683, et il a 11 Pieds de longeur et neuf de hauteur

---

145 Jakub Ludwik Sobieski, *Dyaryusz wyprawy wiedeńskliej w 1683 r*, p.18.

146 Antoni Zygmunt Helcel (ed.), *Listy Jana Sobieskiego do żony Marii Kazimiery*, p.404, Jan III do Marii Kazimiery, 8 Octobris, milę od Grana.

147 Franciszek Kluczycki (ed.), *Akta do dziejów Króla Jana IIIgo*, p.472, Summarium relationum Ablegati Zierowski.

148 Silahdar Mehmed Aga z Fyndykły, 'Diariusz wyprawy wiedeńskiej i kronika związanych z nią wydarzeń w państwie osmańskim od 21 stycznia 1681 do 28 lutego 1684 r.', Zygmunt Abrahamowicz (ed.), *Kara Mustafa pod Wiedniem. Źródła muzułmańskie do dziejów wyprawy wiedeńskiej 1683 roku*, p.181.

149 Husejn Hezarfenn, Historia wyprawy wiedeńskiej', Zygmunt Abrahamowicz (ed.), *Kara Mustafa pod Wiedniem. Źródła muzułmańskie do dziejów wyprawy wiedeńskiej 1683 roku*, p.261.

150 The same number that he mentioned describing the Polish army during the relief of Vienna.

151 Defterdar Sary Mehmed Pasha, 'Wyprawa wiedeńska i związane z nią wydarzenia w państwie osmańskim od lutego do czerwca 1684 roku', Zygmunt Abrahamowicz (ed.), *Kara Mustafa pod Wiedniem. Źródła muzułmańskie do dziejów wyprawy wiedeńskiej 1683 roku*, p.297.

these should be added at least a few hundred wounded, some taken prisoner by the Turks, and those that due to loss of horses and equipment were not combat-ready for the next battle. While such losses were severe, the effect of the defeat on the morale of the army cannot be underestimated. After Vienna they thought that the Ottomans were defeated and that in the rest of the campaign the weather and sickness would be the worst of their problems. Kara Mehmed and his soldiers provided them with a reality check which shook the whole Polish army to the core.

The victorious Turkish cavalry chased after the Poles for a few kilometres and only pulled up on seeing Lorraine's cavalry. The Imperial commander and his cuirassiers allowed the fleeing Polish troops to run between their squadrons, covering their withdrawal. The Polish infantry was close by as well, eager to fight against the Turks and in vengeful spirits, upon hearing rumours that the King himself had died during the battle. They were

Turkish chainmail from the seventeenth century. Such equipment was often used by Polish cavalry, especially *pancerni* (National Museum, Cracow)

encouraging their officers against the Turks, shouting 'all is lost, as our father [King] is gone: lead us, let us all die there'.[152] Sobieski wanted to re-engage the Ottomans with fresh troops, but the cool head of Lorraine prevailed as he understood that the allied forces were in no shape to renew the battle. That evening the combined army camped close to the bank of the Danube, with strong guards protecting the troops and search parties sent out to recover and bury the bodies of the fallen

Kara Mehmed quickly despatched messengers to Kara Mustafa, telling him about the victory and the death of the Polish King. That last rumour was based on the mistaken identity of Denhoff, whose head was delivered to him by one Turkish cavalryman. A companion from Denhoff's unit, Janicki, who was captured by Turks during one of the reconnaissance missions prior to the battle, correctly identified the head as belonging to his *rotmistrz* to the angry reaction of Kara Mehmed.[153] Captured lances, spears and flags were now placed by the Turks around the fortress of Párkány 'like so many Pallisadoes'. On the top of them were heads of Polish soldiers killed during the battle.[154] It seems that some of the captured flags, drums and kettledrums, along with many cut off heads of Polish soldiers, were transported to Buda, to be presented to Kara Mustafa.[155]

152 Antoni Zygmunt Helcel (ed.), *Listy Jana Sobieskiego do żony Marii Kazimiery*, p.405, Jan III do Marii Kazimiery, Przeciwko Strigonium pod Parkanem, 10 Octobris rano.
153 Mikołaj Dyakowski, p.78.
154 Dalerac, *Polish Manuscripts*, p.146.
155 Silahdar Mehmed Aga z Fyndykły, 'Diariusz wyprawy wiedeńskiej i kronika związanych z nią wydarzeń w państwie osmańskim od 21 stycznia 1681 do 28 lutego 1684 r', Zygmunt Abrahamowicz (ed.), *Kara Mustafa pod Wiedniem. Źródła muzułmańskie do dziejów wyprawy wiedeńskiej 1683 roku*, p.181.

The first battle of Párkány showed that the Ottoman army still could be a dangerous opponent, especially when well led and playing to its strengths: utilising shock cavalry, stubbornly attacking the enemy with overwhelming strength and through a long pursuit not allowing a broken enemy to regroup and reform. Overconfidence among the Polish commanders, including the King, Hetman Jabłonowski and (especially) Bidziński who commanded the vanguard, led to their army marching into a trap, fighting piecemeal and quickly losing morale when they faced defeat. Some thought that it was the Almighty that punished Sobieski, as 'God was pleas'd to mortifie this Hero by a contrary Success, and to let him know that the Disposal of the whole was in his Hands; having sav'd his Sacred Person, by a Miracle no less Remarkable than that of the Deliverance of Vienna, the Glory whereof, if unblemish'd, might perhaps have made the Poles too vain-glorious.'[156] Jan III was clearly frustrated with the lack of discipline and poor performance of his army, writing that the defeat was a punishment from God, sent upon the Poles for their behaviour after the relief of Vienna, 'looting churches, greed, adultery'. Another sour, yet realistic comment, was his observation that after Vienna many soldiers left the ranks and were not present with their units, that soldiers were not drilled properly and that their officers were 'stupid, careless, neglectful' – leading to complaints amongst their own troops, especially in the infantry and the badly-affected dragoons.[157]

The second battle of Párkány, 9 October 1683

Sobieski and Lorraine were in agreement, that the joint armies needed to face the Ottoman forces and regain the initiative temporarily lost to Turks. While some of the Polish and Imperial officers were suggesting retreat or to wait for Bavarian reinforcements, the final decision lay in the hands of the Polish monarch and the Imperial commander in chief. They both wanted new battles, 'the Poles being eager to regain their Credit, and the Germans desirous to share in the Glory, which they had in some measure been rob'd of the Day before'.[158] After the success of the first battle, Kara Mehmed was also eager to engage the enemy again, preparing his troops to go on the offensive. The allies estimated the Ottoman army to be around 30,000 men, almost wholly composed of cavalry. Kara Mehmed's force was actually much weaker, with 12,000–15,000 Turkish cavalry, about 1,000 janissaries holding Párkány, and a few hundred Tatars. The Polish researcher Andrzej Witkowicz has put forward the following Order of Battle:[159]

The first line had between 8,000 and 10,000 cavalry:
The right wing under Kara Mehmed, composed mostly of units from Buda

---

156 *Ibidem*, p.140.
157 Antoni Zygmunt Helcel (ed.), *Listy Jana Sobieskiego do żony Marii Kazimiery*, p.404, Jan III do Marii Kazimiery, 8 Octobris, milę od Grana.
158 Dalerac, *Polish Manuscripts*, p.150.
159 Andrzej Witkowicz, *Czerwone sztandary Osmanów*, p.433.

The centre, under Mustaf Pasha, composed mostly of his units from Silistria-Ochakiv

The left wing, under Mehmed Pasha, composed mostly of troops from Karaman and Rumelia. It was supported by artillery and janissary fire from Párkány.

There was a reserve of 4,000-5,000 cavalry, deployed in three lines, composed of units from Rumelia, Bosnia and Sivas.

It is not known where exactly the Tatars were deployed. It seems that a large part of the first line was massed on the right wing, where it was under the direct control of Kara Mehmed. His battle plan seems focused on an attempt to break the left wing of the allied army, which would allow the Turkish cavalry to outflank the enemy, in a similar way as in first battle. The Ottoman general was hoping that large numbers of Tatars and *kuruc* would arrive and strengthen his army, appearing on his right wing, but they did not reach Párkány on time, most probably unwilling to engage in a fight against the strong allied army. The same happened with other Ottoman troops. Prior to the battle, Kara Mustafa despatched some reinforcements to Kara Mehmed, sending him provincial troops from Damascus, Aleppo and Egypt, no more than 3,000-4,000 cavalry in total.[160] They never crossed the Danube and during their march only met the fleeing remnants of Kara Mehmed's army. The deployment of the Turkish troops was unusual, as in case of defeat they did not have clear route to fall back along as behind their lines there were swamps and the river Hron, while the only available bridge nearby was the one in Párkány, over the Danube.

---

160 Andrzej Witkowicz, *Czerwone sztandary Osmanów*, pp.435–437.

Second battle of Párkány.
By Sobieski's court painter,
Martino Altomonte
(Author's archive)

In the meantime the allied armies were strengthened by the arrival of delayed reinforcements, especially those Polish soldiers who had been hanging behind with the baggage train. Now they were back in the ranks, increasing the available manpower. Also, two regiments of cavalry that were marching at the tail-end of the Polish column on the 7 October and did not take part in the battle were now available to fight. Polish historians estimate that Sobieski now had up to 15,000 soldiers, with 7,000-8,000 cavalry, 5,000-6,000 infantry and up to 2,000 dragoons. The Imperial army could deploy a slightly higher number, with up to 6,000 cuirassiers, 3,000 dragoons and around 7,000 infantry.[161] Dupont's and Dalerac's estimates of the joint allied army as 50,000 seems far too high, and is based on the 'paper strength' of the units, not on their actual size.[162] What is interesting is that it appears that at least some part of the Polish hussars had to deploy without their lances, that were lost on 7 October during the fight and subsequent retreat. In his letter to the Queen, Sobieski wrote that when he was deploying his troops on the morning of 9 October, he stood in front of the hussar banners and ordered those that were still in possession of lances to move into the first rank. One of the retainers moved forward with his lance, at which a companion of his retinue wanted to take the weapon off him. The retainer refused, saying 'my lord, I managed to save this lance for myself from the [previous] encounter.

161 Janusz Woliński, 'Parkany (7 i 9 października 1683)', *Przegląd Historyczno-Wojskowy*, volume VI, part 1 (Warszawa: Główna Księgarnia Wojskowa, 1933), pp.56–57, Jan Wimmer, *Wiedeń 1683*, pp.371–372. Thomas Barker, *Double Eagle and Crescent*, p.354, estimated the number of Poles as much lower, as 12,000, while Polish researchers disagreed with such a figure.
162 Dalerac, *Polish Manuscripts*, p.151, Dupont, p.220.

I did not abandon it, like the others [theirs]'. The King praised the brave retainer and gave him an award of five ducats.[163] Unfortunately Sobieski did not write if he allowed him to keep his place in the first rank, normally reserved for companions only. This shows that there were no replacement lances available, even in the baggage train, and considering the short period between both battles, there was no time to prepare new ones. As such, in the forthcoming battle many hussars had to rely on their wide arsenal of personal weapons, from firearms to estocs and pallasches.

The allied battle line was based on a strong centre made up of all the Imperial infantry (deployed in two lines) and artillery, under the command of Ernst Rüdiger von Starhemberg. The left of the centre was protected by half of the Imperial cavalry, led by Johann Heinrich von Dünewald, while the other half, under Ludwig Wilhelm von Baden, was deployed on the right of the centre. Imperial dragoons were placed as a reserve. The whole Imperial force was under the command of the Duke of Lorraine. Unlike at Vienna, the Polish army was this time divided on both wings of the main line. The left wing was led by Grand Hetman Jabłonowski, and he commanded half of the Polish army, with a strong infantry force and artillery under Kątski. Additionally, 10 banners of cavalry (*pancerni*, supported by some light horse) were placed on far left of the line. This detachment, commanded by Stefan Czarniecki, had the task of preventing any outflanking moves by the Turks. The right wing of the allies was under Hieronim Lubomirski, who had the rest of Polish cavalry and infantry, as well as his own auxiliary corps in

Second battle of Párkány in 1683. Published in Milan in 1696 (National Library, Warsaw)

---

163 Antoni Zygmunt Helcel (ed.), *Listy Jana Sobieskiego do żony Marii Kazimiery*, p.406, Jan III do Marii Kazimiery, Przeciwko Strigonium pod Parkanem, 10 Octrobris rano.

Imperial pay. The dragoons, badly mauled at Párkány, were left as a reserve force behind both Polish lines. King Jan III placed himself on the right wing, as in his battle plan it was from here that the allies would start their decisive attack. Both Polish and Imperial infantry carried *chevaux de frise* in the front ranks of their brigades, which were soon to play a crucial role in stopping Kara Mehmed's cavalry. The Ottoman battle line was deployed diagonally towards the allies, with the right wing closest to Jabłonowski's troops and the left wing as far away as possible, covered by fire from Párkány. Thanks to this deployment Kara Mehmed was at least partially able to hide his reserve between the hills and forced the Poles and Imperialists to advance towards his positions. The allies started their slow march forwards just after 9:00 a.m. accompanied by loud music played on drums, trumpets and cymbals. Around noon the allied army stopped about 1.5km from Párkány and by that time both the left wing and centre were much closer to the Ottomans. Noticing that the Poles and Imperialists had stopped their advance and were waiting for the enemy to move, Kara Mehmed led his cavalry forward in the first charge, targeting the left wing and centre of the enemy battle line.

The brave *sipahi,* despite facing infantry protected by *chevaux de frise* and supported by cannons and cavalry, threw themselves at the enemy 'with Impetuosity like Thunder, which cannot be conveiv'd nor describ'd'.[164] The first attacks against the centre and left wing were repulsed but, despite taking heavy losses from the fire of the allied infantry and cannon, they repeatedly charged Jabłonowski's troops. All eyewitnesses mentioned how bold and stubborn was the Turkish cavalry, again and again throwing themselves into the fight. Taaffe wrote of their 'incredible fury',[165] while Dalerac mentions that they kept returning 'with greater Vigour' and praised the Turkish commanders highly as they were leading from the front.[166] Dupont was most impressed with the enemy, who were to charge at least ten times against the Poles. 'It appeared to us that more of them we kill, [then remaining Turks] return towards us with even more energy'. He also praised how easily and quickly they were able to manoeuvre in front of the allied line, as they were riding 'excellent horses'.[167] Dyakowski mentions Mustaf Pasha, of Silistria-Ochakiv, who led his horsemen against the Polish lines, gave Hetman Jabłonowski's hussar banner a hard time.[168] The initial charges against the Imperial centre were easily repulsed, as after opening the salvoes of the German infantry 'a prodigious number of Men and Horses fell to the Ground'.[169] It appears that the Ottomans quickly decided to focus most of their attacks on Jabłonowski's wing. The main role here was played by the Hetman's own regiment of cavalry, under the command of the lieutenant of his hussar banner, Michał Rzewuski. The Hetman's troops were hard pressed by the constant pressure of the attacking enemy cavalry and although the Polish hussars, trying to atone

164 Dalerac, *Polish Manuscripts*, p.151.
165 Franciszek Kluczycki (ed.), *Akta do dziejów Króla Jana IIIgo*, p.462, Francis Taaffe to the Earl of Carlingford, from the camp near Barrakan, 10 October 1683.
166 Dalerac, *Polish Manuscripts*, p.152.
167 Dupont, p.221.
168 Dyakowski, p.82.
169 Dalerac, *Polish Manuscripts,* p.152.

for their poor performance at the first battle, showed great courage leading counterattacks, there was a strong risk that masses of Turkish horse would finally succeed in breaking through. Luckily the Duke of Lorraine kept a close eye on the situation and sent General von Dünewald with five regiments of cuirassiers to help the Poles. Taaffe wrote that Jabłonowski 'received them [Turks] so briskly, that it stopped their fury', while the cuirassiers 'put them totally in disorder'.[170] Heavy fighting finally led the Turks to breaking point and their right wing started to retreat. They were pursued by Polish cavalry, the first line of Imperial cuirassiers and Croats. At the same time the right wing of the allied army, led by Sobieski and Lubomirski, supported by von Baden's Imperialists, started to move towards the Ottoman left. The King wanted to cut off the retreat of Kara Mehmed's army by blocking the bridge across the Danube. Sobieski even ordered his hussars to lower their lances and keep them horizontal, to make the moving cavalry less visible from a distance. At this point the Turkish commanders realised that the battle was lost and ordered a general retreat that quickly turned into panicked flight. Most of the Ottoman cavalry, pursued by the Poles and Imperialists, was desperately trying to get over the bridge in Párkány. Only a few hundred *sipahi*, amongst them a wounded Kara Mehmed, managed to cross the river before the bridge partially collapsed under the weight of masses of men and horses. Thousands of Turks were now crowded in the small space near the Danube, with the allied troops closing in.

Second battle of Parkany in 1683. Justus van den Nijpoort, 1694 (Rijksmuseum)

170 Franciszek Kluczycki (ed.), *Akta do dziejów Króla Jana IIIgo*, p.462, Francis Taaffe to Earl of Carlingford, from the camp near Barrakan over against Gran, 10 October 1683.

Párkány, defended by janissaries, was the next target of the allied attack. Four Polish regiments of foreign infantry, Cossacks, dismounted Imperial dragoons and von Baden's infantry regiment, led by the general himself, assaulted the Turkish *palanka*. The janissaries desperately defended the place but even with the support of artillery from Esztergom they did not stand a chance. The Polish regiments of the Queen and Royal Prince Jakub, led by Stanisław Morstin and Otto Seswegen, broke through the gates and entered the fortification. The janissaries tried to surrender, throwing their weapons on the ground, ripping their clothes and using the cloth as improvised white flags but to no avail. The Polish infantry showed them no mercy, enraged by the sight of their comrades' heads, killed in the first battle and now stuck on the palisade. Most of the garrison were killed, and only 200 that defended a small blockhouse managed to surrender to Imperial dragoons.

After capturing Párkány, the fury of the allied soldiers (especially the Poles) turned towards the Turkish cavalry still stuck on the wrong bank of the Danube. The Polish infantry moved towards them, and there were also orders to bring up the artillery. Some of the *sipahi* attempted to counterattack, but were stopped by Polish pikemen. For the next two hours Polish and Imperial muskets and cannon decimated the Turks, killing thousands. Many Ottoman soldiers jumped into the Danube, trying to swim to the other side. Others risked crossing the damaged bridge, all the time under heavy fire. Some tried to run towards the river Hron but even there they met their end from the hands of vengeful Poles. There were a few groups that fled north between the hills, towards Levice. Many Turks tried to surrender but were killed by the vengeful Poles, who were repaying them for the humiliation they suffered after the first battle. Some Imperial soldiers also took part in this phase of the battle, taking revenge for the siege of Vienna. Jan Chryzostom Pasek mentions that his step-son Stanisław managed to capture a wealthy Turk on a beautiful horse and was taking him towards the Polish lines. Suddenly an Imperial cuirassier appeared next to the prisoner and killed him with one thrust of his sword. Angered, Stanisław Pasek, who had just lost a sizeable ransom, shouted at the Imperial soldier, asking him why he killed his prisoner. The cuirassier just laughed, asking if the Pole was going to keep and feed 'this devil'.[171]

Polish *pancerny* or *petyhorzec* striking Turkish *sipahi*. His mail coif seems far too long. The poses of the soldiers seem very symbolic, like a drawing of St. George defeating the dragon. Engraver's initials G. W. W. B. (Wien Museum Inv.-Nr. 98032, CC0)

171 Jan Chryzostom Pasek, *Pamiętniki*, p.387.

Turkish chronicles tend to focus on the bravery of their soldiers, fighting until the end against overwhelming numbers. Sary Mehmed Pasha provides a brief but colourful depiction of the battle, with highly exaggerated numbers for the allied army.[172]

> Infidels numbering around fifty thousand men suddenly attacked and jumped like dogs on the Muslim troops. Battle and fight was waged for a few hours but, due to such high numbers of dishonourable infidels, also since they attacked from both sides, like a herd of pigs, no matter the losses they took, they could not be stopped.

Silahdar Mehmed Aga described the retreat of Kara Mehmed's army, where 'only one per thousand' of those that jumped into the Danube survived the ordeal. Others were lost on the bank of the river, 'some of the *ghazi* taken prisoners, other cut to pieces with sabres, hit by cannon balls or muskets, all martyred in death'. The waters of the Danube turned red, due to the vast numbers of men killed in it. [173]

It is very difficult to estimate the total losses of the Turkish army during the second battle. Depending upon the sources, there were between 7,000 and 30,000 (sic!)[174] killed and drowned in the Danube, with 1,000–1,500 taken prisoner, including '600 saved from the fury of the Poles'.[175] While Kara Mehmed managed to flee the battlefield, other commanders were not so lucky. Mehmed Pasha from Karaman died dismounted, fighting on the bank of Danube, while Hizir Pasha from Bosnia drowned during retreat. Mustafa Pasha from Silistria and Halil Pasha of Sivas were captured by Jabłonowski's hussar banner. The allies captured the Turkish camp with some tents, baggage wagons and some highly valued camels, and other Poles also recovered some of the equipment and prisoners

Fight for a Turkish flag.
Sebastiano Bianchi, 1684
(Rijksmuseum)

---

172 Defterdar Sary Mehmed Pasza, 'Wyprawa wiedeńska i związane z nią wydarzenia w państwie osmańskim od lutego do czerwca 1684 roku', Zygmunt Abrahamowicz (ed.), *Kara Mustafa pod Wiedniem. Źródła muzułmańskie do dziejów wyprawy wiedeńskiej 1683 roku*, p.297.

173 Silahdar Mehmed Aga z Fyndykły, 'Diariusz wyprawy wiedeńskiej i kronika związanych z nią wydarzeń w państwie osmańskim od 21 stycznia 1681 do 28 lutego 1684 r.', Zygmunt Abrahamowicz (ed.), *Kara Mustafa pod Wiedniem. Źródła muzułmańskie do dziejów wyprawy wiedeńskiej 1683 roku*, p.183.

174 20,000 given by Dupont, p.222, while Krasiński mentions 30,000, see 'Relatia seu descriptia wojny pod Wiedniem, pod Strygoniem i dalszej kampaniej A. 1683', p.167. Jan Wimmer, *Wiedeń 1683*, p.376 and Thomas Barker, *Double Eagle and Crescent*, p.355 estimate approx. 9,000 killed,

175 Franciszek Kluczycki (ed.), *Akta do dziejów Króla Jana IIIgo*, p.462, Francis Taaffe to Earl of Carlingford, from the camp near Barrakan over against Gran, October 10, 1683.

lost after the first battle. As always, valued victory trophies were some Turkish cavalry standards and those of their commanders. The rank and file and marauding servants focused on recovering Turkish horses and stripping the dead and drowned of their weapons, armour and valuables. Despite orders to the contrary, Párkány was also pillaged and set on fire, and it burned to the ground. Allied losses are unknown, but it is more than probable that they were no more than a few hundred killed and wounded. The second battle of Párkány was a crucial victory for the allied cause, as by destroying the remaining Turkish field army they now had opened the way to begin siege operations against Ottoman-held fortresses. Sobieski was so overjoyed with the triumph that he called it greater than the one at Vienna.[176] Soldiers that survived the defeat returned to the Ottoman camp under cover of darkness, 'naked, tearful, in poor shape, mostly without horses and wounded'.[177]

Further operations in Hungary

The allied troops rested and recovered for the next few days in camp near Párkány, while their commanders prepared for the next move: the siege of Esztergom. It was a well-protected fortress, garrisoned by 5,000 Turkish soldiers under the command of Deli Bekir Pasha of Aleppo. His soldiers were well equipped and received a large supply of ammunition and food from Buda. There were also further units stationed in Buda, that could supply added support to the garrison of Esztergom. Kara Mustafa, believing in the safety of the fortress, left the theatre of war and moved to Belgrade.

After a reconnaissance by the Duke of Lorraine in person, it was decided that a new bridge across the Danube would be built by Imperial sappers just above Esztergom, utilising two islands on the river. A stream of orders was issued to Imperial officers in nearby fortresses, ordering them to send siege guns, ammunition and food for the troops. There were also reinforcements on the move. On 12 October the Brandenburg contingent led by Colonel Wolfgang Christoph von Truchsess arrived in the allied camp. It was composed of eight infantry and two dragoon companies, with three small cannon and numbered 1,200 men in total. On 16 October the Bavarian infantry reached the camp as well. Due to sickness and fatigue its ranks were severely depleted, as five regiments and five battalions could only muster 5,233 men. The Bavarian cavalry, with four regiments and one company, had by that time only around half of its normal strength (dropping from 3,100 to 1,500 men) and re-joined the allied army by the end of the month. The Swabian contingent of 4,000 infantry and 1,000 horse was still on the move and it too joined the army at the end of the month. Between 18 and

176 Antoni Zygmunt Helcel (ed.), *Listy Jana Sobieskiego do żony Marii Kazimiery*, p.406, Jan III do Marii Kazimiery, Przeciwko Strigonium pod Parkanem, 10 Octobris rano.
177 Silahdar Mehmed Aga z Fyndykły, 'Diariusz wyprawy wiedeńskiej i kronika związanych z nią wydarzeń w państwie osmańskim od 21 stycznia 1681 do 28 lutego 1684 r.', Zygmunt Abrahamowicz (ed.), *Kara Mustafa pod Wiedniem. Źródła muzułmańskie do dziejów wyprawy wiedeńskiej 1683 roku*, p.184.

21 October Imperial, Bavarian and Brandenburg troops crossed the river and laid siege to the city, building positions for artillery, setting up mines and capturing the outer fortifications. They were also supported by Polish artillery under Kątski, shooting at Esztergom from the other bank of the Danube. Surrounded, under constant fire from allied artillery, without a chance for relief, after some speedy negotiations Deli Bekir Pasha decided to surrender. He received Sobieski's promise that the whole garrison would be allowed to leave freely for Buda. On 28 October the surviving Turkish soldiers (around 4,000 men) were escorted by Imperial cuirassiers to Buda, while the entire civilian population was sent by ship to Pest.[178] Esztergom was then occupied by an Imperial garrison. The Turkish commander and four of his high-ranking officers became victims of Kara Mustafa's wrath for losing such an important fortress. They were strangled on their arrival in Buda and their heads were then sent to Belgrade.[179]

Apart from the Polish artillery, Sobieski's troops did not take a direct role in the siege of Esztergom as they remained on the left bank of Danube. Here they were to protect the allied army against possible *kuruc* attacks but at the same time the Poles were able to rest. The King had to pacify the atmosphere in his camp, as more and more of his officers were advocating an end the campaign and a quick return to Poland. *Rotmistrz* Krasiński went so far that he even announced, 'I will take my banner [of hussars] and return to Poland; [because] as you can see they build here a bridge through the Danube, to lead us to Buda and there doom us all'.[180] The Polish army was still suffering due to the plague, 'we bury many companions, [infantry] soldiers, servants'.[181] The soldiers were tired and, after the success at Vienna and Párkány, more than eager to return to their country. Sobieski was annoyed with their sentiments, as he was hoping to continue the campaign to ensure an important victory over Ottomans and keep the Polish army in winter quarters in Hungary. He bitterly complained in a letter to the Queen '[the army] would prefer to [return to] Poland, to black hearths and poor beer, they [stay] here in palaces and [drinking] best Tokay wine'.[182] On 18 October two Polish soldiers, captured by Turks and brought to Buda, mentioned during questioning, that while Sobieski wanted to march towards Buda, his own officers were against it, pointing out that there would not

Medal celebrating the victory at Vienna in 1683. Made by Jan Höhn in 1683. (National Museum, Cracow)

---

178 Silahdar Mehmed Aga z Fyndykły, 'Diariusz wyprawy wiedeńskiej i kronika związanych z nią wydarzeń w państwie osmańskim od 21 stycznia 1681 do 28 lutego 1684 r'. Zygmunt Abrahamowicz (ed.), *Kara Mustafa pod Wiedniem. Źródła muzułmańskie do dziejów wyprawy wiedeńskiej 1683 roku,* p.193.
179 *Ibidem*, p.193.
180 Antoni Zygmunt Helcel (ed.), *Listy Jana Sobieskiego do żony Marii Kazimiery*, p.408, Jan III do Marii Kazimiery, Nad Dunajem, przeciwko Strygodniu, 15 Octobra.
181 *Ibidem*, p.407.
182 *ibidem*, p.408.

be enough supplies there, so 'our horses will lose their strength and men will die'. Suffering due to sickness and lack of food, the Poles were complaining bitterly that they wanted to return home.[183]

After capturing Esztergom the allies had to decide the next course of action. The campaign season was slowly coming to close, with the armies having perhaps one more month of operations before being forced to find suitable winter quarters. On 20 October the Emperor's Court Council sent orders to Lorraine. The joint armies were to attempt to capture some of the remaining Turkish strongholds: Nové Zámky, Esztergom, Buda and Peszt. After that Lorraine was to march with the Imperial troops into Upper Hungary, to pacify the *kuruc* power base there and to capture Košice, Prešov, Levoča and Tokaj, which would be used for winter quarters. The Polish army was at the same time to move to the border with Transylvania, to capture Szolnok, Debrecen and Oradea.[184] Such plans seemed very ambitious, and did not take into consideration fatigue and losses amongst the allied armies. Lorraine and Sobieski agreed to continue the offensive. They understood that without an Ottoman field army to oppose them, it ought to be easier to progress with any siege operations. The Polish monarch really wanted to keep his army in winter quarters in Hungary. It was very pragmatic approach, as it would save native Polish lands from the massive burden of quartering troops, with instead the whole cost of it being born by recaptured *kuruc* Hungarian and Upper Hungarian territories. Keeping the army abroad would also provide a base for a new campaign in 1684, once the army was be reinforced by new troops and given their pay from taxes raised in Poland. Sobieski also hoped that he could act as the go-between in Imperial-*kuruc* negotiations, which could lead to a ceasefire and safer stay for Polish troops in Hungary. Of course Imperial officials had an opposite view where the *kuruc* were concerned, viewing them as rebels and demanding they surrender without giving many concessions in return. As was often the case, politics and the military clashed again, which quickly led to further disagreements between the allies. Bavarian Elector Maximilian II Emanuel arrived at Esztergom on 26 October and only three days later his army started to march home, leaving a small contingent of 1,000 infantry with the Imperial army. The Swabian contingent under Friedrich Baden-Durlach also left the allied camp and started its way home as soon as it reached Esztergom.[185] Given that now only Imperial and Polish troops were available, it was decided that the armies would be moved into winter quarters. Here Sobieski had a huge disagreement with his allies, as he was against stationing his soldiers on the Transylvanian border. He insisted on locations in Upper Hungary, to the east of Košice, where he was hoping to finally connect with the slow moving Lithuanian army. The Imperialists had to bow to this pressure and gave those areas to the Poles. On 31 October the

---

183 Silahdar Mehmed Aga z Fyndykły, 'Diariusz wyprawy wiedeńskiej i kronika związanych z nią wydarzeń w państwie osmańskim od 21 stycznia 1681 do 28 lutego 1684 r', Zygmunt Abrahamowicz (ed.), *Kara Mustafa pod Wiedniem. Źródła muzułmańskie do dziejów wyprawy wiedeńskiej 1683 roku, pp. 188-189.*

184 Franciszek Kluczycki (ed.), *Akta do dziejów Króla Jana IIIgo*, p.490. Summarium rescripti ex Consilio bellico Imperiali...

185 *Das Kriegsjahr 1683*, p.305.

Polish army started on its slow march, accompanied by the Imperial corps of Johann Heinrich Graf von Dünewald, whose troops had been allotted winter quarters to the west of Košice. Additionally von Truchsess' Brandenburgers were attached to the Polish troops. On 3 November Sobieski said farewell to Lorraine, and after dinner the King presented the Imperial commander with a gift of two horses.[186] The army was marching along the left bank of river Ipel, but it was marching at a very slow pace. As the autumn weather was getting worse, constant rain quickly changing into snow, the baggage train was repeatedly getting stuck on the muddy roads and many horses were dying due to the harsh conditions. The local population was not greeting the Poles with open arms either, which added to the soldiers' misery. Jan Chryzostom Pasek, based on stories of his step-son Stanisław, described this march as follows: 'There, where [the Poles] moved between the mountains, they were attacked from between mountains and forests by *kuruc*, who were really against us, capturing and killing servants, attacking and pillaging wagons, then running away towards the mountains, knowing those places very well. Then the autumn rains started, many of [our] horses died, so men had to abandon many wagons with the spoils of war from Vienna, with many soldiers preferring to burn them rather than leave them for Hungarian rebels'. [187] On 9 November the Poles arrived at Turkish-held Szécsény. While many commanders were opposed to attacking the city, Sobieski insisted on mounting an assault. It is possible that his decision was connected to the arrival of reinforcements that joined the Polish army on 5 November. Mikołaj Daniłowicz brought with him two banners of hussars, a few banners of *pancerni,* one regiment of infantry and a few hundred Cossacks. The King was especially eager to use the latter in combat, finally having them under his command. On 10 November, the allies were getting ready to assault the town, after the Royal Prince Jakub, with a few officers and engineers, after a reconnaissance of the defences, assured the King that an attack would be possible. While Imperial and Brandenburg soldiers started to prepare siege works, the Turks started to burn the outskirts of the town to hinder an attack. Sobieski sent out the newly-arrived Cossacks to try to stop the fires, knowing that the buildings would be useful as quarters for his own troops. In fact the Cossacks were more successful than this, quickly reaching the first palisade, as well as capturing one of the gates. They were then supported by Polish infantry and dragoons, who started to fill in the ditch with fascines. Under increasing fire from Imperial and Polish cannons, and facing overwhelming numbers, the Ottoman defenders decided to surrender. The town was plundered by the Cossacks, after which the Imperialists left three companies of their infantry and one company of ex-*kuruc* (who had changed sides) as a new garrison. The allies lost several dozen killed and wounded, especially amongst the Cossacks.[188] Capturing Szécsény was seen as an important move,

---

186 Jakub Ludwik Sobieski, *Dyaryusz wyprawy wiedeńskliej w 1683 r.*, p.21.
187 Jan Chryzostom Pasek, *Pamiętniki*, pp.388–389.
188 *Das Kriegsjahr 1683*, pp.309–310, Antoni Zygmunt Helcel (ed.), *Listy Jana Sobieskiego do żony Marii Kazimiery,* pp.420–421, Jan III do Marii Kazimiery, W dzień Śgo Marcina, pod Szecinem, Marcin Kątski, 'Diarium Artilieriae Praefecti', Franciszek Kluczycki (ed.), *Akta do dziejów*

Imre Thököly, leader of the *kuruc*. Unknown painter (Wikimedia Commons)

as it led to the isolation of Nové Zámky and gave the allies a new defensive outpost. It also allowed the Polish army some much needed rest and time to gather supplies for the next stage in their march. Finally on 14 November the joint forces left Szécsény and continued with their march towards Upper Hungary.

It was also, finally, an opportunity to link up with the Lithuanian army. The next chapter will focus on the campaign of these troops in more detail, but it is worth noting that on 7 November the Lithuanian Grand Hetman Kazimierz Jan Sapieha met the Duke of Lorraine in Levoča. The Imperial commander wanted to keep the Lithuanians with him, to support his actions against the *kuruc* but Sobieski insisted that Sapieha's troops were to join the Polish army. On 15 November Hetman Sapieha and Hetman Ogiński finally met with the King near Fiľakovo. Their army was still not in a hurry, only meeting the Poles near Rimavská Sobota on 19 November. Here the Lithuanians managed to anger and embarrass King Jan III one more time, when three days later he was supposed to witness the mustering of Sapieha's forces, accompanied by Imperial and loyal Hungarian officers. Vice-Chancellor Krzysztof Jan Gniński, in his letter to the Queen dated 22 November, complained that the Poles waited for six hours in falling snow, 'without any roof and tent' for the arrival of the Lithuanians, who never appeared. The official excuse for Sapieha's men was that they did not know about the planned muster, so they had sent out their retainers and servants to get provisions, and as such, if the Lithuanian army was to show up 'even all companions, without retainers they will look as small number, so such sight cannot be presented to Hungarian and German eyes'.[189]

End of the campaign and the return to Poland.

From 20 November the joint Polish and Lithuanian armies, with the Imperial corps, were marching together to what is today Eastern Slovakia. Despite Sobieski's attempt to mediate between Imre Thököly and Leopold I, the former decided to remain an Ottoman ally. In his letter to the Queen dated 21 November, the King wrote that the leader of *kuruc* 'is leading himself

Króla Jana IIIgo sprawy roku 1683, a osobliwie wyprawy wiedeńskiej wyjaśniające, pp.613–615.

189 Franciszek Kluczycki (ed.), *Akta do dziejów Króla Jana IIIgo*, p.440. Vice Cancellarius Gniński nova quaedam ed exerticu Lithuano nuntiat, et de partium gallicarum machinationibus praemonet.

towards doom (…) moving to Turkish Land' and leaving garrisons in places that were promised Poles as winter quarters.[190] Each town seems to be manned by *kuruc* who were not willing to surrender to the allied troops. Košice was in fact so strongly defended that Sobieski decided to not attack it and carried on marching. From here von Dünewald's corps parted ways with the Poles and Lithuanians, marching to Levoča, which the Imperial troops captured on 11 December.[191] In the meantime Sobieski's army was facing growing resistance from the local population and *kuruc*, leading to the King's bitter complaints that 'from behind every bush they are shooting at us, from each town peasants, nobles and soldiers shouting *kill, kill* like they would be hunting the wolf. They mercilessly murder our sick [in which they are] far worse than Turks, so we had to be on our guard day and night, and march slowly, to not lose men'.[192] On 5 December the army arrived at Prešov but its defenders were very active, making sorties against the invaders and through day and night maintained a steady fire from their cannons. Amongst those killed in the Polish camp was Krzysztof Modrzewski, veteran

Jan III Sobieski in *karacena* armour, lynx pelt and shield, based on a painting representing him as Grand Hetman in the battle of Chocim in 1673. Next to the King is a 'pejk' servant in a Turkish outfit, carrying the monarch's helmet. Painter unknown, after 1683. (National Museum, Cracow)

rotmistrz of a *pancerni* banner, which saddened the King. Sobieski forbade his men to return fire, as he did not want to start new siege operations so late in the year. A small consolation was the success of Polish cavalry and Tatars that managed to defeat a group of *kuruc*, taking some prisoners.[193] As the area was lacking food, on 7 December the army left towards Sabinov. Atanazy Miączyński, led the vanguard, and was able to surprise and defeat *kuruc* cavalry and infantry that tried to intervene and help them. The Polish troops then blockaded the town and the next day Lithuanian artillery that had recently joined the army, opened fire on Sabinov. The garrison quickly surrendered and took service with the Imperialists. Luckily for Sobieski's force, this area had plenty of supplies to offer, so he decided to leave a strong garrison of 800 men under General Altmark. The King was upset as some of his own

190 Antoni Zygmunt Helcel (ed.), *Listy Jana Sobieskiego do żony Marii Kazimiery*, p.423, Jan III do Marii Kazimiery, W obozie pod Chaciem, mile od Ryma Sombat ku Koszycom, 21 Novembris w nocy.
191 *Das Kriegsjahr 1683*, p.312.
192 Antoni Zygmunt Helcel (ed.), *Listy Jana Sobieskiego do żony Marii Kazimiery*, p.425, Jan III do Marii Kazimiery, W dzień św. Mikołaja, pod Preszowem.
193 *Ibidem*, p.425,

soldiers, eager to return to Poland, were 'burning not only grain, villages and towns but even Catholic churches, just so they do not [have to] stay'. Facing growing opposition from the army – especially commanders and companions from the cavalry – Sobieski changed the plans for settling in winter quarters. Only part of the army was to stay in Upper Hungary, mostly drawn from amongst the Lithuanians, some Polish infantry and dragoons, supported by the Brandenburg contingent. The remaining Polish troops were to march to winter quarters chosen by Hetman Jabłonowski. The King and Royal Prince Jakub left the army on 12 December and arrived at Lubowla. Here they said their farewell to dying Field Hetman Sieniawski, who was one of the many sick Polish soldiers transported there ahead of the marching army. Sobieski left Lubowla on 14 December, and Sieniawski died one day later. The King and his son met the Queen in Stary Sącz, after which they all travelled to Cracow, where they arrived on 23 December. In the meantime Jabłonowski led a general 'gathering'[194] of the officers and companions of the Polish cavalry, after which the units marched to their designated winter quarters. The campaign of 1683 was over.

Human cost

It is very hard to estimate the total losses of the Polish army taking part in the relief of Vienna. Jan Wimmer, comparing differences in 'paper strength' of units between 1 August and 1 November 1683, found that the army size decreased by 1,825 horses and portions, with units of the infantry and dragoons especially affected. Some of the cavalry banners did not decrease but even strengthened their numbers. This can be easily explained by the arrival of delayed companions and their retinues or even adding new companions from amongst the volunteers. In total, including those that died of wounds and sickness, Wimmer estimated Polish losses as at least 3,000 dead from all formations and at least 1,000 dead volunteers and camp servants.[195] Losses amongst the latter were probably even higher, as many of them were killed by *kuruc* and died due to sickness, but the exact number will never be known. Lithuanian losses were much lower and mostly occurred due to sickness, so the estimate of losses is no more than few hundred dead. A complete unknown is the total number of deserters, especially as many who at any point in the campaign left their cavalry banners, re-joined their units once the army was back in Poland and Lithuania.

'Hidden' losses, caused by sickness and exhaustion that led to further deaths months after troops returned home should not be forgotten. Jan Tomasz Józefowicz, in his chronicle of the city of Lwów, left a dire picture of the homecoming of the troops. 'Our soldiers were returning (…), some of them laden with loot, [but] many more weakened and tormented with

---

194 As in his earlier book, the author decided to use term gathering, instead of direct translation of Polish word *koło* (circle, as in 'gathering with a circle of equels').

195 Jan Wimmer, *Wiedeń 1683*, p.399.

hunger, cold and the miseries of war, with many lost due to sickness and some killed by the enemies'.[196] As previously mentioned, both Crown Field Hetman Sieniawski and Lithuanian Field Hetman Ogiński died due to sickness at the end of the campaign. There were many more, both officers and soldiers, who followed suit. Lithuanian diarist Jan Władysław Poczobut Odlanicki wrote that his nephew, Michał Kaczanowski, serving in 1683 as a companion in the *petyhorcy* banner of Leon Sapieha, died on 5 February 1684, due to 'heavy illness, after returning from the Hungarian war'.[197] In fact these non-combat losses were so severe that they affected the ability of the Polish army to deploy in the field in 1684. Due to the delays required by the need to rest, rebuild and re-equip the units, Sobieski could not start new military operations until July 1684. 'Many men and horses died from sickness caused by water from the Danube, so we needed time to fill in the ranks. And still the army was weaker than usual'.[198] The returning army not only took losses but also many companions left their units and returned to their homes to rest and recover after such a difficult campaign. Krzysztof Grzymułtowski, voivode of Poznań, did not travel with Sobieski's army to Vienna, as he was leading the Commonwealth's embassy to Moscow. At the beginning of January 1684, he wrote that in letters sent to him by Jan Gniński, Crown Vice-Chancellor, Polish and Lithuanian envoys in Moscow were informed about the very poor shape of the returning army. 'In some banners [of cavalry] there are barely left three horses, not even three companions'.[199] There is also the often ignored financial aspect of the war. When writing about the preparations of the army, it was noted that many companions put themselves into debt, to equip their retinues for the campaign. While some of them were able to recover their financial losses thanks to captured loot, many more were left much out of pocket. Even high-ranking officers could be practically ruined by the campaign. Rafał Leszczyński, Crown Standard-Bearer, was serving as colonel of a cavalry regiment and *rotmistrz* of his own hussar banner. He returned 'without any loot, losing all his horses, with barely any men left under his company [and] losing [almost] all his servants, coming home only with four men [of his retinue and servants]'.[200] As a wealthy man, Leszczyński had to take with him a large retinue of household servants, including some minor nobles, where all their equipment, weapons, horses and tabor wagons were paid for out of his own pocket. For the Polish and Lithuanian magnates, with their constant cash flow problems, an expedition such as this one and the losses incurred led to a major headache for many trying to manage their finances.

---

196 Jan Tomasz Józefowicz, *Kronika miasta Lwowa od roku 1634 do 1690* (Lwów: Zakład Narodowy im. Ossolińskich, 1854), p.420.
197 *Pamiętnik Jana Władysława Poczobuta Odlanickiego* (Warszawa: Drukarnia Michała Ziemkiewicza, 1877) p.164.
198 Dupont, p.244.
199 *Zrzódła do dziejów polskich*, volume II, p.355.
200 *Ibidem*, p.355.

8

The Lithuanian army in 1683

In Chapter 4, when describing plan of increasing the Commonwealth's armies, it was mentioned that the planned 'updated' Lithuanian army was to have 12,000 horses and portions, divided as follow:

1,000 hussars
3,000 *petyhorcy*
1,500 light horse (cossacks and Tatars)
4,400 foreign infantry
1,500 dragoons
600 Hungarian infantry

The final structure of the army shows that it was somewhat different than what was planned, and was mostly based on the units that were already in service prior to 1683. The organisation of the Lithuanian force, based on a list dated on 23 March 1684[1] completed when in winter quarters, and documents presented at the *Sejm* by Grand Lithuanian Treasurer Benedykt Paweł Sapieha,[2] is as follows:

Hussars: six banners with a total of 860 horses

Rotmistrz	Strength	Notes
King Jan III Sobieski	150	Lieutenant Krzysztof Białłozor
Grand Hetman Kazimierz Jan Sapieha	200	Lieutenant Samuel Kmicic
Field Hetman Jan Jacek Ogiński	150	
Marcjan Ogiński	120	Lieutenant Leonard Gabriel Pociej
Benedykt Sapieha	120	Lieutenant Kazimierz Stanisław Dąbrowski
Jan Karol Dolski	120	Lieutenant Kazimierz Michał Pusłowski

---

1   Jan Władysław Poczobut Odlanicki, *Pamiętnik (1640–1684)*, edited by Andrzej Rachuba (Warszawa: Czytelnik, 1987), pp.349–353.
2   Konrad Bobiatyński, 'Skład I liczebność armii litewskiej podczas wojny z Turcją w latach 1683–1686', *Zapiski Historyczne*, volume LXXXVI, 2021, Issue 1 (Toruń: Towarzystwo Naukowe w Toruniu, 2021), pp.30–52.

Petyhorcy: 25 banners with a total of 3,110 horses

Rotmistrz	Strength	Notes
King Jan III Sobieski	120	Lieutenant Jan Kazimierz Wołłowicz
Grand Hetman Kazimierz Jan Sapieha	200	Lieutenant Aleksander Jan Mosiewicz
Field Hetman Jan Jacek Ogiński	150	
Marcjan Ogiński	120	
Michał Dowmont Siesicki	120	
Dominik Radziwiłł	120	Lieutenant Michał Karol Haraburda
Stanisław Kazimierz Radziwiłł	120	
Benedykt Paweł Sapieha	120	Lieutenant Konstanty Michał Paszkowski
Józef Bogusław Słuszka	120	Lieutenant Krustian Felicjan Staszkiewicz
Leon Bazyli Sapieha	120	
Jan Karol Dolski	120	Lieutenant Tomasz Zawisza
Franciszek Stefan Sapieha	120	
Jerzy Karol Chodkiewicz	120	Lieutenant Samuel Narkuski
Andrzej Kazimierz Kryszpin Kirsztensztein	120	
Krzysztof Konstanty Połubiński	120	Lieutenant Florian Leon Kotowski
Kazimierz Władysław Sapieha	120	
Władysław Józefat Sapieha	120	
Dominik Michał Słuszka	120	
Władysław Tyszkiewicz	120	Lieutenant Samuel Jurewicz
Hrehory Ogiński	120	
Jan Krzysztof Pac	120	
Krzysztof Wiktoryn Vorbek Lettow	120	
Hieronim Lacki	120	Lieutenant Stanisław Michał Kozubski
Michał Kazimierz Kociełł	120	
Jan Lipnicki	120	

Hetman Sapieha's banner of reiters under *rotmistrz* Gerard Reinken – 100 horses.
Stefan Czerniawski's banner of cossack cavalry under Lieutenant Jan Kazimierz Korsak – 120 horses.

Tatar light horse: eight banners with a total of 990 horses

Rotmistrz	Strength	Notes
Grand Hetman Sapieha	150	*Rotmistrz* Mikołaj Baranowski
Grand Hetman Sapieha second banner	120	*Rotmistrz* Szczucki
Field Hetman Ogiński	120	*Rotmistrz* Dawid Baranowski
Stanisław Kazimierz Radziwiłł	120	
Benedykt Paweł Sapieha	120	*Rotmistrz* Jerzy Konarzewski
Jan Karol Dolski	120	
Krzysztof Vorbek Lettow	120	
Krzysztof Białłozor	120	

Dragoons: 15 squadrons/companies/banners with a total of 1,750 horses

Rotmistrz	Strength	Notes
Grand Hetman Sapieha	250	Colonel Olszt
Field Hetman Ogiński	150	Colonel Eberhard Fryderyk von Alten Bockum
Marcjan Ogiński	100	
Benedykt Paweł Sapieha	100	
Dominik Radziwiłł	100	Major Jan Bitner
Józef Bogusław Słuszka	100	
Andrzej Kazimierz Kryszpin Kirsztensztein	100	
Leon Bazyli Sapieha	150	
Jan Karol Dolski	100	
Krzysztof Białłozor	100	
Jerzy Karol Chodkiewicz	100	
Samuel Kmicic	100	
Kazimierz Michał Pac	100	
Krzysztof Wiktoryn Vorbek Lettow	100	
Maciej Korwin Gosiewski	100	

Foreign infantry: 15 units with a total of 4,220 portions.

Nominal commander	Strength	Notes
Grand Hetman Sapieha's regiment	800	Six companies/banners, under Captain Jerzy Greben
General-Major Mateusz von Remer	200	Attached to Hetman Sapieha's regiment
Marcjan Ogiński's regiment	500	
Field Hetman Ogiński	500	
Stanisław Kazimierz Radziwiłł	200	
Dominik Radziwiłł	300	
Benedykt Paweł Sapieha	200	
Jan Karol Dolski	400	
Jerzy Józef Radziwiłł	400	
Franciszek Stefan Sapieha	200	
Piotr Rudomino Dusiacki	60	
Jan Andrzej Plater	60	
Krzysztof Konstanty Połubiński	100	
Dominik Michał Słuszka	100	
Maciej Korwin Gosiewski	200	

Hungarian infantry: six units with a total of 700 portions.

Rotmistrz	Strength	Notes
Grand Hetman Sapieha's Hungarian infantry	200	
Grand Hetman Sapieha's janissaries banner	100	
Marcjan Ogiński's Hungaran infantry	100	
Field Hetman Ogiński's Hungarian infantry	100	
Stanisław Kazimierz Radziwiłł's Hungarian infantry	100	
Józef Bogusław Słuszka's Hungarian infantry	100	

Zaporozhian Cossack infantry of Krzysztof Konstanty Połubiński – 100 portions.

The muster list from March 1684 gives the size of the army as 78 units with 10,130 horses and portions but treasury documents give a slightly larger number of 11,950 horses and portions, with same number of units, so very close to the 12,000 agreed in the *Sejm* as the Lithuanian military contribution. There were in fact two separate plans of organisation for the army. One was suggested by Grand Hetman Sapieha, and one was suggested by King Jan III himself. The latter wanted to increase his influence in the army, trying to create new units under his name and establish a Royal regiment in the Lithuanian army. This led to a clash with the newly-nominated Hetman Sapieha, who set himself in political opposition to the King. Sadly it was a pattern found in Polish-Lithuanian relations throughout a large part of the seventeenth century, where the Lithuanian Grand Hetman tended to be engaged in large or small disputes with the Polish royalty. Michał Kazimierz Pac, who held the office of Grand Hetman between 1667 and 1682 was a strong opponent of Jan III, clashing with him on many occasions and having political relationships, of an anti-royal nature, with Muscovy, Brandenburg and the Holy Roman Empire. As per unwritten tradition, the King supported the Field Hetman – in this case Kazimierz Jan Sapieha – as a political ally and to counterbalance the Grand Hetman. Pac died in April 1682 and so Sapieha replaced him as Grand Hetman in February 1683. At the same time Jan Jacek Ogiński became the new Field Hetman. Whatever hopes that Sobieski could have had about good and close cooperation with Sapieha, they very quickly faded in the face of Lithuanian *realpolitik*. The wealthy family of Sapieha now became the new powerhouse in Lithuania, with its strong influence ending only at the start of Great Northern War. Kazimierz Jan Sapieha established close contacts with France, placing himself as an opponent to the political plans of Sobieski. Seeing the defeat of the French party in Poland during the *Sejm* in early 1683, Sapieha went along with a pro-Austrian course of action, although, as will be seen, in practice he did what he could to obstruct and delay Lithuanian involvement in the war. What is most interesting, is that at the end of the campaign of 1683, he wrote and presented at the *Sejm* a diary of the Lithuanian operations, trying to use it as a propaganda tool and to highlight the involvement of his troops. While comparing this source with

Winged hussar from Jakub
Kazimierz Haur's *Skład albo
skarbiec znakomity sekretów
o ekonomiej ziemianskiej*,
published in Cracow in 1693
(National Library, Warsaw)

other documents from the period, it is possible to compare how close, or not, the Hetman's depiction of the events was to reality.[3]

The initial plan assumed that the Lithuanian army led by both the Grand Hetman and Field Hetman would concentrate in Janów Podlaski, from where it would proceed through Małopolska to join the Polish army marching towards Vienna. The troops were gathering very slowly, however. Unpaid soldiers from the regular army were not eager to march to a new war, and an inefficient tax system led to massive delays in delivering money to the army. Magnates, led by Sapieha, put large amounts of their own money into supplementing existing units and creating new ones, with further money provided by Jan III and by Nuncio Pallavicini from Papal subsidies. There was also bickering over attempts to increase Royal influence in the army. What is worse, the existing Lithuanian army was dispersed from the borders with Sweden to Muscovy, and it took a very long time to gather the troops together.[4] On 22 August both Sapieha and Ogiński arrived in the army's camp, but they found only two banners of Tatar light horse and two companies of infantry waiting for them.[5] New units were arriving daily however, and after two weeks all the troops started their march towards Cracow. The cavalry moved first, with the more slowly mustering infantry and artillery to follow. The Lithuanians marched without haste towards Cracow, clearly not eager to be part of the relief of Vienna. What is worse, they were a huge burden on the local Polish population, behaving 'like Tatar raiders'. Of course, according to Sapieha the speed of the march was just fine, and his troops were travelling with good discipline and without any problems. The King was very concerned about the lack of information on the whereabouts of the Lithuanian army and its progress, especially when facing questions from his Imperial allies, who were looking forward to seeing the joint Polish and Lithuanian armies at Vienna. By the end of August Sobieski realised that Lithuanian forces would not arrive in time, so there were at least some hopes that they would march towards Turkish-held Hungary and 'make some diversion against the enemy'.[6] Therefore new orders were dispatched to Sapieha, who with the main Lithuanian army was to invade Upper Hungary (today Slovakia). On 17 September Sobieski wrote to Sapieha redirecting his army to the new theatre of war. The presence of a strong Lithuanian corps there would hopefully force Imre Thököly to abandon the Ottomans and change the overall dynamics of the campaign. His Imperial allies were hoping for the Lithuanians to march into Transylvania and attack Michael I Apafi's lands. Sobieski strongly opposed such an action, as he judged, correctly, that the Lithuanians would be isolated there and could be easily defeated or

3   'Djarjusz kampanji węgierskiej in Anno 1683', pp.259–271.
4   Konrad Bobiatyński, 'Udział Wielkiego Księstwa Litewskiego w kampanii wiedeńskiej 1683 roku', Teresa Chynczewska-Hennel (ed.), *Odsiecz wiedeńska* (Warszawa: Muzeum Pałacu Króla Jana III w Wilanowie 2011), pp.63–64.
5   'Djarjusz kampanji węgierskiej in Anno 1683', p.262.
6   Antoni Zygmunt Helcel (ed.), *Listy Jana Sobieskiego do żony Marii Kazimiery*, p.375, Jan III do Marii Kazimiery, Mila za Bruną, we wsi Modric 29. przed północą.

even destroyed.[7] Sobieski managed to convince the Imperialists to accept his plans, so after marching through Upper Hungary Sapieha's army was to meet the main allied forces. The Hetman received the new orders on 28 September, so it took a courier 11 days to travel between the Polish and Lithuanian armies. Despite the slow tempo of the march, not all units were present with main army. The diary of Aleksander Dionizy Skorobohaty shows how slowly some of the Lithuanian units were preparing to take part in the campaign. He was an experienced soldier, serving in the Lithuanian army since 1655, initially in the Cossack cavalry, then as *pancerny*, finally as a hussar. In 1683 he was a companion in the former banner of Grand Hetman Pac, that was taken over by Jan III as his own Royal banner. Skorobohaty arrived in camp at Onikszty (Anykščiai) on 28 August, but his banner did not leave until 9 September and only on 20 of September did it cross the Neman (Niemien) river near Kaunas. Then the Royal hussars marched slowly through Polish Podlasie and only arrived in Cracow on 31 October. Not surprising then that due to such a delay the banner was then ordered to march to Podolia, to join Andrzej Potocki's force

Lithuanian commander Józef Bogusław Słuszka. He took part in the 1683 campaign in Upper Hungary. Between 1685 and 1701 he was the Lithuanian Field Hetman. Henri Bonnar, 1695 (Author's archive)

there fighting the Turks and Tatars, as by now there was no point sending it to Upper Hungary or Austria. The hussars again took their time during this march, so they only joined the Polish-Lithuanian-Cossack army on 26 November, just in time to take part in the battle at Zienkowo.[8]

Meanwhile, Sapieha's troops were moving slowly towards the border, on their way pillaging lands belonging to Andrzej Potocki, in yet another spiteful act of internal politics between Commonwealth magnates. At the beginning of October the Lithuanian army finally left Poland and entered Upper Hungary which today is Slovakian Orava. After a short battle their vanguard, led by Franciszek Sapieha, defeated a *kuruc* force besieging Imperial-held Orava Castle and forced them to retreat, capturing a few cannons and one mortar. In his diary the Hetman clearly exaggerated the scale of the victory, claiming that 'a few thousand rebels were killed and many captured', while his own troops were to lose only two killed Tatars and a few wounded.[9] After that the Lithuanian troops spread out through Orava, pillaging and looting without mercy. Additionally, a smaller group of cavalry, under Krzysztof Konstanty Połubiński, was detached from the main army and marched to Spiš, to defend it from potential attack by *kurucs*. These soldiers also mercilessly ravaged the territories that they moved through. It seems possible that the

7   *Ibidem*, p.394, Nad Dunajem przeciw samemu Preszburkowi.
8   Aleksander D. Skorobohaty, *Diariusz* (Warszawa: Wydawnictwo DiG, 2004), pp.135–139.
9   'Djarjusz kampanji węgierskiej in Anno 1683', p.263.

Lithuanian High Command allowed or even encouraged their soldiers to do so, to counter Sobieski's negotiations with Emeric Thököly's envoys. In Orava at least 27 villages were burned, and many people were killed. An anonymous Lithuanian companion tried to explain the actions of his army in this gruesome letter: [10]

> Initially the Lithuanian army, on entering Hungary, was full of mercy towards all [local] people, especially with Lutherans, not harming them, not killing or burning. But them [*kuruc*] on the other hand captured few companions from our army, and with all cruelty tortured them, sticking heated skewer through their heads from ear to ear; cutting off noses, lips and mouths; ripping off their private parts with heated pincers, breaking out teeth, gouging out their eyes and after that burning eye holes with fire, filling with tar; hammering pins under their nails, slowly cutting off their fingers; the others [they] cut into pieces, putting their heads on pikes and hanging body parts on gallows.
>
> Seeing that, Lithuanian soldiers changed their mercy into anger, and while before they treated Lutherans as good Christians should, now they were like tyrants, burning villages, taking everything and killing all Lutherans. Other day we had some luck and captured some Lutheran priest, so we skinned him alive, placed some chaff on [his body] and covering him again with skin sent him away to [his] Lutherans, ordering him that, as their shepherd and spirit guide, he need to warn them that as they were laughing [earlier] in such manner at our captured [soldiers], despite [Lithuanians] giving them no reason for it, as causing no harm or cruelty, now we will repay them with the same cruelty. Surely that will scare those Lutherans'.

Sobieski received very delayed reports about the movements and actions of the Lithuanians, as letters had to travel via Poland, a very indirect route. At the same time his orders sent to Sapieha and Ogiński took a long time to reach them. On 7 October, in his letter to both Lithuanian commanders, he described the current military situation in the main theatre of war, advising them that he would soon start to negotiate with Thököly. As such he warned the Lithuanians to 'be cautious: [often] send reconnaissance forces, keep guard and camp [only] in strong[ly defended] and safe places, keep [the army] together and well disciplined, so this nation [in Upper Hungary] is not antagonised and not forced to ultimate desperation'.[11] He could not know that while he was despatching those orders, the Lithuanians were already destroying everything in their path. It led to an end to negotiations with Thököly, as most villages burned in Upper Hungary belonged to him. Sobieski tried to calm down the Hungarian nobleman, explaining that those atrocities were committed without his knowledge and against his orders. Angry, Sobieski wrote to Sapieha and Ogiński, ordering them to stop attacking the local population and to march towards him with all haste. After receiving his letters they continued their very slow journey but, against the King's orders, did not march towards Nové Zámky or toward the

---

10   Władysław Semkowicz, *Udział wojsk litewskich*, pp.10–13.
11   Franciszek Kluczycki (ed.), *Akta do dziejów Króla Jana IIIgo*, pp.449–450.

main *kuruc* force at Levice. Instead, their army marched towards the valley of the river Váh, but at least for the time being they stopped attacking the local population. On 23 October the local commander of the *kuruc*, Georg Illyeshazy, negotiated a temporary truce with Sapieha and his troops started to retreat, avoiding any further fighting with the Lithuanians. Unfortunately some local troops of Captain Franz Pongrácz, unaware of the truce, attacked the Lithuanian baggage train. Sapieha demanded compensation and the return of the captured goods, but the *kuruc* captain was unwilling to oblige him. It led to another outbreak of Tatar-like savagery from the Lithuanian troops, who 'with fire and sword' ravaged the Váh valley.[12] At the same time more and more Lithuanian soldiers deserted, leaving towards Poland or Moravia. By this time Sobieski understood that the Lithuanian campaign was a total failure and that their army was 'dragging itself on the back, away from both Turkish fortresses and the borders'.[13] Sapieha and Ogiński met with the King on 15 November, while their army joined Polish troops four days later. Further actions of the joint armies were described in an earlier chapter, with the disrespect shown by both Lithuanian Hetmen towards the King and the way that their army yet again had no impact on the final phase of the campaign. Sapieha complained that his troops lost many servants due to *kuruc* ambushes, while bad weather 'due to snow and rain costs us many horses'.[14] He also did not want to keep the army in their assigned winter quarters, as the territories were already strained due to previous marches through them by Imperial and Polish troops. When he moved to Spiš, the Lithuanian army had, due to a combination of difficult terrain and bad weather, to abandon a large part of their baggage train. Attacks by *kuruc* and the enraged local population were causing more losses, while sickness and fatigue were taking a further toll amongst men and horses. Sapieha records in his diary that in December many of his companions were forced to march on foot.[15] Soldiers were dying from frostbite, and more and more officers and companions were leaving the ranks and returning home. The Hetman assigned the standard-bearer of his hussar banner, Stanisław Popławski, as *regimentarz*[16] in charge of those Lithuanian units that were to stay on in winter quarters in Upper Hungary (Slovakia). In January Sapieha left the army and returned to Lithuania. Field Hetman Ogiński, in very poor health due to the exhausting campaign, travelled to Cracow, where he died on 24 February 1684.[17] Morale was low, and soldiers were looking forward to the disbandment of the army. For example, all the companions from the *petyhorcy* banner of Benedykt Paweł Sapieha, including his Lieutenant

---

12   Władysław Semkowicz, *Udział wojsk litewskich*, pp.15–16.
13   Antoni Zygmunt Helcel (ed.), *Listy Jana Sobieskiego do żony Marii Kazimiery*, p.421, W dzień Św. Marcina, pod Szecinem.
14   'Djarjusz kampanji węgierskiej in Anno 1683', p.266.
15   *Ibidem*, p.269.
16   The officer in charge of army or a part of it, when the Hetman was not present.
17   His office was vacated until 25 April 1685, when Józef Bogusław Słuszka was nominated as new Field Hetman.

Calendar depicting the allied triumph at Vienna. King Jan III on the white horse, Royal Prince Jakub can be seen on his left. Published in Paris in 1684 (National Museum, Warsaw)

Konstanty Michał Paszkowski wanted to leave the unit at the end of second quarter of their service.[18]

Not all the Lithuanian forces took part in the poorly executed campaign in Upper Hungary. Some of the delayed units, led by Jerzy Karol Chodkiewicz, joined those Polish troops left to defend the country under Andrzej Potocki. Under Potocki's command they took part in an action in Podolia against the Tatars. Among Chodkiewicz's banners was the strong royal banner of hussars, the former unit of the late Grand Hetman Pac, led by Lieutenant Krzysztof Białłozor. These operations will be described in the next chapter..

As has been seen in this chapter, the Lithuanian military effort in 1683 was woefully disappointing. Despite raising and preparing a strong army, they did not play any role in the allied military effort, with just some small-scale diversionary operations that took place in the less important theatre of war. What is more, Lithuanian atrocities in Upper Hungary had a negative effect on political negotiations between Sobieski and Thököly. Combat losses were small, but fatalities due to sickness and fatigue cost the Lithuanians at least a few hundred dead soldiers and hundreds of army servants. Losses in horses were much likely higher and could be counted in the thousands. Sapieha noted that many soldiers lost their equipment, armour and weapons, further affecting how quickly the army could be ready and available for a new campaign in 1684. Despite that, the Hetman was proud of how his army had fought 'for the nobility of His Royal Highness and whole Commonwealth, [for] Christianity'.[19]

---

18   Władysław Skrzydelka (ed.), *Listy z czasów Jana III i Augusta II*, p.49, Jan Kaczanowski do Benedykta Sapiehy, Kraków, 14 stycznia 1684 roku.
19   'Djarjusz kampanji węgierskiej in Anno 1683', p.270.

9

Secondary theatres of war: Podolia and Cossack raids against the Tatars

Podolia was to play a secondary role in 1683, as both sides – Poles and Ottomans – left their minimal forces in the region with the task of defending the larger and smaller fortresses.[1] As of the summer of 1683, between 2,500 and 3,000 soldiers, mostly janissaries and local troops (including ex-Polish Tatars), were garrisoning Kamianets-Podilskyi as the hub of the Ottoman possessions in the region. Other places were held by much smaller forces, so in total the commander of the regional defenders, Halil Pasha, had no more than 4,000 soldiers to call upon. The Poles did not have even that many, with four small infantry regiments based one each in four main locations (Biała Cerkiew, Trembowla, Stanisławów and Lwów), *wybraniecka* infantry and some weak private units defending their master's lands. In a dire situation they could be supplemented by arming the local population, who were hardened by near constant Tatar raids but could only be used defensively. The only force that could, if the situation required it, be used as a rapid strike force, was a group of a few cavalry banners from the regular army, left as a defensive force. This mix of *pancerni* and light horse was led by a veteran of the wars against the Ottomans and Tatars, Andrzej Sierakowski. There was hope that at some point his group would be strengthened by newly raised units sent from Cracow (from those that would be too late to follow the main army into Austria), some Cossacks and private units. For the time being the situation in Podolia was peaceful, with both sides neither having the means nor the will to try any aggressive moves.

This all changed once the Poles and Turks received the news of the battle of Vienna and the triumph of the allied forces. The territory held by Ottoman garrisons was a new addition to their empire, being a new Elayet, or administrative region, for barely 10 years. By the end of September more

---

1 Unless noted, the chapter is based mostly on Tadeusz Urbański, *Rok 1683 na Podolu, Ukrainie i w Mołdawii: szkic historyczny z czasów panowania Jana III Sobieskiego* (Lwów: Akademickie Kółko Historyczne we Lwowie, 1907), *passim*, Jan Wimmer, *Wiedeń 1683*, pp.401–415.

Andrzej Potocki, in 1683 in command of the troops left to defend Poland, from 1684 Grand Field Hetman. Painter unknown (Wikimedia Commons)

and more of the local population, supported by Cossacks and small groups of Polish cavalry, started a guerrilla war against the Turks, attacking smaller outposts and garrisons. Halil Pasha decided to evacuate as many of the weakly-held places as was provident, and gather most of his troops in Kamianets-Podilskyi. He also sent a request for help to the Nogay and Crimean Tatars. A supply convoy, escorted by a mix of Turkish and Tatar troops, was ambushed and defeated at the beginning of October by a Polish-Cossack force under Sierakowski.

Meanwhile, Andrzej Potocki was trying to gather the remaining Polish troops near Lwów. He received warnings from King Jan III that the Crimean Tatars may be returning from Austria and try a diversionary attack against Poland. The defence of the country was inadequate, with an odd mix of regular and private units (*pancerni* and light horse), some infantry units, Cossacks and the delayed Lithuanian units (mostly cavalry). Considering the still weak Ottoman presence in Podolia, Potocki decided to go onto the offensive. It is possible that he wanted to settle a personal score, as by then he already received information that his son Stanisław had died during the battle for Vienna. He led a group of cavalry and infantry, accompanied by Lithuanians under Chodkiewicz, to his own town of Stanisławów, where he reinforced this 'division' by adding some cannons from his privately-owned fortress. His troops were also accompanied by former Moldavian Voivode Ștefan Petriceicu, who had lost his throne in 1674 and since then had lived in exile in Poland. Changes in the political situation opened the door for the return of Petriceicu to Moldavia and to putting this pro-Polish candidate back on throne. Halil Pasha tried to pre-empt Polish actions and sent a strong force under Mustafa Aga, to move reinforcements to Jazłowiec, a small but well-fortified outpost. Mustafa Aga managed to avoid the Polish cavalry under Sierakowski, who was trying to stop the Turkish troops, left some infantry in Jazłowiec and safely returned to Kamianets-Podilskyi. Potocki marched with his soldiers from Stanisławów and besieged Jazłowiec, coming very close to capturing the castle. Unfortunately, while being on the verge of the success, the Poles had to lift the siege. Potocki received information that the main Tatar army was marching, via Upper Hungary, towards Poland, so defending the country became his top priority. All available troops, including the supporting Lithuanians and Cossacks, gathered in the fortified camp at Buczacz, near the river Strypa. This force could defend the country, especially the area around Lwów, from Tatars coming through the Carpathian Mountains. The local population was told to gather in fortified places and prepare to defend them. Potocki, as the de facto regent of the country, issued orders to gather a levy of the nobility. The country was braced for a Tatar attack, but it did not materialise. Khan Muray Giray was removed for his poor performance at the battle of Vienna and replaced with Haji II Giray. The new Khan decided to return to the Crimea via Moldavia, not through Poland, so for now the danger was over.

While Potocki was focusing on the main Tatar forces, there was change in the situation in Kamianets-Podilskyi. Halil Pasha finally received reinforcement from the Crimea, composed of troops that had not gone with the Khan to Austria. Newly-arrived Tatars, supported by the Turkish cavalry of Mustafa Aga and ex-Polish Lipka Tatars under Kryczyński, struck like lighting into Volhynia, destroying villages, capturing many of the local population and gathering supplies for the garrison of Kamianets-Podilskyi. Potocki reacted quickly, marching with all his available cavalry and mounted Cossacks towards Kamianets, hoping to surprise the returning raiders. His vanguard under Sierakowski was sent to find out the size of the enemy force and to capture some prisoners. On 28 November 1683, at Zinkowo (40km from Kamienets), the Polish-Lithuanian-Cossack force defeated the Turkish-Tatar group, recapturing up to 1,000 of their own countrymen held prisoner and all the stolen supplies. The defeated raiders were pursued by light cavalry and Cossacks, and many were also killed in ambushes by the vengeful population. Mustafa Aga survived and managed to return to Kamienets but most of his troops were killed or scattered. Potocki then managed to attack and capture another supply convoy marching to Kamienets, ending the autumn campaign on a high note. It was the end of the campaign season, and the tired soldiers needed some rest and time to replace horses and equipment lost during the fighting. Some units were disbanded due to the end of their service, while Sierakowski with some of the remaining cavalry and Cossacks were protecting the border with Moldavia and keeping an eye on Kamienets. A few banners accompanied Ștefan Petriceicu on his journey to Iași (Jassy), to regain for him the Moldavian throne. Potocki himself travelled to Stanisławów, where he was to spend the winter, waiting for the return of King Jan III and his army.

In 1683 Moldavia was ruled by Voivode George Duca, under Ottoman overlordship. This was his third time sitting on the Moldavian throne, having previously ruled there between September 1665 and May 1666 and November 1668 and August 1672. In November 1678 he replaced Antonie Ruset (Rosetti) and cooperated closely with the Ottomans, relying on their support in expanding the extent of the territory under his rule. He did, thanks to massive bribes, receive in 1681 control from them of the Right-Bank Ukraine, severely ravaged during earlier conflicts. In 1683 he took part in Kara Mustafa's campaign in Austria, leading a contingent of 4,000 men. During his absence, Moldavia was controlled by his wife, Anastasiya Dabizha, while Ukrainian affairs were under the command of governor Draghinici, who deployed some Moldavian garrisons in the region. In case of any trouble, Moldavian rulers could, at least in theory, count on allied Tatars from Budjak, ex-Polish Lipka Tatars that were settled by the Ottomans near the Dniester river and some Turkish garrisons, especially from Bender (Tighina) and Bilhorod. The main threat to Duca's rule was in the person of a former voivode, Ștefan Petriceicu, who, as already mentioned, was living in exile in Poland. Not surprisingly he still had contacts and some support amongst the Moldavian boyars, and what is more, he could count on Polish support as well. As was often the case in Moldavian history, it was an internal conspiracy that led to the change of the monarch. The pro-Petriceicu boyar faction wanted to use the perfect opportunity of the quickly spreading news of the Ottoman defeat at Vienna and the absence of Duca, giving them chance to play on the anti-Turkish mood of the people.

As has been mentioned elsewhere, part of the Papal financial support was to be used to recruit Cossacks to fight against the Turks and Tatars. Prior to his departure from Cracow, Jan III nominated the Polish noble Stefan Kunicki as Cossack Hetman, with orders to gather volunteers from both the Right and Left-Bank Ukraine. Recruitment was slow and only in mid-October did Kunicki have enough troops to march into the Right-Bank Ukraine, forcing Draghinici to quickly retreat and to abandon a few small fortresses held by Moldavian troops. After strengthening his forces with anti-Ottoman Cossacks living in the region, Kunicki reorganised his army, assigning experienced officers like Andrzej Mohyła or Staniecki as colonels in charge of the regiments. After that the Hetman took his growing army against Turkish garrisons at Bar and Medzhybizh in Podolia but was unable to capture them. Facing a stubborn defence, and lacking proper artillery and engineers, Kunicki decided to abandon his attempts to besiege these places, marching into Moldavia instead. Here he was joined by a force of boyars supporting Petriceicu, so by mid-November he had between 20,000 and 30,000 men under his command. He sent 10,000 mounted Cossacks to pacify Budjak, while he led the rest against Turkish-held Bender. The punitive expedition against the Tatars was practically unopposed, as the majority of troops from Budjak were with Crimean Khan in Austria. The first victims of the Cossacks' wrath were the Lipka Tatars, with their settlements razed to the ground, Lipka and their families killed, and prisoners taken on their raids released and recruited into Kunicki's forces. Then 'with fire and sword' the Cossacks marched through Budjak, showing no mercy. Jan Chryzostom Pasek described that time as follows:[2]

> Kunicki with his Cossacks went there [easily], as all better [Tatar] horses were at Vienna. Therefore he had time, [so] he burned and killed anyone that gathered to oppose him; his forces were growing, as he recovered many prisoners that were there, other, from far away, were arriving to him, hearing about this Christian army. Cossacks showed no mercy, killing women, tearing children to pieces and doing the worst things to them; they say that he killed three times a hundred thousand of them, marching everywhere and not afraid of anybody. (…) [After returning] Tatars seen their land destroyed, their wives and children killed, their cattle and sheep taken away [so] they cried because of this tragedy.

The attack at Bender was unsuccessful as the Cossacks were still lacking artillery. What was worse, at the beginning of December Kunicki had to

---

2   Jan Chryzostom Pasek, *Pamiętniki*, p.404.

face a relief force marching towards the fortress. It was an army mostly made of Tatars from Budjak and Bilhorod, supported by Turkish reinforcements. This force was the vanguard of the returning Tatar army and was under command of Ali Girej of the Budjak Tatars, with Ali Bey and Yusuf Aga leading the Turks. Both armies clashed at Kickany (the other names of the battle are Kilia, Filagorna or Filogranum) on 5 December. Heavy snow severely limited the offensive capabilities of the mounted Tatars and Turks, while the Cossacks attacked them 'with great impetus'. The relief force was defeated and quickly fled, chased by vengeful Cossacks. Many Tatar and Turkish leaders, including Ali Girej and Ali Bey, were killed, while 'the roads for four miles were full of killed Tatars, Turks, janissaries and sipahi'.[3] Kunicki, with a certain degree of exaggeration, claimed that none of

Polish or Lithuanian soldiers at the battle of Chocim in 1673. Romeyn de Hooghe, 1674 (Rijksmuseum)

his Cossacks were killed during the fight. The Polish Commissioner with the Cossacks, Druszkiewicz, wrote about the operations in 1683 that '[he] burned Medzhybizh and Bar, recaptured Niemirów from the Turks, Tighina [Bender] besieged, Budjak pacified, killing 10,000 Tatars or more'.[4]

As mentioned before, Petriceicu used this opportunity to regain his throne. With a small Polish contingent send by Andrzej Potocki, he arrived in Moldavia at the end of November. In the town of Botoşani he was welcomed by boyars who had officially deposed Duca and sworn their allegiance to Petriceicu. By the end of December, gathering more and more supporters during his march, the new voivode entered Iaşi (Jassy), capitol of Moldavia. In the meantime Kunicki was still, without much success, attacking Turkish-held fortresses and continued with destroying Tatar settlements. More and more of this troops left the ranks, taking loot back to the Ukraine. The Hetman was counting on Polish reinforcements and money to pay his men, but Potocki was unable to supply either. At the end of December the Cossacks had to face the Tatars again, this time a stronger army led by Hacı II Giray, who allegedly led 10,000 Tatars, a few hundred Turks and seven cannons.[5] Kunicki's Cossack-Moldavian army was at that point was weaker, numbering less than 10,000 men, and Petriceicu, in his letter to Andrzej

3   Tadeusz Urbański, *Rok 1683 na Podolu, Ukrainie i w Mołdawii*, p.39.
4   Stanisław Zygmunt Druszkiewicz, *Pamiętniki 1648–1697*, p.117.
5   Ilie Corfus (ed.), *Documente privitoare la istoria României culese din arhivele polone. Secolul al XVII-lea.* (Bucharest: Editura Adaemiei Republicii Socialiste România 1983), p.304, Petriceicu to Andrzej Potocki, 7 January 1684.

Potocki, mentions that 'Cossacks here told us, that there were no more than 5,000 of them, even though he [Kunicki] many times assured us that he had more than 40,000 under his command'.[6] The allies were surprised by the enemy near the village Tobak. Outnumbered, short of supplies of powder and without cannons, Kunicki's troops managed to set up their famous Cossack tabor wagon fortress, and under its cover started to retreat towards Iași. Unfortunately on the night of 3/4 January 1684 the Moldavian boyars and their troops deserted en-masse and left their allies. What was worse, Kunicki, taking all the mounted troops, abandoned his army and fled across the Prut river. The remaining Cossacks chose Colonel Andrzej Mohyła as the new Hetman and tried to cross the river as well. Taking heavy losses, with many killed, drowned or taken prisoner, the remnants of the Cossack army retreated to Iași. The Tatars did not pursue them but set up a camp near Bilhorod, from which they were planning to continue the campaign. Kunicki, enraged by his erstwhile allies' behaviour, left Iași, moving his remaining troops towards the Polish border. He claimed that he would set up his soldiers there as a defence force and ask Potocki for financial support to re-equip the army and to recruit more men. The Polish commander was unable to support him at that point however. Only once Sobieski returned from his campaign against the Turks, was 100,000zł and cloth for uniforms sent to Kunicki to help him in reorganising his army.[7]

At the same time Petriceicu, now abandoned by the Cossacks, was facing the Tatars with a very small army, composed of a few banners of Polish cavalry and some Moldavian troops. What is more, he was now threatened by the return of Duca, who was travelling through Transylvania with the remnants of his army from Vienna, to take back his throne. There were also internal problems with the boyars, as more and more of them wanted to look towards Muscovy for help instead of the Commonwealth. Petriceicu was desperately looking for help from Potocki but at that time of the year most of the units were already disbanded or settled into winter quarters. The Polish commander did manage to put together a small relief force, composed of a few banners of *pancerni* and light horse. They were led by *rotmistrz* Stefan Andrzej Dymidecki, who was nominated as colonel. This experienced officer, who had served in the army since 'The Deluge' war with Sweden, was nominally in charge of a *pancerni* banner that took part in the Vienna campaign, where it was led by his lieutenant, Aleksander Chomentowski. Dymidecki stayed in Poland though, where he commanded a Wallachian banner (probably a private unit) in Potocki's forces. Now, he was sent to help Petriceic, so he quickly moved against Duca. Receiving news that the returning voivode was in Domnești, near the border with Transylvania, on 25 December 1683 the *rotmistrz* led a group of Polish cavalry in a surprise attack against the Moldavians. As was noted in Pasek's diary '[Dymidecki] was bravely fighting (…), defeating and capturing Duca'.[8] The Moldavian voivode was sent to Poland and died in captivity on 31 of March 1685.

---

6   *Ibidem*, p.304.

7   *Ibidem*, Jan III Sobieski to Petriceicu, 25 January 1684.

8   Jan Chryzostom Pasek, *Pamiętniki*, p.404.

Dymidecki moved to Roman, from where his troops were to fight against the Tatars. At the beginning of 1684, seeing that his support amongst the Moldavian boyars was weakling, Petriceicu decided to leave Iaşi and moved to Suceava (Suczawa). Dymidecki and his soldiers escorted him on his way. The Moldavian capitol was, until April 1684, held by a Polish garrison led by Stanisław Kobielski, lieutenant of Franciszek Dzieduszycki's Wallachian banner from the regular Polish army. His command in Iaşi was composed mostly of *pancerni* and light horse, with some dragoons, gathered into two weak regiments, and cannon sent from the Polish army returning from the Vienna campaign.[9]

Petriceicu now had to face another competitor to the Moldavian throne, Dumitraşcu Cantacuzino, who was supported by the Ottomans. He could not count on Cossack support, as they were busy with their own internal struggles. Kunicki also lost support amongst his own men, who mutinied and killed him at the end of March 1684, and Druszkiewicz was forced to flee for his life.[10] He was replaced as Hetman by Andrzej Mohyła, who was also supported by the Poles but who was unable to return to Moldavia with his troops in time. In mid-April, at the battle at the river Larga, Petriceicu was defeated by Cantacuzino and had to abandon Moldavia and again flee to Poland, where he remained until his death in 1690. The newly triumphant voivode did not enjoy his throne for long, as in 1685, he was replaced by another Ottoman-backed candidate, Constantine Cantemir. Poland lost all its gains in Moldavia, and what is more the weak Polish forces in Podolia were unable to properly defend the region against new Tatar raids in the spring of 1684, nor were they able to block Kamieniets from receiving reinforcements and supply convoys. It seems that due to lack of troops and money, Potocki was unable to support Kunicki during the Cossack campaign in Moldavia. At the same time the Poles did not achieve much success in Podolia, so in the summer of 1684 they had to begin their operations without a new base of operations. Sobieski was unhappy with such an outcome, and at the end of January 1684 was already complaining to Potocki about Kunicki and making attempts to keep Petriceicu on the Moldavian throne.[11]

9   Ilie Corfus (ed.), *Documente privitoare la istoria României*, p.307, Jan III Sobieski to Petriceicu, 16 January 1684.
10   Stanisław Zygmunt Druszkiewicz, *Pamiętniki 1648–1697*, p.111.
11   *Ibidem*, p.310, Jan III Sobieski to Andrzej Potocki, 25 January 1684.

Conclusion

Execution of Kara Mustafa in Belgrade, 25 December 1683. Jan Luyken, 1689 (Rijksmuseum)

The campaign of 1683 was just the beginning of a new period of conflict that was to be waged until 1699. In March 1684, under the patronage of Pope Innocent XI, the Polish-Lithuanian Commonwealth, Holy Roman Empire and the Venetian Republic signed an anti-Ottoman treaty, creating The Holy League (*Sacra Ligua*). Two years later the Tsardom of Russia joined this alliance as well. The war was waged on many fronts, from Hungary, through Moldavia, Podolia, Dalmatia, to Crimea. Sobieski did not see the successful end of the conflict, as he died on 17 June 1696. One year later the Elector of Saxony, Augustus II Wettin, known as Augustus the Strong, was elected as the new King of Poland and Grand Duke of Lithuania. It was him who was able to celebrate the end of the war against the Ottoman Empire, when on 26 January 1699 the Holy League and Ottomans signed the Treaty of Karlowitz. The Commonwealth recovered the territory of Podolia, lost during the 1672–1676 war, including the fortress of Kamianets-Podilskyi. Soon though, the country was plunged into a period of new conflict, both internal and external, known as the Great Northern War, that started a sad period of the Commonwealth's history. As such the war of 1683 became the 'swan song' of Polish military achievements, with the relief of Vienna and the second battle of Párkány counted amongst the final victories of the famous winged hussars. These are the most iconic battles of this formation and the best known in the world, celebrated in books, movies and even songs. In this book an attempt has been made to try and paint a more detailed picture of the Polish army at Vienna, showing the involvement of the hussars only as one element of a much larger army, where all component parts played equally important roles. Jan III Sobieski and his soldiers were a very important element in the allied military effort, which led to the relief of a besieged Vienna and the defeat of Kara Mustafa's army. Considering the political situation in 1683, the decision of the Polish monarch to join forces with the Holy Roman Empire and fight against the Ottomans was the best possible move, especially as the campaign was taking place abroad and was at least partially financed by foreign funds. The Polish army showed considerable skill and stubbornness and relied on its experience when fighting the Turks and Tatars. At the same time there are common negative traits of the Commonwealth's military, such as problems with discipline and internal struggles, especially well illustrated in the actions of the Lithuanian army. Despite all of this, Sobieski's campaign of 1683 should be without doubt treated as a great success, with the relief of Vienna and the defeat of the besieging army being one of the most important battles of seventeenth century.

Appendix I

Polish-Imperial treaty from 31 March 1683

This treaty, signed under the protection of the Pope, is due to last until the final and glorious peace.

It will be guaranteed in front of the Pope by Cardinal Pio[1] and Cardinal Barberini.[2] The Emperor releases the Polish-Lithuanian Commonwealth from the remaining debt for troops sent to support them against the Swedes[3] and gives back the lease of the salt mine in Wieliczka, provided by Poland in lieu of this debt.

Either side [of the treaty] will not sign the peace without agreement of the other. The Emperor, as King of Bohemia and Hungary, in his name and that of his heirs; the Polish King in his name, his successors and the whole Commonwealth, agree to fulfil this treaty.

The Emperor will raise army of 60,000 soldiers, while the Polish King will raise 40,000 soldiers.

In the case of siege of Vienna or Cracow, both armies will combine their forces, if needed.

During the war, each side [of the treaty] will operate in their own theatre of war, trying to capture from the enemy territories in Hungary, Podolia and the Ukraine. The Emperor will supply the Poles with 200,000 thalers to hasten the build-up of the Polish army.

Other monarchs can be invited into this treaty which is, and this needs to be highlighted, signed only against Turks.

This treaty should be signed and confirmed within the next two months.[4]

---

1   Carlo Pio di Savoia, Papal cardinal-protector of Austria.
2   Carlo Barberini, Papal cardinal-protector of Poland.
3   In 1657.
4   Erazm Rykaczewczki (ed.), *Relacye nuncyuszów apostolskich i innych osób* o Polsce od roku 1548 do 1690, volume II (Paryż: Biblioteka Polska, 1864), pp.431–432.

Appendix II

The Polish army in 1683 according to Bernard Brulig

When describing different sources for the description of Polish army in 1683, it was mentioned that a fragment of Bernard Brulig's account would be included as an appendix. Some additional comments were added to both list of troops and to the summary of troops. Unfortunately he rarely made any distinction between types of cavalry, so except for two days when he specifically mentioned winged hussars, all other units are described as cavalry or mounted (*reiter* or *zu pferd*).[1] Besides the main three groups of troops (under the King and both Hetmans) there were soldiers on the Imperial payroll under the command of Lubomirski. After Jabłonowski led the main Polish army into Austria, Brulig's account mentions a steady stream of small groups of banners and companies trying to catch up with the three larger 'divisions'. These stragglers were marching through Moravia well after relief of Vienna, only re-joining the Polish army during the later stages of the campaign.

Date	Formation	Number of banners or companies	Number of soldiers	Additional comments
17/07	Cavalry	9	3000	Lubomirski's auxiliary corps
30/07	Cavalry	2	260	Possibly part of the above
30/07	Musketeers	2	300	Probably Imperial troops
24/08	Cavalry	30	11,000	Field Hetman Sieniawski's avant-garde
24/08	Dragoons	10	5000	
25/08	Cavalry	1	100	Probably delayed units from Sieniawski's group
26/08	Dragoons	1	100	
27/08	Cavalry	2	140	
28/08	Cavalry (and dragoons)	30	10,000	King Jan III Sobieski, Royal Prince Jakub and few other important court officials

---

1   Bernard Brulig, 'Pat. Bernard Brulig's Bericht über die Belagerung der Stadt Wien im Jahre 1683. ', pp.424–426.

30/08	Cavalry	34	6000	Main army under Grand Hetman Jabłonowski
30/08	Dragoons	18	5000	
30/08	Infantry	80	14,000	
30/08	Artillery	-	30 large cannons	
30/08	Haiduks	1	100	Royal Guard (private troops)
30/08	Janissaries	2	200	
30/08	'Different troops'	7	700	Possibly other guard units?
31/08	Cavalry	3	260	
01/09	Cavalry	1	100	
01/09	Dragoons	3	240	
01/09	'Polish Tatars on foot'	-	120	Brulig noted that they were carrying horse-tail tug (buńczuk)
02/09	Dragoons	2	140	
02/09	Infantry	8	1000	
03/09	'Polish Tatars on foot'	-	150	Also with horse-tail tug (buńczuk)
04/09	Cavalry	2	130	
04/09	Infantry	2	160	
05/09	Cavalry	1	70	
05/09	Dragoons	2	130	
05/09	'Polish Tatars on foot'	-	130	Also with horse-tail tug (buńczuk)
06/09	Cavalry	2	100	
06/09	Dragoons	1	60	
06/09	Infantry	4	200	
06/09	'Polish Tatars on foot'	-	100	Also with horse-tail tug (buńczuk)
07/09	Cavalry	2	140	
07/09	Dragoons	2	120	
08/09	Calvary	4	250	
08/09	'Polish Tatars on foot'	-	150	Also with horse-tail tug (buńczuk)
09/09	Dragoons	4	250	
09/09	Infantry	1	100	
09/09	Mounted Cossacks	1	100	Zaporozhian Cossack on Polish service
09/09	'Polish Tatars on foot'	-	100	Also with horse-tail tug (buńczuk)
10/09	Winged hussars	6	1000	'With eagle wings and fully armoured'
10/09	Cavalry	10	700	
10/09	Dragoons	2	120	
11/09	Cavalry	5	250	
11/09	Dragoons	1	50	
11/09	'Polish Tatars on foot'	-	130	Also with horse-tail tug (buńczuk)
12/09	Cavalry	2	100	
12/09	Infantry	3	120	
13/09	Cavalry	1	70	
13/09	'Polish Tatars on foot'	-	120	Also with horse-tail tug (buńczuk)
14/09	Cavalry	1	60	

15/09	Cavalry	1	60	
15/09	Dragoons	1	50	
16/09	Cavalry	2	100	
17/09	Cavalry	2	100	
18/09	Cavalry	1	70	
19/09	Winged hussars	6	1000	'With eagle wings and fully armoured'
19/09	Infantry	4	400	
20/09	Mounted Cossacks	2	200	Zaporozhian Cossack in Polish service
21/09	Mounted Cossacks	4	400	Zaporozhian Cossack in Polish service
22/09	Mounted Cossacks	2	200	Zaporozhian Cossack in Polish service
23/09	Mounted Cossacks	1	100	Zaporozhian Cossack in Polish service
24/09	Mounted Cossacks	1	100	Zaporozhian Cossack in Polish service
25/09	Mounted Cossacks	1	100	Zaporozhian Cossack in Polish service
26/09	Mounted Cossacks	2	200	Zaporozhian Cossack in Polish service

Brulig then gives a total summary of troop numbers; 37,360 cavalry, 11,260 dragoons and 17,280 infantry, making a total of 66,000 men. They were accompanied by a tabor (wagon) train of 32,000 with the total number of horses in the army estimated as 400,000. As the number of troops mentioned are far higher than expected, it seems that soldiers' servants have been included as well. It is probable that, especially when witnessing larger groups of cavalry, he in fact added the numbers of mounted servants to the overall strength of the units. They were carrying weapons, usually sabres and long firearms, so for a non-military eyewitness the fact that they rode after the main body of the cavalry unit could suggest they were part of it.

Rather confusing is the fact that on both 10 and 19 September Brulig mentions a group of six banners of winged hussars, numbering 1,000 men. In both cases he provides the same description of those soldiers, but he counts them as separate troops. Polish researcher Radosław Sikora points out that none of the Polish sources from the campaign mentions such large reinforcements like the group travelling past Brulig's monastery on 19 September (already after the battle), suggesting that it may be in fact the same group, that on 10 September was travelling towards Vienna and then returned nine days later.[2] Such a theory does not explain why a group of six winged hussar banners should be 120 miles from Vienna on 19 September, while the main Polish army was at that time marching in a completely different direction? It is possible that on 19 September Brulig did in fact see reinforcements marching towards the Polish army. Thanks to the research of Zbigniew Hundert we know that *rotmisrz* Władysław Denhoff was late for the battle of Vienna and that he joined main army with his 80-men strong, newly raised, banner of winged hussars prior to battle of Párkány. Of course there is a huge difference between one and six banners, but it is possible that Brulig (or the nineteenth century editor of his account) made a mistake while copying the text.

---

2   Raosław Sikora, *Husaria pod Wiedniem*, p.54.

Appendix III

Recruitment letter for hussars banner of Marcin Zamoyski from 1683

In 1683 Marcin Zamoyski, Voivode of Lublin, was already nominal *rotmistrz* of the 100-horse strong banner of hussars and nominal colonel of a 180-portion strong regiment of foreign infantry. As a part of raising the army for the relief of Vienna, he was to a create new unit, a 120-strong banner of *pancerni*, and to strengthen the existing ones. The hussar banner was to increase from 100 to 150 horses, while the infantry regiment increased from 180 to 340 portions. Presented below is an attempt to translate the recruitment letter for the strengthened hussar banner. It was originally edited and published in Polish by Zbigniew Hundert.[1] While the original document, in the style of many Polish documents from the period, had a large number of Latin words included in the text, for the purpose of this translation into English these have been translated as part of the overall text, making the whole letter easier to read, especially as the Latin words were often used to highlight original Polish sentences and they could make the whole document confusing if translated directly. All comments in brackets are part of editing the translation or come from the original Polish edit.

Jan III, by grace of God the King of Poland, Grand Duke of Lithuania, Ruthenia, Prussia, Masovia, Samogitia, Kiev, Volhynia, Livonia, Podolia, Podlasie, Smoleńsk, Seversk and Chernihiv.

[To] His Excellency [space][2] Zamoyski, Voivode of Lublin, our cherished, [we show] our Royal favour. Our cherished Excellency. It is uneasy peace and times when the Commonwealth, our motherland, is in growing danger due to the approaching Turkish war, which can be only stopped by our brave knights.

---

1   Zbigniew Hundert, 'Listy przypowiednie dla Marcina Zamoyskiego z lat 1656, 1679 i 1683 na chorągwie jazdy i regiment pieszy w wojsku koronnym', *Res Historica*, no 43 (Lublin: Instytut Historii UMCS 2017), pp.331–333. Original document: AGAD, AZ, no 463, pp.71–72.

2   The original document had a space, called 'window' (*okienko* in Polish), where normally the full name, dates, details, etc. could be added when the document was officially issued.

Because of this, we are doing our best to make sure that the Commonwealth is well defended and that we can live in the peace that we desire. During our reign we [already] many times experienced how much [good] can be done by Polish hussars[3] against such a powerful enemy. [It is] Flower of our Polish cavalry and great support of our small army. Through the years we had many occasions to witness the bravery, prowess and courage of Your ancient noble family. We also know that in public service you are not afraid to risk your life and belongings. [Because of this] We decided to give Your Honourable [command of] 150 horses of hussars, which we order with this letter. They are due to start service on day [space] of month [space] in this current year. This banner [of cavalry] will receive pay as per the agreed regulation from voivodeships and lands. Make sure Your Honour, with all your diligence, to have this unit always at the prescribed strength, [made of] experienced men, well equipped with all that is needed for warfare. Any of the men that will commit any crimes, can be punished by Your Honour as per military regulations. You are due to march with those men to [army camp], following our orders and orders of our Crown Hetmen; wherever such orders tell you to go, you are due to march and take part in all military affairs. During recruitment and while en route, Your Honour should ensure the safety of our citizens, [so] that soldiers and their servants do not hurt them with their actions; that no provisions are taken by them [without agreement] but that all is done as per military regulations and orders [and] that soldiers are behaving modestly and are content with their agreed pay. [We hope that] With this all and further good service you will work, by your courage and prowess, for the fame and honour of yourself and your family, to earn our and the Commonwealth's respect. And we will not forget about Your Honour in future.

Given in Warsaw, on day [blank] of the month June and July[4] [space] on the Year of Our Lord MDCLXXXIII, year [blank] of our reign[5]

King Jan

[royal seal]

[Signed by] Stanisław [Antoni] Szczuka, Deputy Cup-bearer, secretary of His Royal Highness

---

3   The Latin term used here, *robur Polonae militia*, could mean both military force (army) but also specifically hussars, that during Sobieski's reign was sometimes called *Polonae militia*.
4   Both months are mentioned, so it is not exactly certain in which month Zamoyski received this letter.
5   Jan Sobieski was elected as King on 1673, so despite the later date of his coronation in 1676, his reign was calculated since the election year.

Appendix IV

Polish cavalry during the Vienna campaign, based on winter quarters list from 1684

One of the most interesting sources that can be used to reconstruct the organisation of the Polish cavalry during campaign of 1683 is the list from the distribution of so called *hiberna*[1] from early 1684. It gives details of all cavalry regiments, units of *arkabuzeria,* all light horse banners still in service and all *pancerni* banners that were left as part of the defence force in Poland. Unfortunately the original of this document does not exist, only a copy survives, from 1724,[2] made at the request of then Crown Grand Hetman Adam Mikołaj Sieniawski (1666–1726), son of Crown Field Hetman Mikołaj Hieronim Sieniawski. As such, a copy could contain a certain degree of errors, due to imprecise clerical work, which is especially noticeable in the list of light horse banners. Where possible, such errors have been corrected or comments placed in the footnotes.

Regiment of His Royal Highness Jan III Sobieski: 11 banners of hussars and 10 banners of *pancerni*.

	Name of *rotmistrz*	Paper strength at the start of campaign of 1683	Paper strength at the beginning of 1684
Hussars			
	King Jan III Sobieski	200	200
	Royal Prince Jakub	200	200
	Royal Prince Aleksander	200	200
	Marcin Zamoyski	150	150
	Samuel Prażmowski	120	120

---

1   Known also as winter's bread (*chleb zimowy*), it was a special tax from the Royal estates, that was distributed to accommodate cavalry troops (but not dragoons and infantry) during the winter. Earlier in the seventeenth century *hiberna* was delivered as provisions, and since 1667 paid in cash and then distributed by special commissioners to the troops.

2   Biblioteka Czartoryskich, no 2589, pp.97–102, *Komput wojska koronnego z aktów dystrybuty hybernowej…*

		150	150
	Jan Wielopolski	150	150
	Michał Warszycki	150	150
	Józef Lubomirski	150	150
	Stefan Branicki	150	120
	Jan Cetner	100	100
	Marcin Cieński	100	100
	King Jan III Sobieski	200	200
	Marcin Zamoyski	120	120
Pancerni			
	Mikołaj Sapieha	120	120
	Stanisław Druszkiewicz	120	120
	Mikołaj Daniłowicz	120	120
	Michał Warszycki	150	150
	Wojciech Prażmowski	120	120
	Józef Lubomirski	150	150
	Jan Koniecpolski	120	120
	Andrzej Rzeczycki	120	120

Regiment of Crown Grand Hetman Stanisław Jabłonowski: five (or seven)[3] banners of hussars and 11 banners of *pancerni*.

	Name of *rotmistrz*	Paper strength at the start of campaign of 1683	Paper strength at the beginning of 1684
Hussars			
	Hetman Jabłonowski	200	200
	Jan Małachowski	120	120
	Wacław Leszczyński	120	120
	Franciszek Bieliński	120	123
	Jan Dobrogost Krasiński	150	150
	Hetman Jabłonowski	200	200
	Franciszek Dzieduszycki	120	120
Pancerni			
	Józef Słuszka	120	120
	Stefan Czarniecki	150	150
	Stefan Grudziński	60	120
	Józef Szumlański	100	120
	Aleksander Chodorowski	120	120
	Michał Rzewuski	120	120
	Andrzej Sierakowski	120	120
	Jan Stadnicki	120	120
	Stefan Ledóchowski	100	100

3 The list is missing the banner of Jan Gniński, omitted by mistake by whoever made a copy of it. Considering that before and after 1683 this banner served as part of Jabłonowski's regiment, it should be placed here as well. There is also a strong possibility that Władysław Denhoff's unit was deployed as part of this regiment. See: Zbigniew Hundert, 'Organizacja husarii koronnej na wyprawę wiedeńską', pp.192–194.

Regiment of late Crown Field Hetman Mikołaj Sieniawski: five banners of hussars and 10 banners of *pancerni*.

	Name of *rotmistrz*	Paper strength at the start of campaign of 1683	Paper strength at the beginning of 1684
Hussars			
	Hetman Sieniawski	200	200
	Stanisław Dąbski	100	100
	Stanisław Herakliusz Lubomirski	120	120
	Wojciech Urbański	120	112
	Jan Myszkowski	100	100
	Hetman Sieniawski	200	200
	Michał Jerzy Czartoryski	100	150
Pancerni			
	Karol Łużecki	150	150
	Melchior Grudziński	120	120
	Franciszek Koryciński	120	120
	Stanisław Cetner	100	100
	Stanisław Opaliński	120	120
	Franciszek Makowiecki	100	100
	Adam Mikołaj Sieniawski	150	150
	Marcin Bogusz	120	120

Regiment of Andrzej Potocki: one banner of hussars and five banners of *pancerni*.

	Name of *rotmistrz*	Paper strength at the start of campaign of 1683	Paper strength at the beginning of 1684
Hussars			
	Andrzej Potocki	150	150
	Andrzej Potocki	150	150
	Andrzej Modrzewski	150	120
Pancerni			
	Stanisław Potocki	120	120
	Nikodem Żaboklicki	120	120
	Wiktoryn Bykowski	100	100

Regiment of Andrzej Potocki: one banner of hussars and three banners of *pancerni*.

	Name of *rotmistrz*	Paper strength at the start of campaign of 1683	Paper strength at the beginning of 1684
Hussars			
	Szczęsny Potocki	120	120
	Szczęsny Potocki	150	150
Pancerni			
	Hieronim Lanckoroński	100	100
	Michał Wasilkowski	100	100

Regiment of Konstanty Wiśniowiecki: five banners of *pancerni*.

Name of *rotmistrz*	Paper strength at the start of campaign of 1683	Paper strength at the beginning of 1684
Konstanty Wiśniowiecki	150	115
Stanisław Witwicki	100	100
Józef Mniszech	120	120
Adam Radliński	120	120
Jan Stanisław Giżycki	100	100

Regiment of Stefan Bidziński: five banners of *pancerni*.

Name of *rotmistrz*	Paper strength at the start of campaign of 1683	Paper strength at the beginning of 1684
Stefan Bidziński	150	150
Mikołaj Szczawiński	100	100
Stanisław Tarło	120	120
Stanisław Sariusz Łaźniński	120	120
Marcin Ubysz	100	100

Regiment of Hieronim Lubomirski: six banners of *pancerni*.

Name of *rotmistrz*	Paper strength at the start of campaign of 1683	Paper strength at the beginning of 1684
Hieronim Lubomirski	150	200
Second banner of Hieronim Lubomirski	68	100
Władysław Morstin	120	120
Felicjan Białogłowski	100	100
Franciszek Dunin	100	100
Wojciech Dąbski	100	100

Regiment of Rafał Leszczyński: one banner of hussars and three banners of *pancerni*.

	Name of *rotmistrz*	Paper strength at the start of campaign of 1683	Paper strength at the beginning of 1684
Hussars			
	Rafał Leszczyński	150	150
	Jakub Rokitnicki	100	100
Pancerni			
	Wojciech Łubieński	100	100
	Dymitr Jełowiecki (Jełowicki)	100	100

Regiment of Michał Zbrożek: two banners of *pancerni.*

Name of *rotmistrz*	Paper strength at the start of campaign of 1683	Paper strength at the beginning of 1684
Michał Zbrożek	150	150
Jerzy Skarżyński	100	100

Regiment of Tomasz Karczewski: two banners of *pancerni.*

Name of *rotmistrz*	Paper strength at the start of campaign of 1683	Paper strength at the beginning of 1684
Tomasz Karczewski	150	150
Stefan Andrzej Dymidecki	100	100

Regiment of Atanazy Miączyński: three banners of *pancerni.*

Name of *rotmistrz*	Paper strength at the start of campaign of 1683	Paper strength at the beginning of 1684
Atanazy Miączyński	150	150
Andrzej Miączyński	100	100
Stanisław Miączyński	100	100

Regiment of Mikołaj Radecki: three banners of *pancerni.*

Name of *rotmistrz*	Paper strength at the start of campaign of 1683	Paper strength at the beginning of 1684
Mikołaj Radecki	120	120
Dymitr Żabokrzycki	100	100
Wojciech Stępowski	100	100

Arkabuzeria

Name of *rotmistrz*	Paper strength at the start of campaign of 1683	Paper strength at the beginning of 1684
King Jan III Sobieski	300	300
Hetman Jabłonowski	100	100
Hetman Sieniawski	100	100

Light horse[4]

Name of *rotmistrz*	Paper strength at the start of the campaign of 1683	Paper strength at the beginning of 1684
Hetman Sieniawski under Marcin Rykaczewski	150	100
Hetman Sieniawski under Janaki	80	60
Andrzej Potocki under Leon Eysmont	70	70
Andrzej Potocki under Szaniawski	?	90
Andrzej Potocki under Marcjan Gostkowski	70	70
Józef Słuszka	?	80
Tomasz Karczewski	100	100
Stefan Górski under Zachariasz Olszamowski	?	80
Andrzej Dobraczyński	80	80
Aleksander Zaborowski	80	80
Damian Ruszczyc	80	80
Stefan Nicki	100	100
Mikołaj Zbrożek	100	100
Andrzej Jeżowski	100	100
Paweł Florian Drozdowski	100	100
Jerzy Frąckiewicz	80	80
Szymon Zawisza	100	100
Andrzej Sierakowski under Ochocki	70	70
Marcin Bogusz	90	90
Józef Modzelowski (Modzelewski)	80	80
Balcer Wilga	70	80
Andrzej Michał Wardyński	70	70
Tomasz Gdeszyński	60	60
Jerzy Huzdewen	70	70
Samuel Krzeczowski	60	120
Ilia Drogoszkuł	70	70
Korycki	120	120
Mikołaj Daniłowicz	100	100
Jan Wołczyński	100	100

---

4   In documents described as Wallachian.

Pancerni **banners that 'did not go to Ungvár' (stayed in Poland as a defence force): 10 banners**

Name of *rotmistrz*	Paper strength at the start of campaign of 1683	Paper strength at the beginning of 1684
Jerzy Wielkorski	150	100
Marcjan Ścibor Chełmski	150	150
Aleksander Drzewicki	100	120
Jan Łącki	120	120
Tomasz Kazimierz Głuski	100	100
Kazimierz Grudziński	120	120
Bogusław Potocki	100	100
Jakub Czarnowski	120	120
Hieronim Siemiaszko	100	100
Konstanty Czeczel	100	100

Appendix V

Lists of trophies

There are a number of lists of the main trophies captured by the allies in the Ottoman camp, focusing on siege equipment and weapons used during the siege. In this appendix two of them are presented, as they were in circulation in Europe in the form of pamphlets and letters, describing the scale of the victory. The first was published in Polish[1] but seems to be a translation of 'An Account of such things as upon the flight of the Turks were brought and to be brought out of the Turkish Camp into the Arsenal of Vienna' from the official chronicle of the siege, written by Johan Peter von Vaelckeren.[2] Of course it does not mentioned horses, tents, weapons, etc. captured directly by the soldiers, instead focusing on the large quantities of siege equipment and supplies.

4,000 hundredweight (cwt) of powder
4,000 cwt of lead
6,000 cwt of match
20,000 fire balls
18,000 hand grenades
18,000 pickaxes and spades
50 cwt of saltpetre
5 cwt waxed cloth for tents
50 cwt of Turkish horseshoes and *hufnal*[3]
1,100 planks
400 saws
1,000 empty woollen sacks
100 cwt of tallow and others used as unguent
2,000 leather bags for bullets
50 cwt of iron
8,000 empty ammunition wagons

---

1   *Biblioteka starożytna pisarzy polskich*, volume II (Warszawa: S. Orgelbrand, Księgarz, 1834), pp.287–289.
2   English version published as John Peter a Valcaren, *A relation or diary of the siege of Vienna* (London, 1684), pp.107–108.
3   Large nail used by blacksmiths to fasten horseshoes.

18,900 large and small cannonballs of all kinds
50 cwt of tar and resin
500,000 pounds of linseed oil
300,000 different items used to prepare mines
20,000 empty bags used to be filled with earth and sand to be thrown into moats
50 cwt of *bratnal*[4]
4,000 sheep skins
20 cwt of string made from camel's and oxen's fur
500 janissary handguns
50 *kip*[5] of cotton
2,000 iron shields and hand-guards
1,000 powder horns for janissaries
4,000 large bellows used to heat up fire balls
200 wooden lifts used for moving cannons
2,000 large bombs
Four very large cannons
160 large and small cannons
A huge number of different ropes used for cannons
16 large anvils
20,000 large handguns used to shoot heated large and small grenades

A similar but more detailed version of this list was printed in Delarac's book. [6] It was entitled 'List, or State of the Ammunitions of War, that was found untouched, after the Defeat of the Turks, as Count Staremberg himself confessed; besides what was embezzled'. Below is the full list, as per the original text of the English edition:

400,000 Weight of Powder, besides the like Quantity that was burnt by our Men after the Battle.
400,000 of Lead.
18,000 Hand-Granadoes, of mixed Mettle.
20,000 Hand-Granadoes of Iron.
10,0000 Pickaxes.
30,000 several Instruments for the Mines.
4,000 Spades.
4,000 Baskets.
600 Pounds of Match.
5,000 Pounds of Pitch.
1,000 Pounds of a kind of Oil for Workmanship, and a Quantity of Linseed-Oil.
5,000 Pounds of Cordage of different sizes.
200,000 Sacks made of Hair.
100,000 Sacks made of Cloth.

---

4   Large nail.
5   One *kipa equals 453,59 kg.*
6   Francois Paulin Dalerac, *Polish Manuscripts*, pp.365–366.

6,000 Pounds of Nails for Horse-shoes.
5,000 Pounds of several sorts of Nails for the Cannon.
20,000 Powder-Bags.
16 large Anvils; a Quantity of great Cordage for the Carriages of the Artillery.
1,000 Caldrons to boil the Pitch and Gums in.
20,000 Pounds of Thread made of Hair and Lint.
20,000 Halberds.
4,000 Scythes.
5,000 Muskets of the Janissaries.
600 Sacks full of Cotton, spun and unspun.
30,000 Pounds of Grease or Suet.
20,000 Powder Horns for the Janissaries.
4 Pair of Great Bellows.
5,000 Pounds of new Iron.
200 Waggons for the Artillery.
4 huge Bars of Iron for the great Cannon.
8 Great Iron Wheels for the same use.
8,000 Waggons for Ammunition.
1,000 Great Bombs.
18,000 Ball for the Cannon of a Middle bore.
20,000 red Bullets.
160 Pieces of Canon, among which were many 48 and 24 Pounder

As an addition to those lists, there is the following passage from the diary of Jan Chryzostom Pasek, who based his description on the accounts of eyewitnesses. During his military career Pasek many times mentioned looting defeated enemies, so one can only think how his imagination was moved by the stories told by veterans of 1683 campaign:[7]

[Turks] Left all their cannons [and] camp with all its riches. It was full of gold, horses, camels, oxen, cattle, sheep. There were beautiful tents, with chests full of all exotic items, even with money left in, that [Turks] did not take away. The Vizier's tents were so big, it looked as large as the whole of Warsaw,[8] all of which were taken by our King; even large sacks full of coins were left on the ground; there were golden and silver carpets; a bed with sheets worth several dozen thousands thalers. There were additional chambers hidden in those tents, that only on the third day after the battle they found there one of the vizier's concubine, while another, very well dressed, was lying beheaded in front of the tent. They said she was killed by the vizier himself, as he did not want her to be captured.

There was so much riches, that other tents were standing there even for up to two weeks [after battle]. Our Polish soldiers took so much loot, that when they were ordered to march to Hungary, they throw it out from their wagons or when their cart-horses were stuck in mud, they used those tents worth thousand or even more, to put under [wheels] to help quickly get the wagon out.

---

7   Jan Chryzostom Pasek, *Pamiętniki*, p.378.
8   He means that the area of vizier's camp was as big as Warsaw's Old Town.

Appendix VI

Letters of Leopold I to Jan III

When depicting the relief of Vienna the disagreements between Leopold and Jan, that started almost at once after the battle have already been mentioned. It should be remembered that their relations prior to September 1683 were, at least in the diplomatic channels, much warmer and polite. As an example, presented here are two letters sent by the Emperor to Poland in August 1683, showing how Leopold I was reminding Jan III of the allied obligation and urging him to arrive in Austria with his army Both are quoted *in extenso* from the English translation of Dalerac's *Polish Manuscripts*.

Leopold, by the Favour of the Divine Clemency, chosen Emperor of the Romans always Augustus, King of Germany, Hungary, Bohemia, Dalmatia, Croatia and Slavonia; Arch-Duke of Austria, Duke of Burgundy, Styria, Carinthia, Carniola and Württemberg, and Count of Tirol. To the most Serene and most Potent Prince, John III. King of Poland, Great Duke of Lithuania, Russia, Prussia, Masovia and Samogitia, our most dear Brother and Neighbour, greeting and mutual Friendship.

Most Serene and most Potent Prince, our most dear Brother and Neighbour. In this most calamitous Condition, into which the Treachery of the Hungarians and the most impetuous Barbarity of the Turks, hath cast our Country of Austria. Your Serenities most kind Letters wrote to us on the 7th of July, have wonderfully refreshed us. It was indeed a most joyful Message to us, when we understood, that your Serenity having laid aside all other Military Expeditions, was marching your Army with utmost Diligence to rescue Vienna, which is so closely besieged, out of the Jaws of the Barbarous Enemy. With how grateful and true a Sense we accept this Readiness to aid us, (as not going ahead only from the League betwixt us, but from your Serenities kind Affection, and Inclination which you have towards us and our Interests) and with what Returns of Kindness, we shall acknowledge this obligation, which tends to the safety of Christendom. We have given Orders, to our faithful and beloved John Christopher Free Baron of Zieroua Ziorouski, our Envoy, and magnificent Counsellor to us, and to the Sacred Empire, to explain more at large. He hath also Instructions to acquaint and submit to your Serenities sublime Prudence, what we have thought necessary and useful on the present Occasion for the more vigorous carrying on of the War, and raising the Siege of the said Town: Wherefore out of friendly and brotherly confidence, we obtest your

Serenity, to give entire Credit unto our said Envoy, in everything he shall say to you in our Name, and that you would cheerfully prosecute what you have begun, whereas by this Assistance and delivering and rescuing the City of Vienna, you will purchase Glory and eternal Fame, and more and more engage our Affection, (which hath long ago been fixed upon your Serenity) unto your Royal Off-spring. To which end we pray, That God would vouchsafe you the height of all sorts of Felicity.

Given at Passaw, 3 August 1683. of our Reigns over the Roman Empire the 26th, over Hungary the 29th and over Bohemia the 27th.

Your Serenity's Brother and Neighbour.[1]

***

A Letter from the Emperor, to the King of Poland, wrote by his own Hand.

Dated at Passaw, 24 Aug 1683.

To the most Serene Lord, the King of Poland, my most dearly beloved Brother and Neighbour.

I Have seen, by Your Majesty's Letter wrote with Your own Hand, dated the 15th Instant, how that You have already sent a good part of Your Army before; and given order that they shall join very speedily with the Troops of Lithuania and the Cossacks; and that You had begun Your march on that great Day of the Feast of our Lady, with Your whole Army, to come and succour with all Your might, my City of Vienna; which is ready to surrender, being closely besieged by the most powerful Army of the Turks. So puissant and opportune a Succour, makes me sufficiently to see the brotherly Love You have for me, to preserve my Dominions; as well as the Zeal You have for the Good of Christendom. So I return You most hearty Thanks, and shall endeavour upon all Occasions to acknowledge Your brotherly Love. I have been also willing to confess the same by this my devout Acknowledgment, which will be presented by the Count de Schafsgoutz, who will acquaint You, that I am to set out to Morrow for Lintz, to be nearer the City, and have News of it the sooner, and to have an Opportunity to consult more easily with You; to whom I wish a perfect Health and all Prosperity.

Your Majesty's most Affectionate Brother, and Neighbour, Leopoldus.[2]

---

1   Dalerac, *Polish Manuscripts*, pp.348–349.
2   *Ibidem,* pp.352–353.

Appendix VII

Letters of Charles Lorraine to Jan III

The Duke of Lorraine, as field commander of the Imperial army, was in constant communication with Polish King, sending him letters and copies of the communications from the besieged garrison in Vienna. This correspondence provides a very interesting insight into the relations between both allies, indicating how skilfully Lorraine was appealing to Sobieski's pride and honour, in order to hasten the arrival of the Polish army to Austria. In this appendix are translations of those letters. The first one is taken from the English translation of Dalerac's work; all the others are attempted translations into English from Dupo and do not quite work, therefore their language is not be as stylish as in first one.

In the Imperial Camp near Mayerech, dated 31 of July 1683[1]

Most Serene King,

I received, with a due Respect, the Letters which your Majesty was pleased to do me the honour to transmit to me; dated the 25th Inst. And from them I understood how much your Majesty's Royal Mind is moved, to accelerate the Succour of the City of Vienna, and how much inclined to the Defence of the Christian Empire, and Austrian Territories: Of which, indeed, I have been always so much persuaded, that in relation hereunto, I have received, from your Majesty's Letters, nothing new, nor what I did not before believe. In the meantime, I esteem it a great Favour and honour to me, that your Majesty does not vouchsafe to trust to your own most prudent Judgment in these things that are still to be done. I have hitherto endeavoured to guard myself against the Watchfulness of the Enemy by the Situation of my encampments; which though indeed I did not look upon as walled about, yet I have thought them to be as good as such from the Situation of the Rivers and the disposition of the Ground they take up. I have provided for the Security of the Bridge of Crems, and am advising the building of a second about Tulm, a Place nearer to Vienna, and which is reckoned to be secure. That which is hardest to me is, that I can scare send any Person into the Town; nor on the other

---

1   Dalerac, *Polish Manuscripts*, pp.340–342.

hand, receive any News from the besieged. But seeing I understand, from the magnificent Marshal of the Court of the Kingdom of Poland, that the particular Relations of what things are acted in the Imperial Army, do not displease your Majesty, I have communicated something to your Majesty in Writing, which hath Relation to the same; from which and from the said Marshal's Letters, your Majesty may distinctly understand everything; particularly what was done against the flying Rebels and Turks, about Pressburg, on the 29th Instant, by Prince Lubomirski and his Polish Officers and Soldiers alone, most prudently, valiantly, and with the natural Vigor of the renowned Polish Nation. Your Majesty will also understand in what Condition this Army is, and also the Progress of the German Auxiliaries. It is my Hope and Prayer to see the Christian Army defeat this most inveterate Enemy, and deliver the Austrian Territories under your Majesty's Conduct, being sensible that in such a Field, I shall have an Opportunity of further deserving your Royal Majesty's Favour and Benevolence, to whom I wish a healthful and long Reign, from the very Heart of,
Your Majesty's, most Humble and most Obedient Servant and Allie, Charles, Duke of Lorraine.

In the Imperial Camp near Enzersdorff, dated 5 August 1683[2]

Most Serene King,
I thought that I answered in full all questions asked by Your Majesty in letters dated 22 of the previous month, which I only received on the first day of this month [and] that all my previous letter, and those of Prince Lubomirski, explained everything. Therefore I hesitated to send further information, worried that I can bore Your Majesty with unnecessary repetitions. I was able [at the time] add some news, especially description of the area around Vienna, which can be find on attached pages.[3] Those things were not discussed yet. I ensure that none [information] that Your Majesty should know is missing here.

I did not receive any news from town [Vienna] since 22 of last month. Of many men, that I each day send to town and Turkish camps, none returned so far. As such I do not know anything for sure regarding the situation of the defenders. I will admit that it makes me uneasy, especially when thinking about [how long will be] period of the siege. I appeal to Your Majesty, to hasten the movement of Worthy Field Hetman Sieniawski and noble General Łaziński. It's because I need [them] to defend against [kuruc] rebels, who now, after reinforcements from Grand Vizier, have 12,000 men. Therefore I would like to know, if Your Majesty is marching towards us with your army. Once we are strengthened with the presence of Your Majesty, your bravery and great experience in military matters, we will together be able to defend common enemy, as defenders of Christian Empire and for the greater glory of Your Majesty's name, to whom I wish good health and all of the best.
Your Majesty's most humble servant and friend, Charles, Duke of Lorraine.

---

2   Dupont, pp.149–150.
3   He refers to relation written by his secretary. As it covers events in besieged Vienna, we will not be presenting it here.

In the Imperial Camp, dated 7 August 1683[4]

Most Serene King,

To fulfil Your Majesty's wishes, to be informed about everything [happening here], I would like to inform, that yesterday we camped at the river Morava, near Angern, and I noticed lots of fire and smokes in the area. I realised it had to be [*kuruc*] rebels, who were pillaging and burning neighbourhood villages. It was confirmed by the colonels [from the command] of Duke Herman Lichtenstein, who estimated that there were 400 enemies there. I immediately sent against them unit of Poles, with order to chase the rebels away. Once [our] unit was two miles away [from the camp], it encountered the enemy, but not in the number of 400, as by previous reports, but in the number of 4,000. Small group of Poles, despite being so severely outnumbered, charged with such energy and bravery, that they force them [enemy] to retreat, saved all Austrian prisoners, recaptured whole loot, killed three hundred enemies and captured few hundreds Hungarian horses and ten standards, that they brought to the Imperial camp.

When at dusk I received news about the real strength of the enemy, I quickly marched with unit of cavalry, hoping to save Poles. Instead, I met them returning to the camp after the fight ended.

What is amazing is that, despite the number of the enemy, who surrounded the Poles, [Lubomirski's troops] their strength and courage was so unyielding that they lost no more than twenty dead and wounded. Your Majesty will hear more about it from the report, that will be sent by Prince Lubomirski.

As for me, I just want to praise this amazing action and pay tribute to the natural zeal of the Polish nation and its generosity, always ready to be revealed on each occasion.

From the letters of the [Imperial] commander in Pressburg I know that 15,000 Turks camped next to this town and denied crossing, [move] to Altemburg and crossed the Danube there, moving on the island *Schütt* and then down the river to the bridge at Esztergom. Therefore I beg Your Majesty, to not think ill of me, when I repeat my plea, mentioned yesterday, for Your Majesty to hasten the march of troops of brave general Łaziński, and also your own with your army, so we can as quickly as possible relief Vienna from the enemies and raise the glory of His Majesty, with all my best wishes.

Your Majesty's most humble cousin, Duke of Lorraine.

In the Imperial Camp at Angram, dated 15 August 1683[5]

Most Serene King,

From the two attached letters, sent from Vienna on the 8th and 12th of this month,[6] Your Majesty will gain knowledge of the state of the city and how badly they need

---

4   Dupont, pp.154–156.

5   *Ibidem*, p.161.

6   Lorraine refers to two letters sent from the besieged town by Count Zdeněk Kašpar Kaplíř (1611–1686). He was a Bohemian noble and former soldier, nominated by the Emperor as the head of the Secret College of Deputies, dealing with the civilian affairs of Vienna during the siege. Dalerac called him Count de Capliers.

quick relief action. Many officers, including main engineer[7], were killed. We can start to worry that the city is in more danger than we thought, as it can be seen in relation of Count [Antonio] Caraffa and Prince Lubomirski. Therefore I strongly beg Your Majesty, to hasten his arrival and [quickly] arrive here with your troops to help us. So under Your Majesty's command, weakening folks of Vienna can be supported and Christian world [to be] saved from the tyranny of pagans. Also from aforementioned Count Caraffa Your Majesty will hear our plans, regarding the defence of the besieged Vienna and actions we want to take to help with the operations of the Christian armies. In this way there will be no secrets from Your Majesty, to whom I wish luck, success and more glory of his name, thanks to happy and successful relief of Vienna.

Your Majesty's most humble and obedient servant and friend, Charles, Duke of Lorraine.

In the Imperial Camp at Angram, dated 19 August 1683[8]

Most Serene King,

Only today I received letter of Your Majesty, written of the 11th of this month. I read [there] how much Your Majesty is taking care of that House of Austria can keep their lands, and your anxiety observing the situation of the besieged Vienna. I sent to Your Majesty news, that I received from town on the 8th and 12th of this month. And to provide more detailed information to Your Majesty, I ordered Count Caraffa to explain everything in my name, and to especially beg Your Majesty to hasten the march of the army. Just your presence [here] will be more important than large number of troops. I allow myself to present you all the dangers and problems that we currently encounter, so you can realise how big is the danger and how we do not have time to spare. From the signal noticed the day before yesterday from the tower of Saint Stephen I realised, that at least one [messenger] sent by me to the Turkish camp, managed to slip into town. I hope that thanks to this, the defenders received some hope and encouragement to stubbornly resist [the Ottomans]. I do not hide that I'm worried by the illness of the Count von Starhemberg, especially due to his vigilance and great trust put in him by people of Vienna. I am also worried by the death of the chief engineer [Rimpler], as I cannot think how those two [officers] could be ever replaced.

Many times I wrote to the Emperor and the Imperial quartermasters, to ensure preparation of the forage for horses for the march through the Vienna Woods. I do not doubt then, that there will be [prepared] everything that is needed.

As far as I know, *Thököly*'s soldiers relocated their camp near the island *Schütt*, to have easier access to the part of Tatar troops. I'm still waiting for the confirmation of those news though.

Since the departure of Count Caraffa I have no news about the movement of [allied] German troops, I think though that they left Frankfort and Saxony, easily reaching Linz. We need Your Majesty here, so we can start necessary and immediate actions in the defence of Christianity. Therefore I will yet again ask for Your Majesty and his famous army to hurry up.

---

7   Johann Georg Rimplier, who died on 3 August.
8   Dupont, pp.162–163.

In the meantime, in next three days, I will send infantry units [regiments] of [Herman] Grana and [Ludwig Wilhelm von] Baden to Tulln, to protecting construction of the bridge over the Danube, while I will move my camp into area of Krems, so from there I can better protect the roads, places for camps and other matters, so necessary in the relief of Vienna. According to the wishes of our people, since the first days of siege, [command of] this relief is reserved to Your Majesty.

Wishing Your Majesty best luck, I remain your most humble and obedient servant and cousin,

Charles, Duke of Lorraine.

In the Imperial Camp at Vogelsdorf, dated 21 August 1683[9]

Most Serene King,

When I was preparing for Your Majesty reports about the besieged Vienna and [ordering] copies of the letters of Count Kaplíř and Count Starhemberg, I received, to my great joy, letter of Your Majesty dated the 16th of this month. I do not doubt, that with God's help and under command of Your Majesty everything will fine, and we will succeed against the enemy of Christianity.

Your Majesty will easily realise, that situation of the defenders require quick action and arrival with help. Despite fighting bravely, with each day they lose more and more officers and soldiers, during 40 days of siege their supplies of ammunition were severely depleted, people are ravaged by dysentery, [while] enemy facing bastions, as soon as it heard about march of the relief force, increased their effort, building trenches and setting up mines. [I am sure] Your Majesty will agree, that [defenders] immediately needs help.

From my previous letters Your Majesty understands, why I decided to move my camp near Tulln and what information I had about camp of [*kuruc*] rebels and arrival of German [allies] troops. Therefore I do not need to add anything here, besides my wishes of save journey and better glory for Your Majesty.

Your most humble and obedient servant and cousin, Charles, Duke of Lorraine.

In the Imperial Camp at Korneuburg, dated 26 August 1683[10]

Most Serene King,

From the letter of Count Caraffa I know, how quickly Your Majesty is marching with his army to help the besieged town. It is indeed effort worthy of your Royal heart and much needed for the wellbeing of all Christianity.

Since the 19th of this month I did not receive any further news from the defenders. Letters of Count Kaplíř and Count Starhemberg, written on the same day, I [already] sent to you, so Your Majesty can judge himself how long town can survive the siege.

Both people fleeing from the town and prisoners captured since then claims that for last few days Turks deployed in the moat and dig in two places under

---

9   *Ibidem*, p.165.
10   *Ibidem*, pp.170–172.

bastions. Your Majesty will understand, how we are running out of time to save besieged and weakening town.

As I mentioned before, I planned to move to Tulln and check the state of the road. Area there is the most suitable to set up camp and build bridges. When on 24th of this month I wanted to move the camp away from Vogelsdorf, I received news that [kuruc] rebels stopped at river Morava and sent out numerous groups of Tatars towards Viennese bridges. It forces me to change my plans. I order general [Jacob] Leslie, who is in command of Imperial artillery, to coordinate construction of the bridge in Tulln, while myself marched the same day towards Viennese bridges, to secure area for approaching Polish troops under command of Voivode of Volhynia [Field Hetman Sieniawski]. On my way I received the news that the enemy set up camp near the bridges. Therefore I decided to attack them. Turks, seeing our Imperial soldiers, decided for pre-emptive charge and three or four thousands of their vanguard troops (rest, as we were informed later by the prisoners, stayed in camp) attacked us on left and right wing. They broke through first and second line and reached the baggage train. But their escape route was much more difficult, they managed to retreat but with great losses. Rest of their army, seeing this, decided to flee. Part retreated towards [river] Morava, others, abandoning weapons, wagons and horses, tried to swim to the other bank of Danube. We captured 25 flags and few hundred Turkish horses. Knowing that on the other bank of Morava there's rebel camp, I asked Voivode of Volhynia to join [his forces] with our camp on the 27th of this month, so we can decide on the plan of the attack on the rebels. From previous experience I already knew bravery [shown] by of the Polish soldier in fight, which yet again was confirmed in the yesterday's battle, and I knew that even when facing more numerous enemy, [while] joining our efforts we can attack.

I plan to move by the 29th of this month, then to set up camp to Tulln and there impatiently awaits the arrival of Your Majesty.

On 24th of this month Count Pálffy returned from the Imperial Court. He brought news, that auxiliary troops from Swabia and Franconia are due to set up camp near the bridgehead at Krems, on the other bank of Danube, on 29th of this month. Saxons troops are do join them there around 30th of this month.

He also brought assurances, that everything that is needed is ready: food, forage, weapons supplies. He also confirmed that Emperor is looking forward to Your Majesty's presence and allowed me to ask you to arrive here with first soldiers of the Polish army to help us. Glorious name of Your Majesty and your experience in fighting against Turks reassure me that we can be certain of the relief of the town.

Praying for Your Majesty's success, I signed as Your most humble and obedient servant and cousin, Charles, Duke of Lorraine.

P.S. While I was describing to Your Majesty all the current affairs, Count Caraffa arrived [in the camp] and informed me about everything that Your Majesty advised him of. I'm grateful, that within next few days I will be able to stand in Your Majesty's presence and under your command march with relief of Vienna.

In the Imperial Camp at Korneuburg, dated 28 August 1683[11]

Most Serene King,

I just received letter from Count Starhemberg, commander of Vienna, and I attached it to this correspondence.[12] I wish to forward it to Your Majesty as quickly as possible, as it contains information about situation in besieged town, deployment of the siege army, attacks made the enemy and the plan of the enemy's camp. I'm sure that Your Majesty will find it right to ensure that [all] allied armies move immediately towards the besieged town. I would also like to point out, that matters seems to be even more urgent, as this letter was not written in cipher, which indicates that [Starhemberg] sent it in hurry.

I will also add that Turks are working on repairing Viennese bridges, so, in attempt to stop them, I sent thousand soldiers with few cannons to the bridgehead. From all my heart I wish Your Majesty a good journey, success and relief of the Vienna under Your Majesty's command.

Your most humble and obedient servant and cousin, Charles, Duke of Lorraine.

---

11   *Ibidem*, pp.174–175.

12   In his letter Starhemberg described many Turkish attempts to set up mines and their attacks towards Imperial bastions. He advised of heavy losses, especially due to sickness. Garrison run out of hand grenades and lost few cannons. Imperial general asking Lorraine for quick relief action, mentioning there was no time to lose.

Colour Plate Commentaries

Plate A

A1. King Jan III Sobieski

While most of the paintings commemorating the victory at Vienna show King Jan III Sobieski in the style of a triumphant monarch in his *karacena* armour and helmet, in reality during the battle the Polish monarch was dressed in more ordinary attire. Kochowski provides us with a detailed description of the royal outfit. The King was wearing a white silk *żupan* with a dark blue *kontusz* outer garment over it. On his head he had a fur hat called a *kołpak*, with a heron's feather attached to it. He is presented here in slightly different attire, partly based on a contemporary painting by Adam Frans van der Meulen. It can be imagined that while travelling from Poland to Austria during the hot summer months, the King would prefer something comfortable, especially as he was suffering due to his obesity and other health problems. In this reconstruction he is wearing a red żupan with a yellow *kontusz* (linen with fur) over it. His boots are made from yellow Morocco leather known as saffian, a type very popular amongst Polish nobility serving in the military –similar types are shown on a few other illustrations. A small cross-like medal seen on a belt worn over the left shoulder is a symbol of the *L'Ordre du Saint-Esprit,* the French Order of the Holy Spirit. As a French ally, Jan III received this award on 30 November 1676. While the King is presented here without armour, he still has a sabre, which is worn in the scabbard connected via a leather belt on his left side.

A2. Crown Grand Hetman Stanisław Jan Jabłonowski

After King Jan III, Crown Grand Hetman Stanisław Jan Jabłonowski was the most important Polish commander during the campaign of 1683. He led the main army in the march from Poland to Austria in relief of Vienna, in command of the Polish right wing. He was well liked and respected by his soldiers, as he often shared the miseries of their campaign life and supported his troops in lean times. Unlike Jan III, we can see him here in full battle panoply, as he may have looked when he led Polish soldiers in the 1683 and later campaigns against the Ottomans and Tatars. He has *karacena* armour and helmet, that gained in popularity – especially amongst the hussars – during Sobieski's reign. The red material used as the base of *karacena,* as seen over hetman's arm and under the armour, was either deer or elk hide. In his right hand he is carrying his badge of office, the hetman's mace (*buława hetmańska*). Over the armour, as was customary with hussars, we can see the pelt of an exotic cat: in this case a leopard. Like the King, his clothing is red, as it was the colour often associated with nobility serving in the army. His long boots are made from yellow saffian. His military attire is completed by a sabre, seen on his left side.

Plate B

B1. General of Artillery Marcin Kątski

Marcin Kątski was one of the key Polish commanders during 1670s and 1680s, from 1667 holding the office of the Crown General of Artillery. He was also a very experienced infantry officer, with his most famous action commanding the rear-guard during the retreat from Bukovina in 1685. Kątski was responsible for many fortification works during Sobieski's reign and, as it was proved during 1683 campaign, was a very able commander of artillery. It was the determination of the general and his soldiers that allowed the Poles to drag all their cannons through hills and forests, so they were able to support the allied troops in the relief of Vienna. Surviving portraits always shows him dressed in Western-style clothing, usually with full armour, even though such equipment was by that time long abandoned in European armies. He is instead presented with the far more commonly used set of breastplate and backplate, worn over his coat (yet again in typical Polish 'army red'). One can only wonder how such dashing clothes looked like after passing through the Vienna Woods. His fashionable attire of course includes the periwig, with many dark curls.

B2. *Rotmistrz* of *pancerni*

Pancerni were the mainstay of the Polish cavalry and, unlike with the hussars, many of their *rotmistrz* were not just nominal commanders of the banners but also led them in person. His equipment is very similar to the companion from Plate C2: chainmail, *misiurka* helmet, sabre and bow. He has different arm-guards however, providing him with better protection. In his hand he is carrying a type of the mace called *buzdygan.* It was a symbol of his rank and, if needed, could be used as weapon. Chainmail is worn over a yellow *żupan,* while shoes – yet again made from saffain – are red, which next to the yellow was the most popular colour for them.

Plate C

C1. Hussar companion

Companion (*towarzysz*) from one of the hussar banners getting ready to mount his horse. He is well equipped, with a proper set of armour, arm-guards and *szyszak* helmet. The pelt of an exotic cat is worn over the armour, although he does not have wings attached to his back. From his large arsenal, only his sabre is visible. The *kopia* lance would be carried once in the saddle, while the other weapons: estoc or pallasch and two pistols, are with his horse. The combination of a green *żupan* and red saffian boots is based on the painting of battle of Khotyn (Chocim) in 1673, painted between 1674 and 1679 by Andreas Stech and Ferdinand van Kessel the Elder.

C2. *Pancerny/petyhorzec*

A well-equipped companion (*towarzysz*) of *pancerni* cavalry, and as already mentioned, very similar in his armament to the *rotmistrz* from Plate B2. He seems to be one of the lucky ones, as his banner is equipped with *rohatyna* spears, with a white and blue pennant. While it wasn't a common occurrence, it seemed to happen in certain banners, as shown on the engraving in Jakub Kazimierz Haur's *Skład albo skarbiec znakomity sekretów o ekonomiej ziemianskiej*, published in Cracow in 1693. The companion has chainmail with fairly short sleeves, worn over his *żupan*. His head is protected by *misiurka* helmet with a chainmail hood. As a symbol of his status as a noble he is carrying a bow; we can see the quiver with arrows worn on the right side and part of the bow case on the left side. Of course there is also a sabre, used as the main weapon after the *rohatyna*. The spanner-like tool on his belt indicates that he also has wheellock pistols, that would be kept with horse in holsters. Lithuanian *petyhorzec* would have the same equipment but in his case the spear would be replaced with a light *kopia* lance, similar to those used by hussars.

Plate D

D1. Light horseman

Companion from one of the light cavalry banners, serving 'Walachian style *alias leviori*', without any armour. He is equipped with a bow, which could show he is a Tatar cavalryman, although such a weapon could also be found amongst Wallachian horse. As with the *pancerni* figures, he has a quiver with arrows on his right side and the bow case on his left side. He is also armed with horseman's pick (*nadziak*), which he is wearing on the back of his belt - the handle is visible next to his left leg. He is wearing blue *kontusz*, tight red trousers and yellow saffian boots. Another red element can be seen on his fur-brimmed cap.

D2. *Arkabuzer*/reiter

Polish *arkabuzer*, in reality a reiter/cuirassier, very similar in his equipment to those serving in the Imperial army or in the regiments raised by Lubomirski as a part of the auxiliary corps for the Imperial forces. There were three units of Polish *arkabuzeria* present during the 1683 campaign: the Guard squadron under Jan Górzyński, the company of Grand Hetman Jabłonowski and the company of Field Hetman Sieniawski. All units took an active part in all the battles and Colonel Jan Górzyński died on 12 September 1683 during relief of Vienna. It was soldier like the one presented here who sacrificed his life during the first battle of Párkány to save King Jan III Sobieski.

He is well protected, with *szyszak* helmet, breast and backplate. Brulig mentioned seeing cavalry armed with handguns and 'beautiful long buff-coats', so we can see such a coat under the soldier's armour. Weapons are a sword at his side and wheellock musketoon worn on a leather belt across his chest, known as a *bandolier*. Such soldiers would normally be also equipped with two pistols, part of their requirement to own 'three firearms' (the musketoon being the third). They were, like the other cavalrymen, kept in holsters next to the saddle.

Plate E

E1. Musketeer of foreign infantry

The Polish style of the clothing for the foreign infantry has been covered in the main text, which would make this plate very similar to the dragoon next to it. Instead, the infantryman is shown in Western-style clothing, more like his Austrian or Bavarian counterparts that he will fight side-by-side with in 1683. A few surviving paintings depicting Sobieski's victories from 1672-1676 show blue-uniformed regiments of pike and shot, while a painting of battle of Khotyn (Chocim) in 1673, by Andreas Stech and Ferdinand van Kessel the Elder shows troops with Western-European style coats and hats. Blue-uniformed clothing is based on the painting of the battle of Lwów/Lesienice from 1675. Surviving documents related to the Foot Guard regiment and Marcin Zamoyski's foot regiment from 1680s and 1690s indicates the purchase of hats and clothing called *liberie*, *płaszcze* and *sukienki*, which is enigmatic enough to leave it open to risk the hypothesis of at least the partial presence of the Western clothing in the infantry. Amongst the fashionable uniform of this soldier is a wide felt hat and white cravat. It could be that his regiment was raised in a region with a stronger German influence, like Prussia or next to the border with Silesia, hence the availability of Western-style clothing. He is armed with musket and sword, but he does not have a berdiche axe. On his belt is his powder horn and leather powder bag, known as *pulwersak*. He also has a belt called a *bandolier* worn over the left shoulder. His coat is blue, a colour that through the whole of the seventeenth century was associated in the Commonwealth with infantry. As his clothing is in good shape, he may be a soldier from the Guard or Queen's regiment, as these could always count on favourable treatment and better supplies.

E2. Dragoon

Another soldier in typical 'infantry blue' clothing, a dragoon with more Polish-type of garment (*żupan*) with the characteristic fur cap but also, like the infantryman, with a white cravat. He has also managed to acquire long black cavalry boots. Polish cavalry traditionally did not use gloves but dragoons, like *arkabuzer*, had a pair of leather ones. His sabre is worn on one leather belt across his right shoulder, and on other there is a smaller belt with *antaba* used to attach his musket during horse ride. The axe is a very important part of his equipment, used both as an engineering tool and as weapon. Dragoons played vital role in Sobieski's campaigns, as they were able to accompany his cavalry and provide them with fire support, which was especially useful against Tatar raids.

Plate F

F1. Haiduk

Reconstruction of haiduk is based on Caspar Luyken's drawing from the early eighteenth century. The red colour of his clothing is taken from the description of the household haiduks of Jan III Sobieski from the 1680s. His hat is a Hungarian *magierka,* very popular in Poland since the reign of Stephen Bathory – while often black, here is an example of a better quality green one, with attached feathers. He also has shoes made from yellow leather. This haiduk may be on the ceremonial guard duty, as he is equipped only with sabre and short axe, lacking his musket. We know that both Hetman Jabłonowski and Hetman Sieniawski took their haiduk banners on campaign, but there is no confirmation that the Royal haiduks left Poland. It is possible that they stayed with the Queen's court or were deployed to protect one of the royal estates.

F2. Royal Guard Janissary

The company of the Household Janissaries accompanied King Jan III Sobieski to Austria, marching as a part of his guard unit. One can only imagine how surprised Silesians or Moravians were, seeing such Ottoman-style troops in the army of the Polish king. The colour of this clothing is based on painting of the battle of Khotyn (Chocim) in 1673, by Andreas Stech and Ferdinand van Kessel the Elder. This Polish janissary-like soldier wears red clothing with yellow lining and with a white hat. His blue trousers are not as tight as those worn by Polish troops, although the soldier has chosen long black boots instead of short shoes. He is armed with musket and sabre.

Plate G

G1. Cossack

Despite Sobieski's wishes, only a small contingent of Cossacks took part in the relief of Vienna, with further units joining the Polish army in later stages of the campaign. His clothing is based on written sources, describing the cloth issued to Cossacks as part of their pay. This one is wearing a white *żupan*, made of white wool called *kir*. Over the *żupan* he has a green caftan (*chekmen*) made from thick simple cloth called *paklak* (*pakłak*). He also has tight red trousers, long black boots and a blue cap. He is armed with a flintlock musket and sabre, with the powder horn attached to his belt.

G2. Polish Tatar

Tatars were favourites of Jan III Sobieski, settling many of them on his private land and taking many of them to Austria. Brulig seems rather shocked, noting hundreds of them marching on foot with the baggage train of the Polish army. He was appalled by their culinary habits, writing that 'their favourite dish [is] horse meat, which they throw on the fire like we do with pigs [but make] not half roasted [and] with great lust they eat it, unsalted and with blood [from meat] running over their mouth'. The Tatar that can be seen here would be serving mounted though, either in one of light horse banners or as one of the mounted servants. He is carrying a whip, as he would not wear spurs on his leather boots. This Tatar has a lower quality blue *żupan*, with a fur *burka* worn over left arm. He also has the characteristic cap, often seen amongst Tatars on paintings by Johan Philip Lemke. He is armed with a bow and sabre.

Plate H

H1. Artilleryman

Polish artillery played vital part in the relief of Vienna; its soldiers with stubborn determination transporting their cannons through the difficult terrain of the Vienna Woods to support the allied troops. Modern reconstructions usually present artillery crew in blue clothing, as used by infantry. To be different, this artilleryman's red clothing is based on the painting of the battle of Lwów/Lesienice from 1675, where there are many artillery crews shown, with most of them in what seems to be a combination of red garments and brown hats. Many amongst Kątski's men, especially the trained crews operating the guns, were foreigners, explaining the more Western-style of uniform shown here.

H2. Cavalry servant (*czeladź*)

One look at this servant, normally mounted on some lower-quality horse, could indicate why for many Western European eyewitnesses it was so easy to exaggerate the numbers of Polish troops on campaign. As one of main tasks of such men was to gather provisions and forage, so they were well armed, this one with a handgun and axe (again, as with dragoons, used both as a tool and a weapon), and many could also have sabres. Good quality clothing and boots shows that this servant is from a well-financed retinue, perhaps serving a winged hussar companion. During their supply missions *czeladź* could meet many dangers: from Tatars and *kuruc* rebels, to local armed peasants not willing to share food with a foreign army. Servants could be also seen defending camps and garrison towns, sometimes even taking part in assaults on fortresses. At the same time they were also a dangerous element on the battlefield, as after the fighting was over they would be found robbing dead and wounded, from both sides without mercy or remorse .

Bibliography

Archival Sources

Archiwum Główne Akt Dawnych (AGAD) w Warszawie
Archiwum Radziwiłłów (AR), VII, no 229
Archiwum Skarbu Koronnego (ASK), II, 64, 67, 68
Akta Skarbowo-Wojskowe (ASW), 85
Archiwum Zamoyskich (AZ), 463, 3112
Biblioteka ks. Czartoryskich (BCzart) w Krakowie
2589, 2755
Biblioteka Zakładu Narodowego im. Ossolińskich we Wrocławiu
337

Printed Primary Sources

'Djarjusz kampanji węgierskiej in Anno 1683', Otton Laskowski (ed.), *Przegląd Historyczno-Wojskowy*, volume VI, part 2 (Warszawa: Główna Księgarnia Wojskowa, 1933)

'Dziennik Franciszka Tannera', Jan Ursyn Niemcewicz (ed.), *Zbiór pamiętników historycznych o dawnej Polszcze*, volume V (Lipsk: Bretikopf i Haertel, 1840)

'Relatia seu descriptia wojny pod Wiedniem, pod Strygoniem i dalszej kampaniej A. 1683', Otton Laskowski (ed.), *Przegląd Historyczno-Wojskowy*, volume II, part 1 (Warszawa: Główna Księgarnia Wojskowa, 1930)

'Relatio a comitiss anni 1683 biennalium gestorum et laborum exercitus…', Andrzej Chryzostom Załuski (ed.), *Epistolarum historico-familiarum,* volume I, part 2 (Brunsberge, 1710)

'Sposoby i porządek obrony Rzpltej podczas wojny tureckiej (marzec 1676 r.)', *Przegląd Historyczno-Wojskowy*, volume II, part 1 (Warszawa: Główna Księgarnia Wojskowa, 1930)

A true and exact relation of the raising of the siege of Vienna, and the victory obtained over the Ottoman army. The 12th of September 1683 (Dublin: Joseph Ray, 1683)

Abrahamowicz, Zygmunt (ed.), *Kara Mustafa pod Wiedniem. Źródła muzułmańskie do dziejów wyprawy wiedeńskiej 1683 roku* (Kraków: Wydawnictwo Literackie, 1973)

Akta grodzkie i ziemskie z Archiwum Ziemskiego we Lwowie. Lauda sejmikowe halickie 1575–1697, volume XXIV (Lwów: Towarzystwo Naukowe, 1931)

Akta grodzkie i ziemskie z czasów Rzeczypospolitej Polskiej z archiwum tak zwanego bernardyńskiego we Lwowie, volume X: *Spis oblat zawartych w aktach grodu i ziemstwa lwowskiego* (Lwów, 1884)

Akta grodzkie i ziemskie z czasów Rzeczypospolitej Polskiej z archiwum tak zwanego Bernardyńskiego we Lwowie, volume I (Lwów: Drukarnia Zakładu Narodowego im. Ossolińskich, 1868)

Akta grodzkie i ziemskie z czasów Rzeczypospolitej Polskiej z archiwum tak zwanego bernardyńskiego we Lwowie, volume X: *Spis oblat zawartych w aktach grodu i ziemstwa lwowskiego* (Lwów, 1884)

Biblioteka starożytna pisarzy polskich, volume II (Warszawa: S. Orgelbrand, Księgarz, 1834)

Brulig, Bernard, 'Pat. Bernard Brulig's Bericht über die Belagerung der Stadt Wien im Jahre 1683.', *Archiv für Kunde österreichischer Geschichts-Quellen,* volume IV, year 3, issue III and IV (Wien, 1850)

Compendiosa e veridical relazione di quanto ha operato nella scorsa campagna l'armata del re di Polonia contro quelle de'Turchi e Tartari nella Podolia (Bologna, 1685)

Connor, Bernard, *The history of Poland. vol. 2 in several letters to persons of quality, giving an account of the antient and present state of that kingdom, historical, geographical, physical, political and ecclesiastical ... : with sculptures, and a new map after the best geographers : with several letters relating to physick / by Bern. Connor ... who, in his travels in that country, collected these memoirs from the best authors and his own observations ; publish'd by the care and assistance of Mr. Savage* (London: J.D., 1698)

Corfus. Ilie (ed.), *Documente privitoare la istoria României culese din arhivele polone. Secolul al XVII-lea.* (Bucharest: Editura Adaemiei Republicii Socialiste România 1983)

Count Taaffe's letters from the imperial camp to his brother the Earl of Carlingford here in London giving an account of the most considerable actions, both before, and at, the raising of the siege at Vienna, together with several remarkable passages afterward, in the victorious campagne against the Turks in Hungary : with an addition of two other letters from a young English nobleman, a volunteir in the imperial army. (London: printed for T.B, 1684)

Dalerac, Francois Paulin, *Pamiętniki kawalera de Beaujeu* (Kraków: Władysław Markowski, 1883)

Dalerac, Francois Paulin, *Polish Manuscripts: or the secret history of the reign of John Sobieski* (London: H. Rhodes, T. Bennet, A. Bell, 1700)

Druszkiewicz, Stanisław Zygmunt, *Pamiętniki 1648–1697* (Siedlce: Wydawnictwo Akademii Podlaskiej, 2001)

Dupont, Phillipe, *Pamiętniki historyi życia i czynów Jana III Sobieskiego* (Warszawa: Muzeum Pałacu Króla Jana III w Wilanowie, 2011)

Dyakowski, Mikołaj, *Dyaryusz wideńskiej okazyji Jmci Pana Mikołaja na Dyakowcach Dyakowskiego podstolego latyczewskiego* (Warszawa: Wydawnictwo MON, 1983)

Fredro, Andrzej Maksymilian, *Potrzebne consideratie około porządku woiennego y pospolitego ruszenia* (Słuck: Drukarnia Radziwiłłowska, 1675).

Friedman, Filip (ed.), 'Nieznana relacja o batalii wiedeńskiej 1683 roku', *Przegląd Historyczno-Wojskowy*, volume VII, part 1 (Warszawa: Główna Księgarnia Wojskowa, 1935)

Helcel, Antoni Zygmunt (ed.), *Listy Jana Sobieskiego do żony Marii Kazimiery* (Kraków: Biblioteka Ordynacji Myszkowskiej, 1860)

Journal de tout ce qui s'est passé entre les Impériaux et les Turcs: durant la campagne de l'année 1683 et 1684 (Leyden: Pierre Du Marteau, 1684)

Kluczycki, Franciszek (ed.), *Akta do dziejów Króla Jana IIIgo sprawy roku 1683, a osobliwie wyprawy wiedeńskiej wyjaśniające* (Kraków: Fr. Kluczycki i SP, 1883)

Kluczycki, Franciszek Ksawery (ed.), *Pisma do wieku i spraw Jana Sobieskiego*, volume I, part 1 (Kraków: Akademia Umiejętności, 1880)

Kluczycki, Franciszek Ksawery (ed.), *Pisma do wieku i spraw Jana Sobieskiego*, volume I, part 2 (Kraków: Akademia Umiejętności, 1881)

Kochowski, Wespazjan, *Commentarius belli adversus Turcas* (Kraków: Albert Górecki, 1684)

Lipowski, Błażej, *Piechotne ćwiczenie albo wojenność piesza* (Kraków: Nakładem Jerzego Forstera, 1660)

Listy Jana III Króla Polskiego, pisane do krolowy Maryi Kazimiry w ciągu wyprawy pod Wiedeń w roku 1683 (Warszawa: N. Glucksberg, 1823)

Pasek, Jan Chryzostom, *Pamiętniki* (Warszawa: Państwowy Instytut Wydawniczy, 1963)

Poczobut Odlanicki, Jan Władysław, *Pamiętnik (1640–1684)*, edited by Andrzej Rachuba (Warszawa: Czytelnik, 1987)

Poczobut Odlanicki, Jan Władysław, *Pamiętnik Jana Władysława Poczobuta Odlanickiego* (Warszawa: Drukarnia Michała Ziemkiewicza, 1877)

Pułaski, Franciszek (ed.), *Źródła do poselstwa Jana Gnińskiego wojewody chełmińskiego do Turcyi w latach 1677–1678* (Warszawa: Druk Rubieszewskiego i Wrotnowskiego, 1907)

Rykaczewczki, Erazm (ed.), *Relacye nuncyuszów apostolskich i innych osób o Polsce od roku 1548 do 1690*, volume II (Paryż: Biblioteka Polska, 1864)

Sauer, Augustin, *Rom und Wien in Jahre 1683* (Wien: K. Hof- und Staatsdruckerel, 1883)

Singer, Samuel Weller (ed.), *The Correspondence of Henry Hyde, Early of Clarendon*, volume I (London: Henry Colburn, 1828)

Skorobohaty, Aleksander D., *Diariusz* (Warszawa: Wydawnictwo DiG, 2004)

Skrzydelka, Władysław (ed.), *Listy z czasów Jana III i Augusta II* (Kraków: Drukarnia Wincentego Kirchmayera, 1870)

Sobieski, Jakub Ludwik, *Dyaryusz wyprawy wiedeńskiej w 1683 r.* (Warszawa: edited and published by Teodor Wierzbowski, 1883).

Sprawy wojenne króla Stefana Batorego. Dyjaryusze, relacyje, listy i akta z lat 1576–1568 (Kraków, 1887)

Tende, Gaspard de, *Relacja historyczna o Polsce* (Warszawa: Muzeum Pałacu Króla Jana III w Wilanowie, 2013)

True Relation of the Manner of the Coronation of the present King of Poland (London, 1676)

Valcaren, John Peter a, *A relation or diary of the siege of Vienna* (London, 1684)

Wagner, Marek (ed.), *Źródła do dziejów wojny polsko-tureckiej w latach 1683–1699* (Oświęcim: Wydawnictwo Napoleon V, 2016

Werdum, Ulryk, *Dziennik podróży 1670–1672. Dziennik wyprawy polowej 1671* (Warszawa: Muzeum Pałacu Króla Jana III w Wilanowie, 2012)

Wierzbowski, Stanisław, *Konnotata wypadków w domu i kraju zaszłych od 1634 do 1689* (Lipsk: Księgarnia Zagraniczna, 1858)

Zawadzki, Adam, Przeździecki, Aleksander (ed.), *Zrzódła do dziejów polskich*, volume II (Wilno: Józef Zawadzki, 1844)

Secondary Printed Sources

Barker, Thomas, *Double Eagle and Crescent: Vienna's second Turkish siege and its historical setting* (Albany: State University of New York Press, 1967)

Bobiatyński, Konrad, 'Skład I liczebność armii litewskiej podczas wojny z Turcją w latach 1683–1686', *Zapiski Historyczne*, volume LXXXVI, 2021, Issue 1 (Toruń: Towarzysztwo Naukowe w Toruniu, 2021),

Bobiatyński, Konrad, 'Udział Wielkiego Księstwa Litewskiego w kampanii wiedeńskiej 1683 roku', Teresa Chynczewska-Hennel (ed.), *Odsiecz wiedeńska* (Warszawa: Muzeum Pałacu Króla Jana III w Wilanowie 2011

Brzezinski, Richard *Polish Armies 1569–1696,* volume 2 (London: Osprey Publishing Ltd, 1987)

Das Kriegsjahr 1683: nach Acten und anderen authentischen Quellen dargestellt in der Abtheilung für Kriegsgeschichte des K.K. Kriegs-Archivs (Wien, 1883)

Hnilko, Antoni, 'Przygotowanie artylerji koronnej na wyprawę wiedeńską w 1683 r.', *Przegląd Historyczno-Wojskowy,* volume VI, part I (Warszawa, 1933)

Hundert, Zbigniew, 'Jeszcze o organizacji husarii koronnej na kampanię wiedeńską 1683 r.', *Przegląd Historyczno-Wojskowy,* no 3 (269) (Warszawa: Wojskowe Biuro Historyczne, 2019)

Hundert, Zbigniew, 'Kilka uwag na temat chorągwi petyhorskich w wojskach Rzeczypospolitej w latach 1673–1683', *W pancerzu przez wieki. Z dziejów wojskowości polskiej i powszechnej,* Marcin Baranowski, Andrzej Gładysz, Andrzej Niewiński (ed.) (Oświęcim: Napoleon V, 2014)

Hundert, Zbigniew, 'Komputowe oddziały rodziny królewskiej w kampanii mołdawskiej 1686 roku w świetle rozkazów i sprawozdania sejmowego hetmana wielkiego koronnego Stanisława Jabłonowskiego', Dariusz Milewski (ed.), *Jarzmo Ligi Świętej? Jan III Sobieski i Rzeczpospolita w latach 1684–1696* (Warszawa: Muzeum Pałacu Króla Jana III w Wilanowie, 2017)

Hundert, Zbigniew, 'Listy przypowiednie dla Marcina Zamoyskiego z lat 1656, 1679 i 1683 na chorągwie jazdy i regiment pieszy w wojsku koronnym', *Res Historica*, no 43 (Lublin: Instytut Historii UMCS 2017),

Hundert, Zbigniew, '*Organizacja husarii koronnej* na *kampanię wiedeńską 1683 roku*', „*W hetmańskim trudzie". Księga Pamiątkowa ku czci Profesora Jana Wimmera* (Oświęcim: Wydawnictwo Napoleon V, 2017)

Hundert, Zbigniew, 'Pozycja Jana III w wojsku koronnym w latach 1674–1683. Utrzymanie czy też utrata wpływów wypracowanych w czasie sprawowania godności hetmańskiej?', Dariusz Milewski (ed.), *Król Jan III Sobieski i Rzeczpospolita w latach 1674–1683* (Warszawa: Muzeum Pałacu Króla Jana III w Wilanowie, 2016)

Hundert, Zbigniew, 'Projekt organizacji i finansowania "wojska JKM i Rzptej Zaporoskiego" z 1683 roku. Przyczynek do badań nad funkcjonowaniem wojsk kozackich w strukturach sił zbrojnych Rzeczypospolitej w dobie wojny z Imperium Osmańskim 1683–1699', *Saeculum Christianum,* volume XXIII (Warszawa: Wydawnictwo Naukowe Uniwersytetu Kardynała Stefana Wyszyńskiego, 2016)

Hundert, Zbigniew, 'Projekty komputów wojska Wielkiego Księstwa Litewskiego z lat 1683–1684. Przyczynek do badań nad problemem rywalizacji Jana III z Sapiehami o wpływy w wojsku litewskim w latach 1683–1696.', *Rocznik Lituanistyczny,* volume 3, year 2017 (Warszawa: Instytut Historii Polskiej Akademii Nauk, 2017

Hundert, Zbigniew, 'Strażnicy koronny i wojskowy w dobie Jana Sobieskiego (1667–1696). Kilka uwag o osobach odpowiedzialnych za organizowanie przemarszów armii koronnej', *Acta Universitatis Lodziensis, Folia Historica 99* (Łódź: Wydanictwo Uniwersytetu Łódzkiego, 2017)

Hundert, Zbigniew, 'Wykaz koronnych chorągwi i regimentów w okresie od 1 V 1679 do 30 IV 1683. Przyczynek do organizacji wojska koronnego w dobie pokoju 1677–1683, *Studia Historyczno-Wojskowe*, Volume V (Zabrze-Tarnowskie Góry: Wydawnictwo Inforteditions, 2015)

Hundert, Zbigniew, *Husaria koronna w wojnie polsko-tureckiej 1672–1676* (Oświęcim: Wydawnictwo Napoleon V, 2012)

Hundert, Zbigniew, *Między buławą a tronem. Wojsko koronne w walce stronnictwa malkontentów z ugrupowaniem dworskim w latach 1669–1673* (Oświęcim: Wydawnictwo Napoleon V, 2014),

Józefowicz, Jan Tomasz, *Kronika miasta Lwowa od roku 1634 do 1690* (Lwów: Zakład Narodowy im. Ossolińskich, 1854)

Konarski, Kazimierz, *Polska przed odsieczą wiedeńską 1683 roku* (Oświęcim: Napoleon V, 2017)

Kopiec, Marcin, *Król Sobieski na Śląsku w kościołach w drodze pod Wiedeń* (Mików: Spółka Wydawnicza Karola Miarki, 1920)

Kosowski, Miron, *Chorągwie wołoskie w wojsku koronnym w II poł. XVII wieku* (Zabrze: Inforteditions, 2009

Kroll, Piotr, 'Hetmanat lewobrzeżny wobec Rzeczypospolitej i Prawobrzeże w dobie Ligi Świętej', Dariusz Milewski (ed.), *Jarzmo Ligi Świętej? Jan III Sobieski i Rzeczpospolita w latach 1684–1696* (Warszawa: Muzeum Pałacu Króla Jana III w Wilanowie, 2017)

Kroll, Piotr, 'Jan III Sobieski wobec Kozaczyzny w latach 1676–1683', Dariusz Milewski (ed.), *Król Jan III Sobieski i Rzeczpospolita w latach 1674–1683* (Warszawa: Muzem Pałacu Króla Jana III w Wilanowie, 2016)

Millar, Simon, *Vienna 1683. Christian Europe repels the Ottomans* (Oxford: Osprey Publishing, 2008)

Nagielski, Mirosław, 'Organizacja rajtarii i arkebuzerii koronnej w XVII wieku, Karol Łopatecki (ed.), *Organizacja armii w nowożytnej Europie. Struktura-urzędy-prawo-finanse* (Zabrze: Inforteditions, 2011)

Newald, Johann, *Beiträge zur Geschichte der Belagerung von Wien durch die Türken im Jahre 1683.* Part II (Wien: Verlag von Kubasta und Voigt, 1884)

Rauchbar, Johann Georg von, *Leben und Thaten des Fürsten Georg Friedrich von Waldech (1620–1692)* (Arolsen: Speyer, 1872)

Semkowicz, Władysław, *Udział wojsk litewskich Sobieskiego w kampanii 1683*, (Wilno: Zakłady graficzne Znicz, 1934)

Sikora, Radosław, *Husaria pod Wiedniem* (Warszawa: Instytut Wydawniczy ERICA, 2012)

Smolarek, Przemysław, *Kampania mołdawska Jana III roku 1691* (Oświęcim: Wydawnictwo Napoleon V, 2015),

Sowa, Jan, '"Ludzie niezwalczeni". Rejestry chorągwi jazdy autoramentu narodowego w Okopach Św. Trójcy, 1693–1695, *Studia nad staropolską sztuką wojenną*, volume II (Oświęcim: Wydawnictwo Napoleon V, 2013)

Stoye, John, *The Siege of Vienna* (London: Birlinn, 2000)

Urbański, Tadeusz, *Rok 1683 na Podolu, Ukrainie i w Mołdawii: szkic historyczny z czasów panowania Jana III Sobieskiego* (Lwów: Akademickie Kółko Historyczne we Lwowie, 1907)

Wagner, Marek, 'Formacje dragońskie armii koronnej w czasach Jana III Sobieskiego. Lata 1667–1696', Aleksander Smoliński (ed.), *Do szarży marsz, marsz... Studia z dziejów kawalerii*, volume 5 (Toruń: Wydawnictwo Naukowe Uniwersytetu Mikołaja Kopernika, 2014

Wagner, Marek, *Słownik biograficzny oficerów polskich drugiej połowy XVII wieku*, volume I (Oświęcim: Wydawnictwo Napoleon V, 2013)

Wagner, Marek, *Słownik biograficzny oficerów polskich drugiej połowy XVII wieku,* volume II (Oświęcim: Wydawnictwo Napoleon V, 2014)

Wheatcroft, Andrew, *The enemy at the gate. Habsburgs, Ottomans and the Battle for Europe* (New York: Basic Books, 2009)

Wimmer, Jan, *Wyprawa wiedeńska 1683 roku* (Warszawa: Wydawnictwo MON, 1957)

Wimmer, Jan, 'Błażeja Lipowskiego pierwszy polski regulamin piechoty', *Studia i Materiały do Historii Wojskowości*, volume XX (Warszawa: Wydawnictwo Czasopisma Wojskowe, 1976)

Wimmer, Jan, *Wiedeń 1683. Dzieje kampanii i bitwy* (Warszawa: Wydawnictwo MON, 1983

Wimmer, Jan, *Wojsko polskie w drugiej połowie XVII wieku* (Warszawa: Wydawnictwo Ministerstwa Obrony Narodowej, 1965)

Witkowski, Andrzej, *Czerwone sztandary Osmanów. Wojna roku 1683 opisana na nowo* (Warszawa: Muzeum Pałacu Króla Jana III w Wilanowie, 2016)

Woliński, Janusz, 'Parkany (7 i 9 października 1683)', *Przegląd Historyczno-Wojskowy*, volume VI, part 1 (Warszawa: Główna Księgarnia Wojskowa, 1933)

Wrede, Alphons von, *Geschichte der K. Und K. Wehrmacht*, volume III, part 2 (Wien: W. Seidel und Sohn, 1901)